Human Skeletal Remains

Human Skeletal Remains is a step-by-step field guide to teach proper recovery techniques when a forensic anthropologist is unavailable for immediate scene responses. In the absence of a forensic anthropologist, the investigator assumes the responsibility of ensuring the complete and accurate recovery of skeletal materials from scenes. This could be problematic if the investigator has not had specialized training in human remains recoveries. To help investigators carry out this task, the authors developed this guide using 328 full-color demonstrative photos with easy-to-follow instructions on how to identify and recover human skeletal remains using scientifically defensible methods. It is an excellent resource for law enforcement, medicolegal death investigators, CSIs, anthropologists, medical examiners, coroners, evidence recovery technicians, students, and other forensic professionals.

Features

- Side-by-side photographic comparisons of adult and juvenile human remains with nonhuman bones
- Start-to-finish demonstration of proper recovery techniques involving scenes with surface scattered and buried human remains
- Preservation considerations with respect to cultural sensitivity and ethical practices

Human Skeletal Remains is an illustrative tool designed to accompany you on scene. Use it to identify the bones you locate, then follow the instructions to recover them. Get it dirty!

Human Skeletal Remains

A Field Guide to Identification, Recovery, and Preservation

Teresa A. White,
Hillary R. Parsons,
and Samuel S. White

CRC Press
Taylor & Francis Group
Boca Raton London New York

CRC Press is an imprint of the
Taylor & Francis Group, an **informa** business

Designed cover image: Teresa A. White and Hillary R. Parsons

First edition published 2026
by CRC Press
2385 NW Executive Center Drive, Suite 320, Boca Raton FL 33431

and by CRC Press
4 Park Square, Milton Park, Abingdon, Oxon, OX14 4RN

CRC Press is an imprint of Taylor & Francis Group, LLC

ISBN: 9781032622163 (hbk)
ISBN: 9781032621951 (pbk)
ISBN: 9781032623320 (ebk)

DOI: 10.4324/9781032623320

Typeset in Minion
by codeMantra

Contents

About the authors

Teresa A. White is a forensic and cultural anthropologist. In 2013, she and her husband, Dr. Samuel S. White, established Bone and Stone Anthrosciences, LLC, where they provide anthropological and archaeological consulting services and educational workshops to federal, state, county, Tribal, and international law enforcement agencies and other medicolegal professionals. She received her M.A. in forensic anthropology in 2013 and her Ph.D. in anthropology in 2019 from the University of Montana.

From 2015 to 2018, Teresa created and facilitated the Medicolegal Death Investigation Conference at the University of Montana, where she provided continuing education to hundreds of attendees. She is a medical investigator and DMORT Region VIII team member with the Department of Health and Human Services (HHS) and the National Disaster Medical System (NDMS). She is also an instructor for Tri-Tech Forensics Training, where she teaches webinars and short courses to law enforcement personnel and forensic practitioners. She has worked as an adjunct instructor at the University of Montana, teaching *Fundamentals of Forensic Science.*

Hillary R. Parsons is a forensic anthropologist and sole proprietor of Odyssey Anthropology, LLC, providing domestic and international forensic anthropology consulting for governmental and nongovernmental agencies including attorneys, law enforcement, medical examiners' offices and coroners, and private clients. She instructs educational short courses and workshops for the medicolegal community, work she has been involved with for over 17 years. She currently holds the forensic anthropology contract at the Laboratoire de sciences judiciaires et de médecine légale in Montréal, Québec, and the contract as the senior scientific recovery expert (SRE) with Shoulder 2 Shoulder, assisting the Defense POW/MIA Accounting Agency (DPAA) with their mission to search, recover, and repatriate America's fallen soldiers.

Dr. Parsons received her undergraduate degree in anthropology from Montana State University, her M.A. in anthropology from the University of Montana, and her Ph.D. in anthropology from the University of Tennessee. She is an associate member of the American Academy of Forensic Sciences (AAFS) and a member of the American Association of Biological Anthropologists (AABA) and the Society of American Archaeologists (SAA).

Samuel S. White is an archaeologist, working for Vantage Point Solutions as an assistant manager for their environmental services department. He recently retired from FEMA where he reviewed projects in the process of disaster recovery to facilitate consistent compliance with local, state, federal, and Tribal laws as they pertained to environmental and historic preservation. He received his M.A. in cultural anthropology in 2015 and his Ph.D. in applied anthropology in 2019 from the University of Montana. He is a co-owner, instructor, and consultant at Bone and Stone Anthrosciences, LLC, with his wife, Dr. Teresa A. White.

Samuel has participated in numerous archaeological projects, surveys, and excavations in Yellowstone National Park; at various United States Air Force bases across the continental United States; on the island of Saipan in the CNMI; and in the Aysén region of Chilean Patagonia.

Preface

Death scenes involving human skeletal remains are unique from other types of scenes. First, the investigator is tasked with the challenge of differentiating human from nonhuman bones. Then, if the bones are identified as human, the investigator must properly recover and preserve those remains, just as they would other items of evidentiary value.

In a perfect world, a forensic anthropologist would attend every scene where human remains exist, to assist the investigator. Unfortunately, that is neither practical nor feasible. Therefore, forensic anthropologists have been on the ground teaching professionals how to conduct proper recoveries to preserve the integrity of unidentified remains. Years of co-instruction of hands-on scene recovery methods have given us the opportunity to interact directly with investigators, listen to their feedback, and incorporate their needs into our short courses.

We teach these courses to diverse groups of professionals including national and international law enforcement personnel, coroners and medicolegal investigators, crime scene investigators, evidence recovery technicians, and other forensic scene investigators. Despite the abundant experience and education these professionals bring to the table, we recognized a training gap between death scene recovery courses with and without skeletal remains. Therefore, we sought to fill that gap with our hands-on courses. Unfortunately, not every scene investigator will be able to attend these courses. The alternative to acquiring this experiential information from our course, or others like it, is to read a book about the processes.

Although there are several great books available on human remains recovery methods, many are written for the academic audience and are narrative-heavy. Few written resources cater to the professionals who do this work on a day-to-day basis. Therefore, we wanted to create something for them – for YOU: A visual guide to show the bones investigators may encounter in the field and to demonstrate the logical sequence of steps in the recovery process emphasizing documentation and preservation. We believe this field guide will not only fill that gap in knowledge but also do so in an easy-to-comprehend, demonstrative way.

Finally, the goal is the same for all professionals involved in human remains recoveries: Provide answers to the loved ones left behind, provide justice to victims or fair adjudication to the accused, and preserve the honor and dignity of the person you have found. Their lives mattered.

Thank you for trusting us! We hope you enjoy our field guide!

Acknowledgments

The authors would like to express their deep appreciation to all the law enforcement officers, crime scene specialists, medical examiners, coroners and medicolegal death investigators, evidence recovery and forensic technicians, special agents and military personnel, anthropologists and archaeologists, fire investigators, and college students who attended our courses and helped us grow. We are especially thankful for those who allowed us to photograph them for this field guide. It would not have been possible without you!

We want to thank the following agencies and institutions for hosting our short courses: Bellingham WA Police Department, Kootenai County Sheriff's Office (Hayden, ID), Martin County Sheriff's Office (Stuart, FL), MCAS Miramar Forensic Investigation Center (San Diego, CA), New York State Police (Albany, NY), and the Center for Applied Forensics at Jacksonville State University (Anniston, AL).

The authors would also like to thank the following people:

Dr. Sharon Plotkin who introduced Dr. Teresa White to Mark Listewnik, senior editor at CRC Press, who gave the authors the awesome opportunity to write this field guide. She also provided advice from her many years of experience as a certified crime scene investigator and faculty member at Miami Dade College in Florida.

Dr. Rick Snow who gave sage advice for the manual and mentored Dr. Parsons throughout her graduate career teaching her fundamentals of scene recovery and effective communication with medicolegal personnel.

Phil Sanfilippo and Tri-Tech Forensics Training for facilitating many of our short courses, where we met such amazing people.

Sergeant Tony Dodd and the Blount County Sheriff's office for improving our azimuth mapping handout.

Finally, we would like to thank Dr. Michael Finnegan for not only his mentorship but also for donating part of his anatomical teaching collection to Dr. Teresa White and Dr. Samuel White. Several photographs featuring human skeletal remains, in Part one of this field guide, were possible because of Dr. Finnegan's thoughtfulness and generosity.

Introduction

The thorough, legally defensible recovery of human skeletal remains is an important skill set for the forensic investigator. Scenes involving suspected human bones pose several challenges: (1) the investigator must differentiate human from nonhuman bones, (2) if human, the remains must be properly documented and recovered, and (3) the remains must be preserved to facilitate further scientific analysis. If the investigator lacks training for these types of scenes, the evidence may not be identified or recovered and may become damaged. Furthermore, without proper training, scene investigators may unintentionally compromise the integrity of the civil or criminal case.

Fortunately, there are a number of outstanding continuing education short courses geared toward these topics. Unfortunately, not everyone has access to or funding for such training. This field guide is designed to support the need for training and is written for all law enforcement personnel, crime scene investigators, medical examiners and coroners, evidence technicians, medicolegal death investigators, anthropologists, and more at all levels of experience. The forthcoming pages are filled with photographs of human and nonhuman skeletal elements detailing the recovery processes from start to finish as demonstrated by actual forensic professionals. From the author's experience, it is more effective to show the materials and processes instead of just describing them. The materials and methods outlined in this field guide can be used for all types of scenarios including indoor, outdoor, rural, and urban settings, as well as other challenging environments.

An essential member of the medicolegal community is the **forensic anthropologist**, who specializes in the analysis of human skeletal remains for the purposes of personal identification and reconstructing the circumstances surrounding death. Additionally, forensic anthropologists are trained in the recovery of surface scattered and buried bones including those where the examination of fleshed, decomposed, and burned remains is required. They are also instrumental in search, recovery, and investigations of deaths at mass disaster scenes and where human rights violations have occurred.

It is often the case that forensic anthropologists are asked to perform scientific analyses on skeletal remains *after* the recovery has occurred without their assistance. Consequently, the anthropologist may be left without a comprehensive overview of the **context** from which those remains were recovered. And, if the context is compromised, it could lead to undesirable outcomes.

As the expertise of a forensic anthropologist is unfortunately not always available, this field guide is designed to provide investigative personnel with straightforward, scientifically defensible strategies to recover human skeletal remains. The goal of this manual is to prevent the unintentional destruction of a scene or misidentified evidence by well-meaning personnel. This is not a book with the intention to teach anyone how to be a forensic anthropologist, **archaeologist**, or **osteologist**. Rather, it provides instructions in plain language to identify human skeletal materials, conduct basic recovery operations, and preserve evidence for scientific analysis in the absence of a forensic anthropologist. Overall, the goal is to process these types of scenes correctly the first time. Remember, the context of the scene is altered when the first piece of evidence is collected. There is only one chance to get it right.

This field guide is divided into three parts: (1) identification, (2) recovery, and (3) preservation. Part one is an introduction to bone identification providing photos of skeletal materials including adult and **subadult** (juvenile) bones as well as various animal bones. This section can be used as a reference guide in the field to help when human bones are suspected. Part two demonstrates search, recovery, and preservation methods for human skeletal remains and other items of evidentiary value. It details accurate, meticulous recovery methods for **surface scatter** scenes and **clandestine graves**. Part three discusses the preservation of human skeletal remains when collected and packaged for transport. It also emphasizes the relevance of legal issues concerning the treatment of human remains, by breaking down several laws into digestible content. Finally, this section asserts why investigators should strive to recognize and understand the moral and ethical responsibility to preserve human dignity, not only in consideration for the deceased individual but also to show deference for their surviving loved ones. These efforts will help to instill and preserve public confidence in the medicolegal death investigation system.

The appendices in the back of this guide include equipment lists, documentation paperwork, and a variety of suggested readings and additional resources. The documentation paperwork can be photocopied for use on scene. The recovery methods in this field guide are designed to integrate into any agency's existing scene protocols and adapted as needed.

DOI: 10.4324/9781032623320-1

Identification

1

HILLARY R. PARSONS AND TERESA A. WHITE

Contents

Adult human osteology

Introduction

Osteology is the study of bones and the foundation for the work of forensic anthropologists. Forensic anthropologists are skilled practitioners of all areas of osteology including:

- Bone formation.
- Bone growth and development.
- Pathological conditions.
- Differentiating human from nonhuman bones.
- Determining contemporary remains from archaeological human remains.
- Estimating the minimum number of individuals (MNI) present.
- Identifying individualizing characteristics and creating a **biological profile**.
- How bone responds to external forces such as trauma.
- How bone deteriorates over time (**taphonomy**).

The goal of this section is to introduce basic human osteology for the medicolegal professional for identification purposes only. Distinguishing human from nonhuman skeletal remains is the first step when suspected human skeletal remains are encountered on a scene. Correct bone identification at the beginning of an investigation will determine if scene recovery is required. If the bones are not human and a poaching situation is not suspected, a scene response will not be necessary, and the bones can be disposed of according to agency protocols.

When a bone is encountered, first ask, does the bone look human? Not sure? No problem. Reference this guide and reach out to a forensic anthropologist by text or email with clear photographs of the bone from multiple angles with a measurement scale for reference. Their expert opinion should be considered to prevent the unintentional misidentification of remains. When possible, do not remove bone from the scene without proper documentation, just as you would not remove a piece of evidence/weapon from a scene.

Anatomical terminology

There are approximately 206 bones in the adult human skeleton. The first step in identifying them is to know their position in the human body. Figure 1.1 shows the

DOI: 10.4324/9781032623320-2

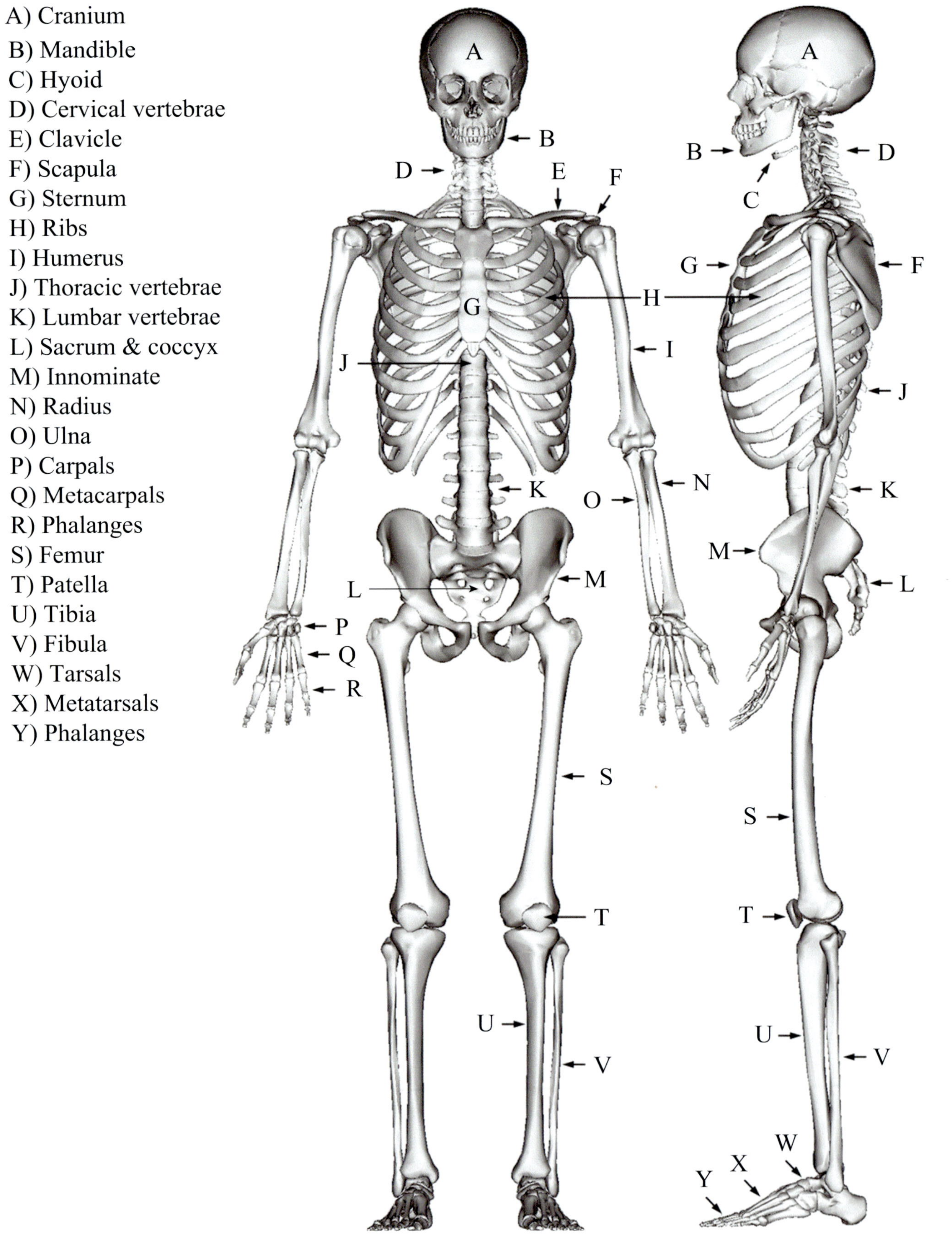

Figure 1.1 The adult human skeleton in anatomical position (from Dupras et al., 2012, CRC Press, Taylor & Francis, Boca Raton, FL).

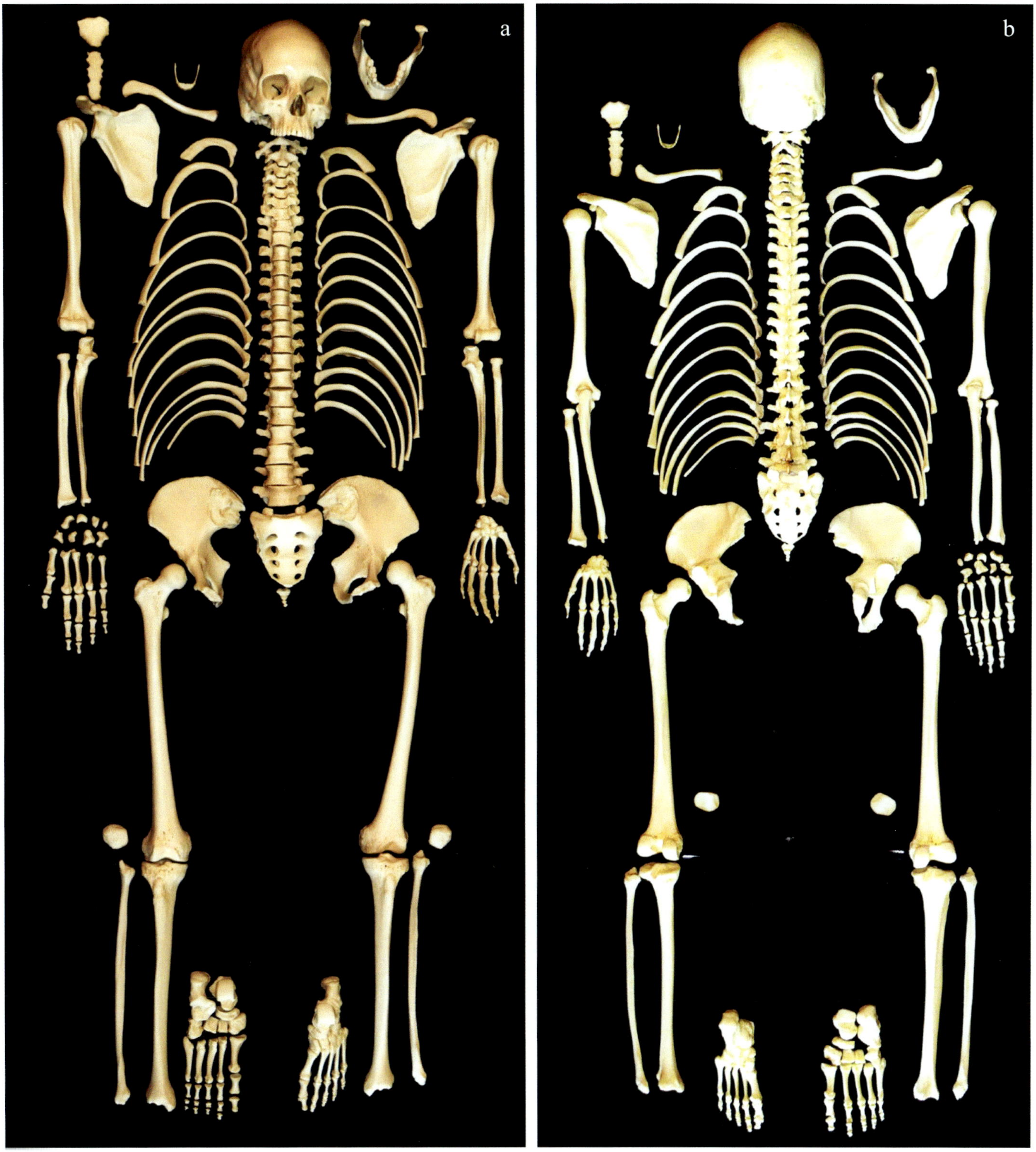

Figure 1.2 Adult human skeleton. (a) Anterior view. (b) Posterior view.

adult human skeleton in **anatomical position**; that is, the way the bones appear in the human body in their correct location and orientation. When in anatomical position, the body is forward facing with arms to the side and palms forward. In this position, the bones are visible from the front and the long bones are uncrossed.

Figure 1.2 shows the adult skeleton from the **anterior** perspective (from the front) and from the **posterior** perspective (from the back).

Figure 1.3 shows the directional terms in relation to the human body versus a nonhuman animal standing on all four limbs. The human directional terms are defined as follows:

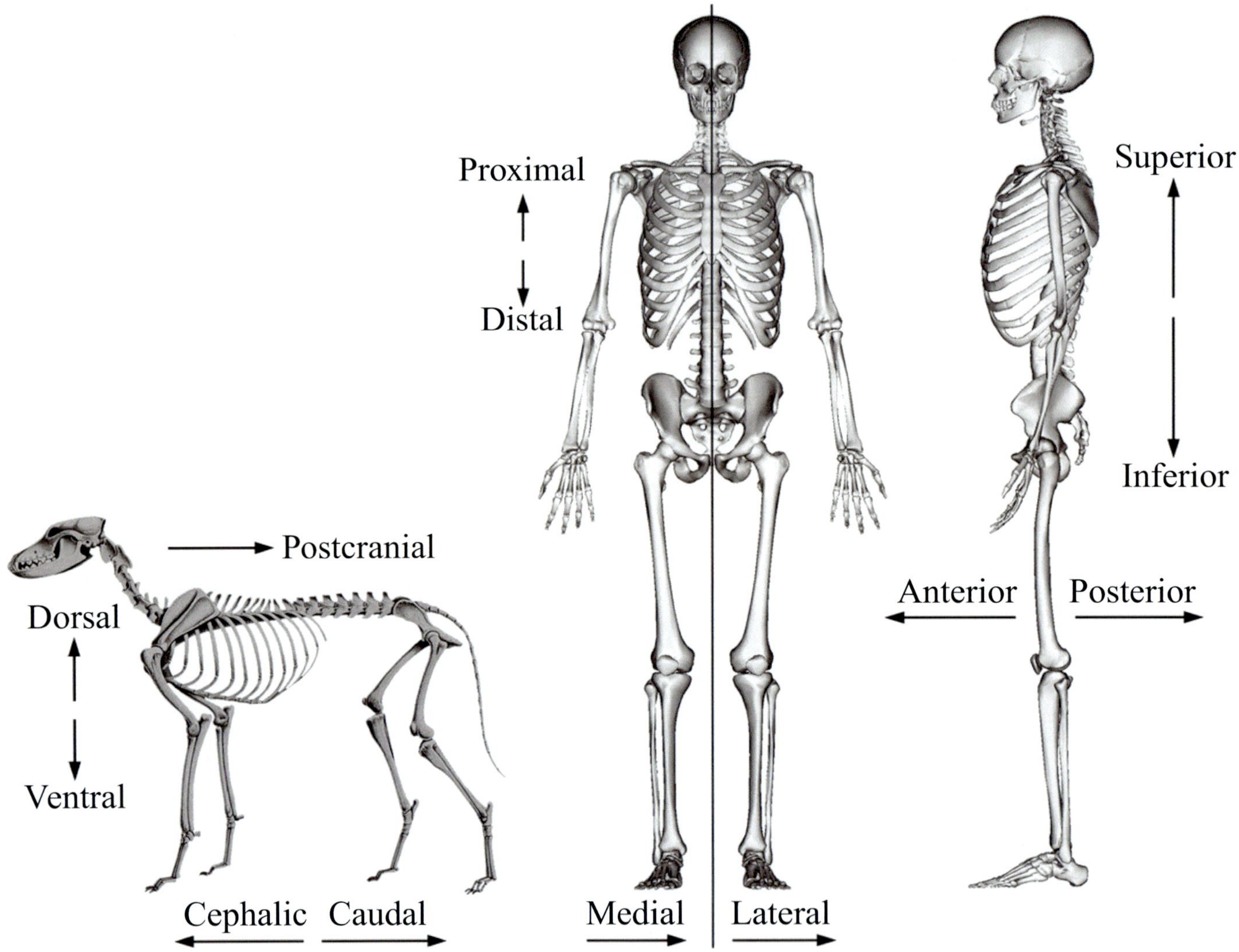

Figure 1.3 Directional terms to describe the position of skeletal remains (from Dupras et al., 2012, CRC Press, Taylor & Francis, Boca Raton, FL).

- **Anterior**: the position of a bone or portion of the bone oriented toward the front of the body when in anatomical position.
- **Posterior**: the position of a bone or portion of bone oriented toward the back of the body.
- **Medial**: the position of a bone or portion of the bone toward the **midline** of the body.
- **Lateral**: the position of a bone or portion of the bone away from the midline of the body.
- **Superior**: the position of a bone or portion of the bone above or toward the cranium.
- **Inferior**: the position of a bone or portion of the bone below or away from the cranium.
- **Proximal**: the portion of a bone positioned nearest to the trunk (midline) when in anatomical position.
- **Distal**: the position of a bone or portion of the bone furthest from the trunk (midline) when in anatomical position.
- **Dorsal**: the position of a bone or portion of the bone toward the back of the body. Sometimes used in place of posterior.
- **Plantar**: a bone or portion of bone oriented toward the bottom of the foot. Used only when describing bones of the foot.

There are different types of bones that serve a particular function in the body. Some examples include:

- **Flat bones**: bones of the cranium and ribs.
- **Long bones**: bones that are longer than they are wide typically found in the limbs.
- **Short bones**: bones found in the wrists and ankles.
- **Irregular bones**: vertebrae bones and pelvic bones.
- **Sesamoid bones**: bones that lie within ligaments near a joint.

Some bones are **paired**, meaning there are two, a left and a right. An example is the left and right humerus (bone of the arm). Examples of **unpaired** bones include the vertebrae (bones of the spine) and hyoid (a bone in the neck). **Cranial bones** are bones of the head, and **postcranial bones** describe bones of the skeleton except those of the head.

Bones of the adult human skeleton

The skull

The human **skull** is made up of 28 bones when the three pairs of ear ossicles are included. The skull includes the mandible (jaw) and is called the **cranium** when the mandible is absent. The external surface of flat cranial bones is called the **ectocranial** surface while the internal surface is called the **endocranial** surface. Figure 1.4 shows the **articulated** skull from six views. Figure 1.5 shows the **disarticulated** skull and the ear ossicles. Figure 1.6 shows the paired bones of the skull and the unpaired bones of the skull.

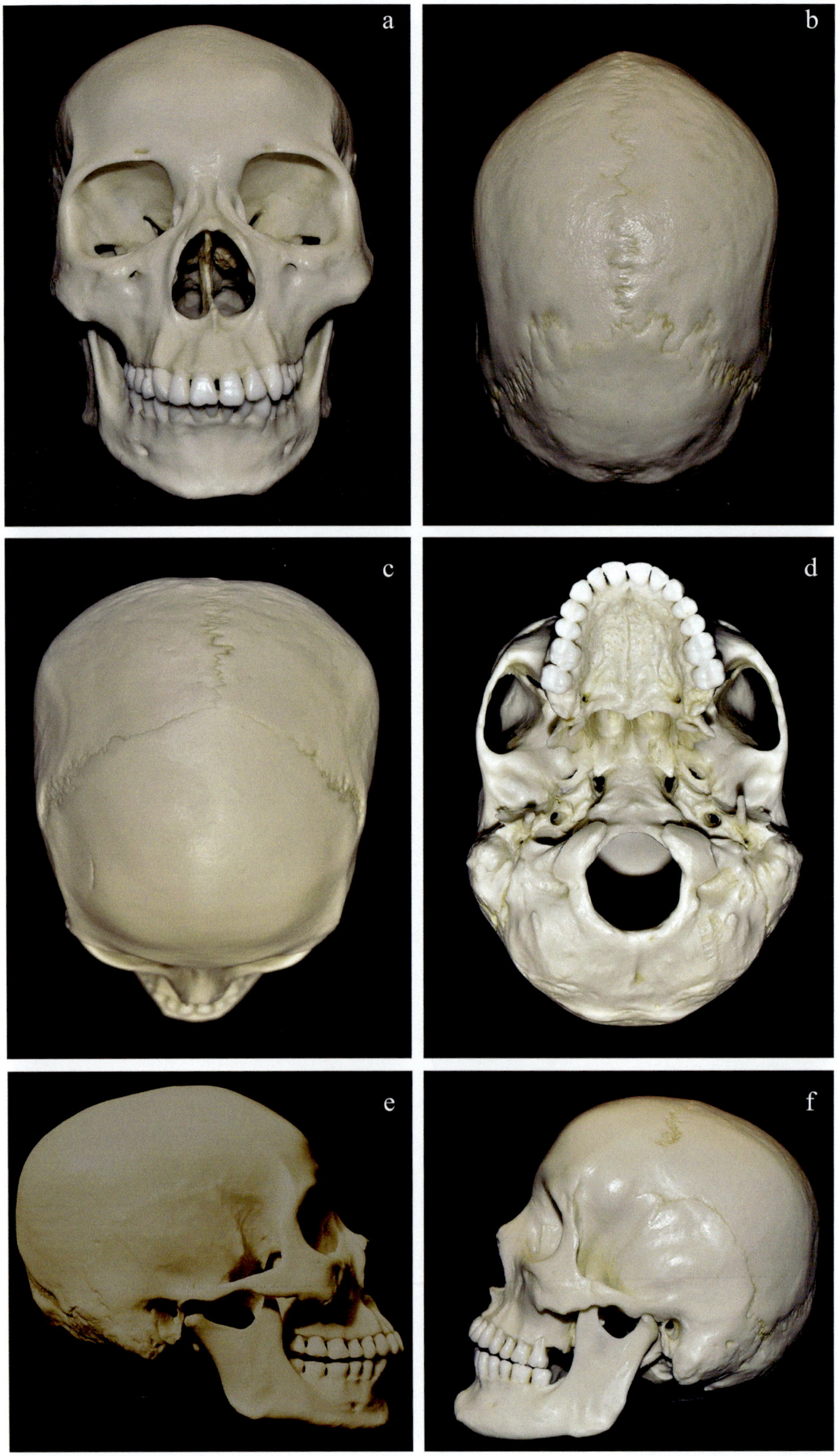

Figure 1.4 The skull. (a) Anterior view. (b) Posterior view. (c) Superior view. (d) Inferior view. (e) Right lateral view. (f) Left lateral view.

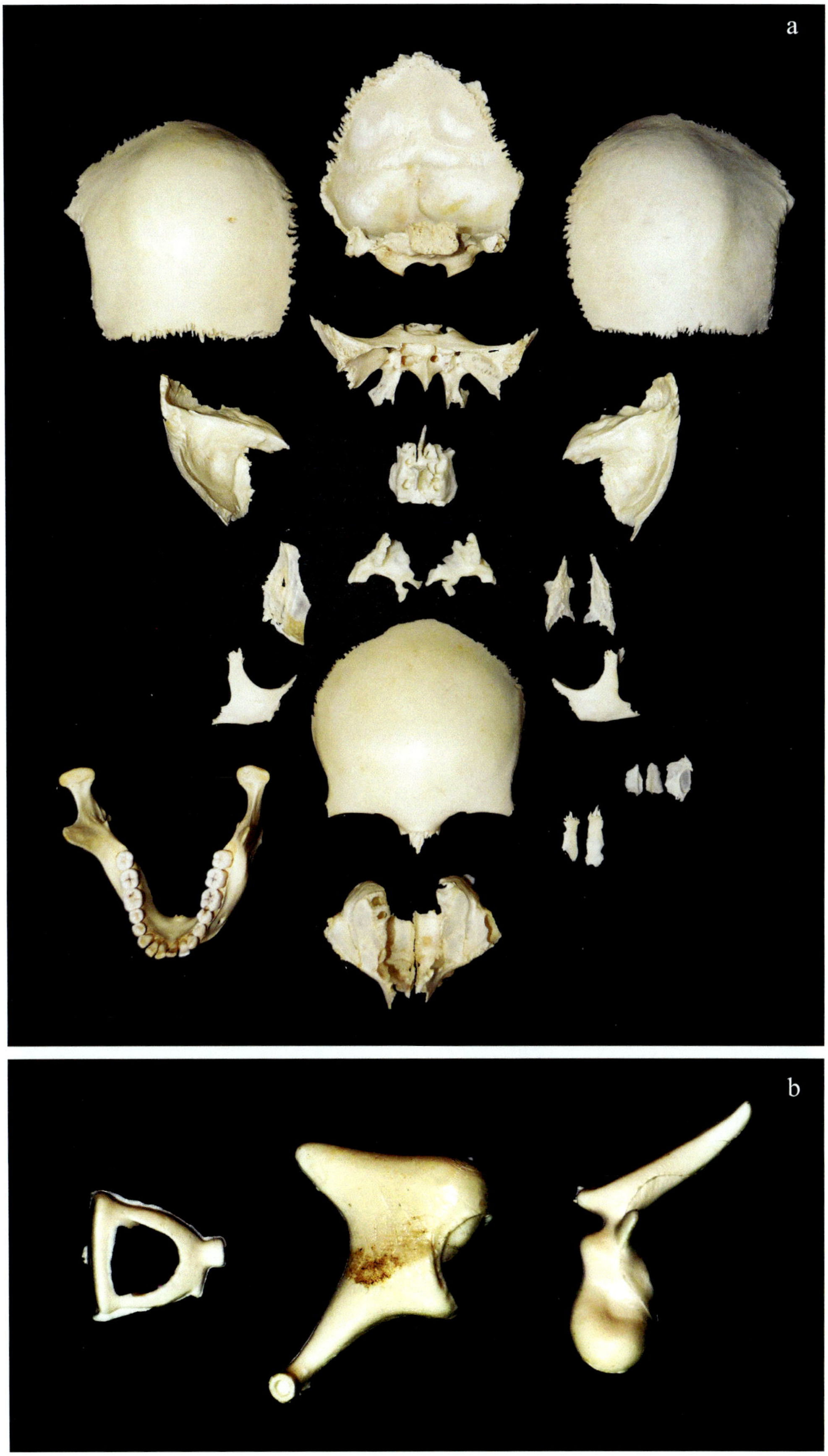

Figure 1.5 (a) Disarticulated skull. (b) Auditory ossicles from left to right: stapes, incus, and malleus.

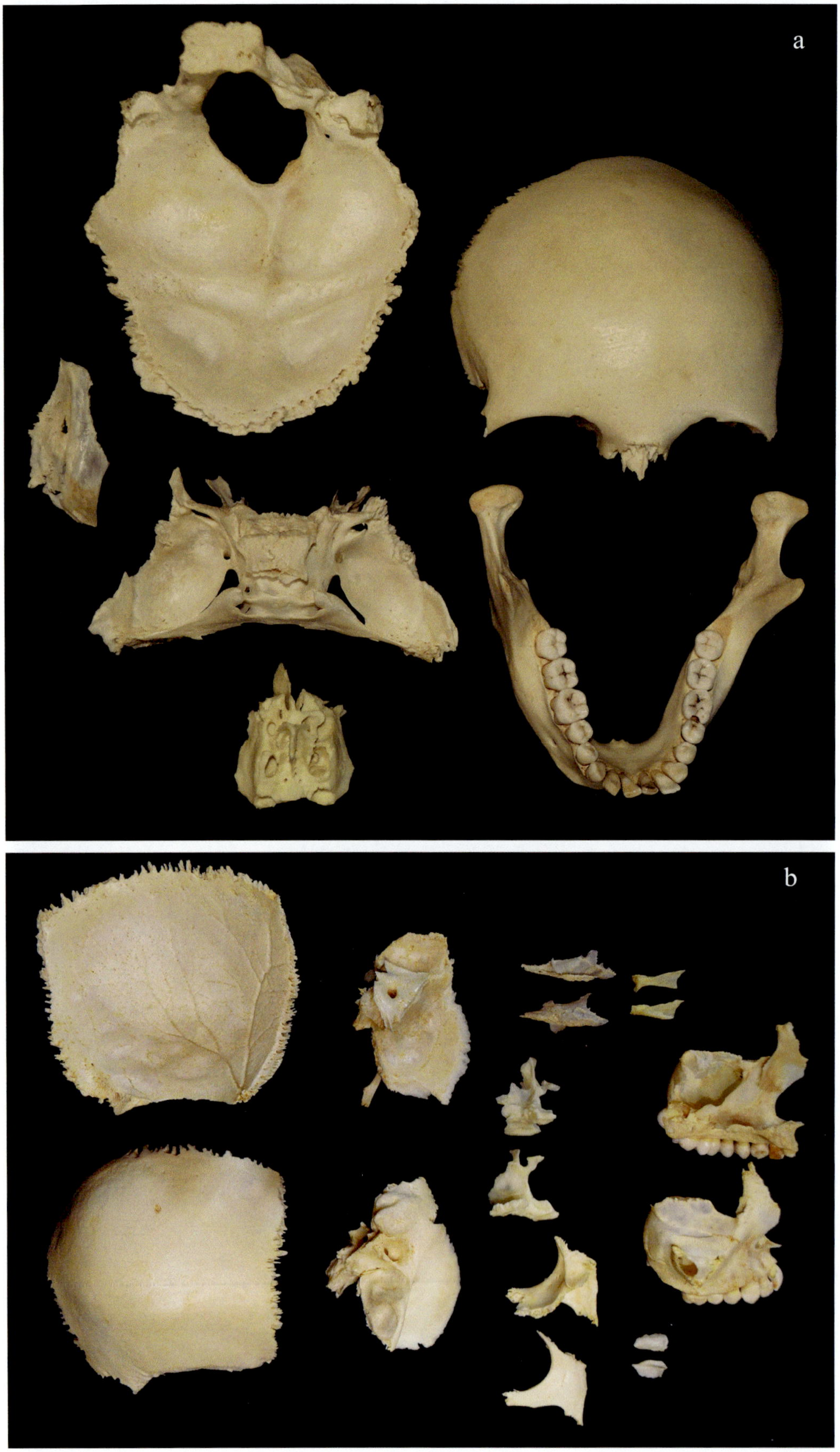

Figure 1.6 (a) Unpaired skull elements. (b) Paired skull elements.

The frontal bone The frontal is an unpaired cranial bone that makes up the forehead and the top of the eye orbits (Figure 1.7). The orbital plate on the endocranial surface has a bumpy or wavy appearance unique to the frontal bone. The sinuses located in the frontal bone (frontal sinuses) have been found to be a unique identifier among individuals and can provide positive identification when antemortem radiographs or imaging can be compared.

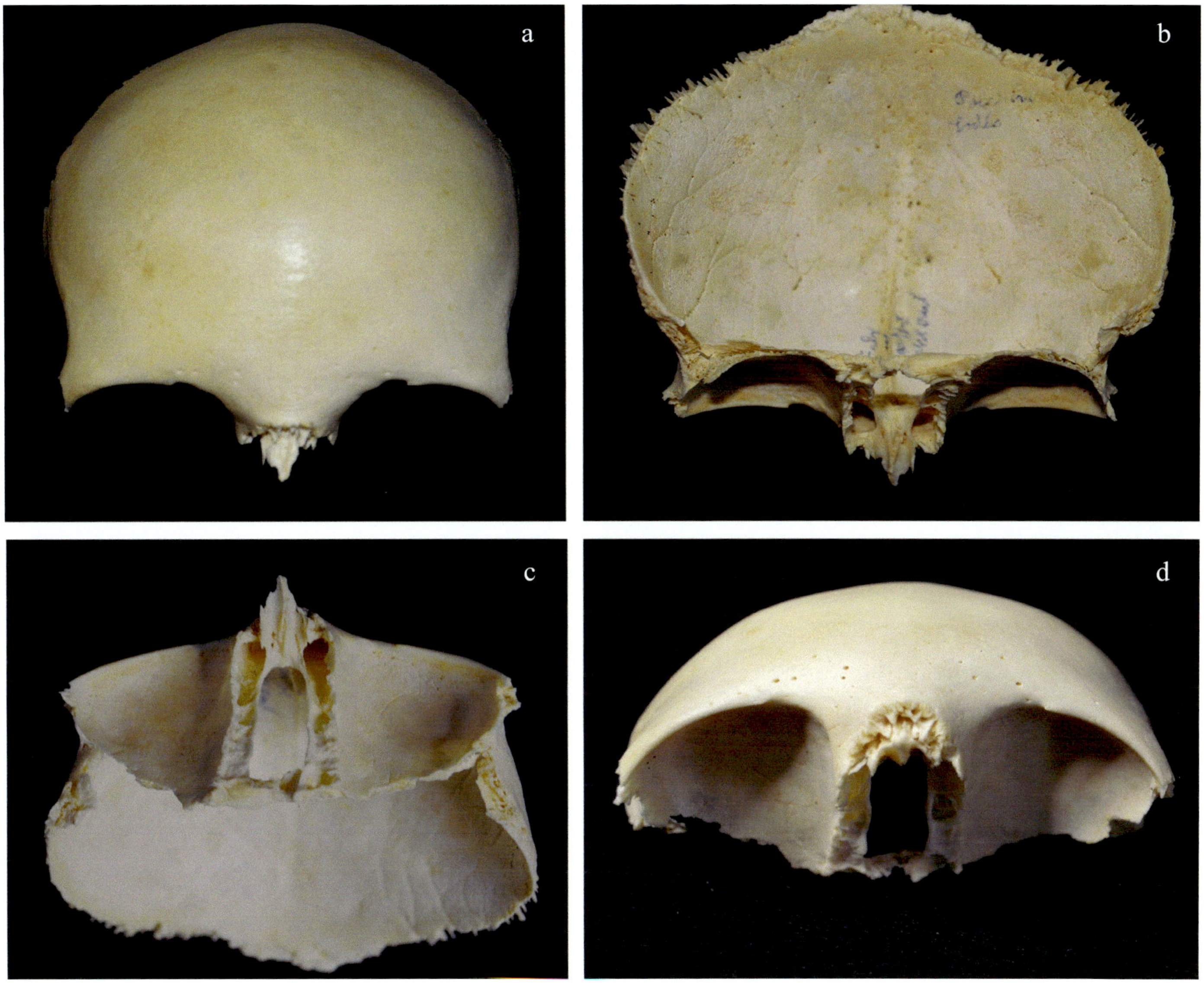

Figure 1.7 The frontal bone. (a) Anterior (ectocranial) vertical view. (b) Posterior (endocranial) vertical view. (c) Inferior view. (d) Anteroinferior view.

The parietal bones The parietals are paired bones that make up large portions of the top and sides of the cranium (Figure 1.8). The endocranial surface has a distinctive pattern of carvings that look like tree branches created by the middle meningeal arteries.

Figure 1.8 The parietal bone. Left parietal bone, endocranial view. Right parietal bone, ectocranial view.

The occipital bone The occipital is a thick unpaired bone that makes up the back and underside of the cranium. There is a large hole **(foramen)** in the base of the occipital where the spinal cord passes through from the brain to the spine (Figure 1.9). This hole is called the **foramen magnum**.

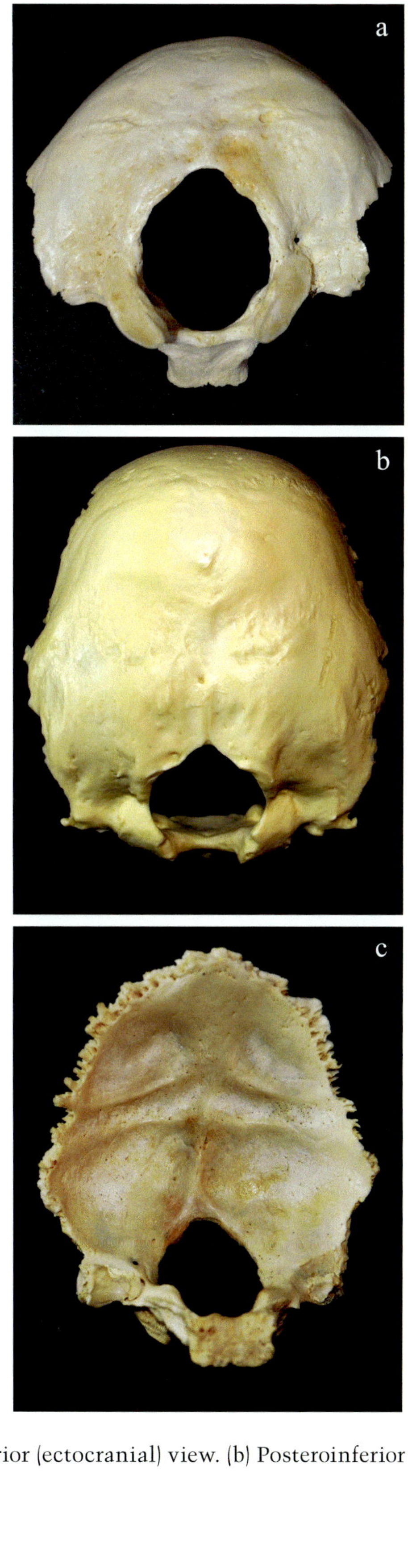

Figure 1.9 The occipital bone. (a) Inferior (ectocranial) view. (b) Posteroinferior (ectocranial) view. (c) Anterior (endocranial) view.

The temporal bones The temporals are paired bones that comprise the sides of the cranium and house the ear (Figure 1.10). The portion that contains the inner ear is called the **petrous portion (pyramid),** and it is the densest bone in the human body. It usually preserves longer than other bones in buried and archaeological contexts.

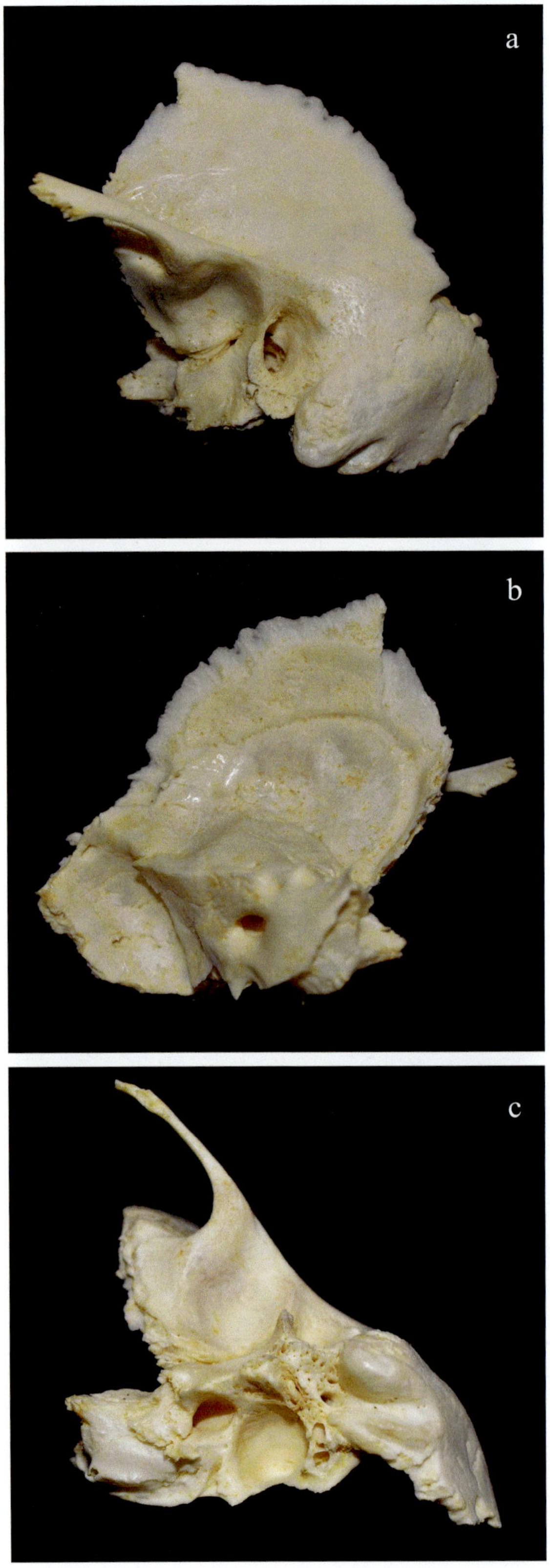

Figure 1.10 The temporal bone. (a) Left ectocranial view. (b) Left endocranial view. (c) Left inferior view.

The sphenoid bone The sphenoid is an unpaired bone situated in the middle of the cranium behind the face making up the back of the eye orbits (Figure 1.11). It is an irregularly shaped bone having the appearance of a bat or butterfly. Due to its location and connections with many bones of the cranium and face, it is rarely found in isolation.

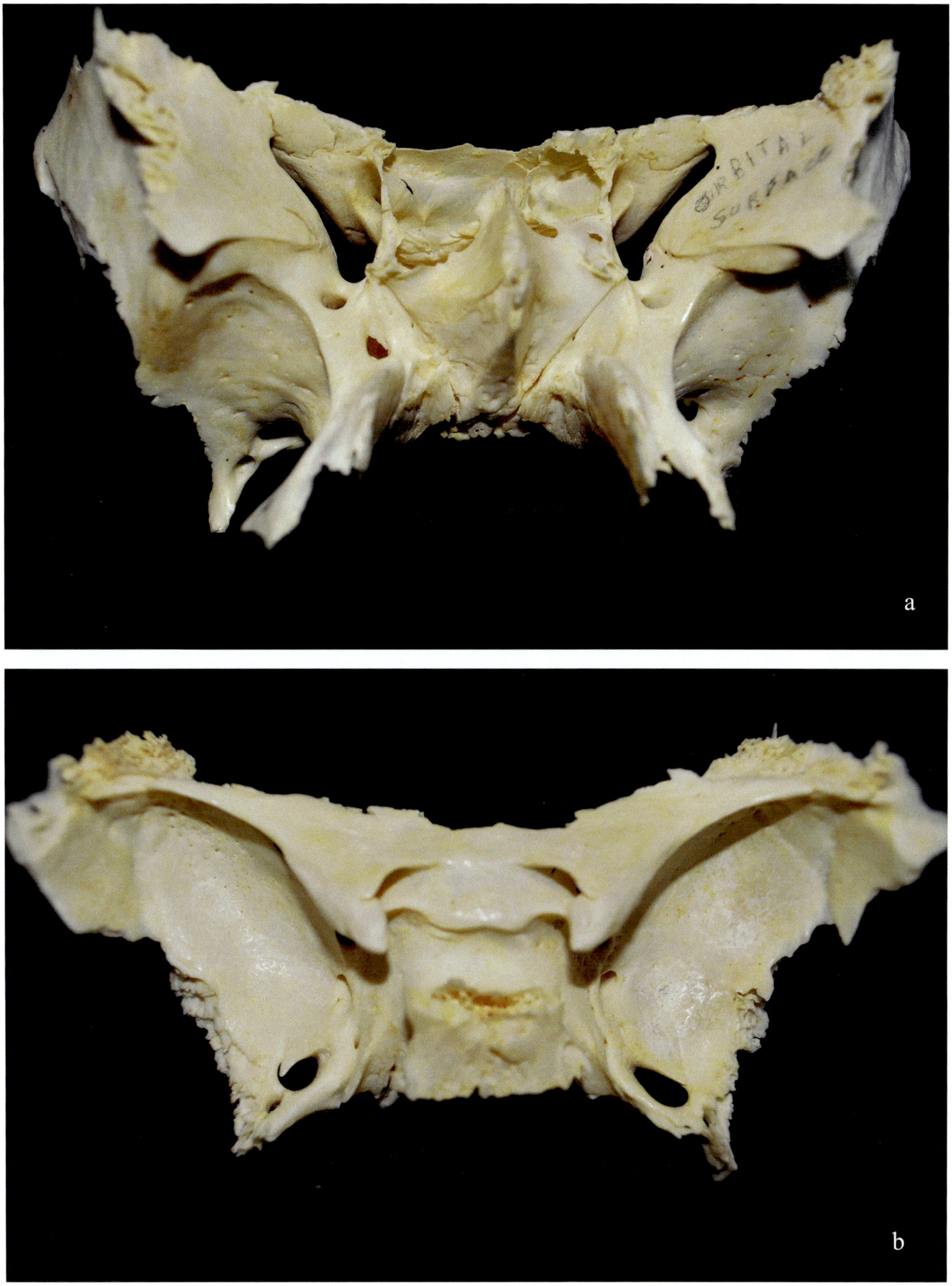

Figure 1.11 The sphenoid bone. (a) Anterior view. (b) Posterior view.

Bones of the face (facial bones) The facial bones consist of both paired and unpaired elements (Figures 1.12 and 1.13). These bones are more delicate than the cranial bones and break easily when exposed to harsh environmental conditions, improper handling, and inadequate packaging and transport of remains. The bones of the face include:

- Maxilla (paired) the upper jaw. It contains tooth sockets to hold the top teeth. It forms the nasal opening the bottom of the eye orbits, and a portion of the roof of the mouth.
- Lacrimal bones (paired): these bones include the canal for the tear duct.
- Nasal bones (paired): bones of the nasal bridge.
- Inferior nasal conchae (paired): housed on the interior edges of the nose.
- Ethmoid (unpaired): centrally located behind the eye orbits. It is a spongy, fragile bone with numerous air pockets.
- Vomer (unpaired): located inside the nose and connects the maxilla to the ethmoid.
- Zygomatic bones (paired): the cheekbones.
- Palatine bones (paired): back portion of the roof of the mouth.

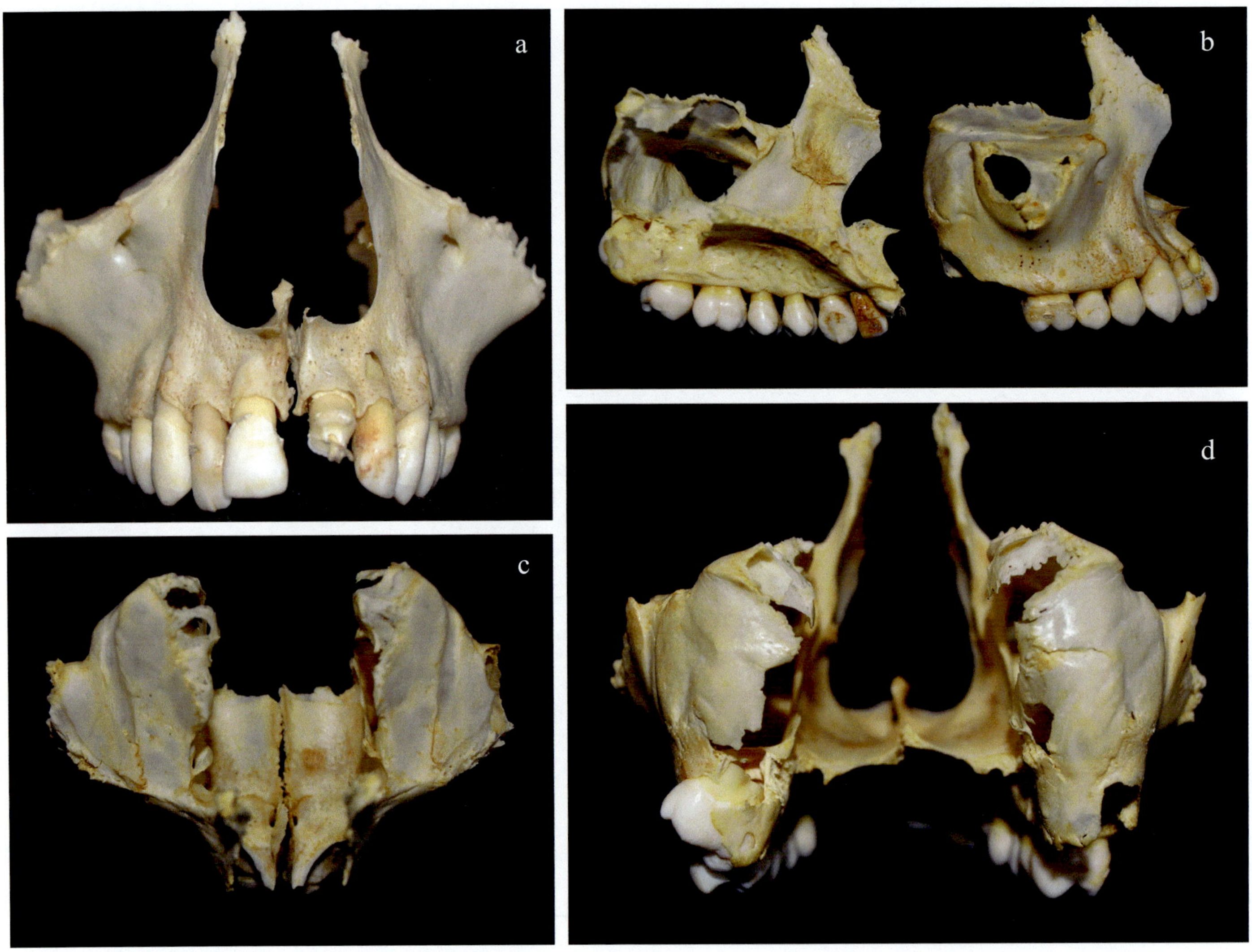

Figure 1.12 The maxilla. (a) Anterior view of the articulated right and left maxillae. (b) Medial view of the left maxilla (left) and lateral view of the right maxilla (right). (c) Superior view of the articulated maxillae. (d) Posterior view of the articulated maxillae.

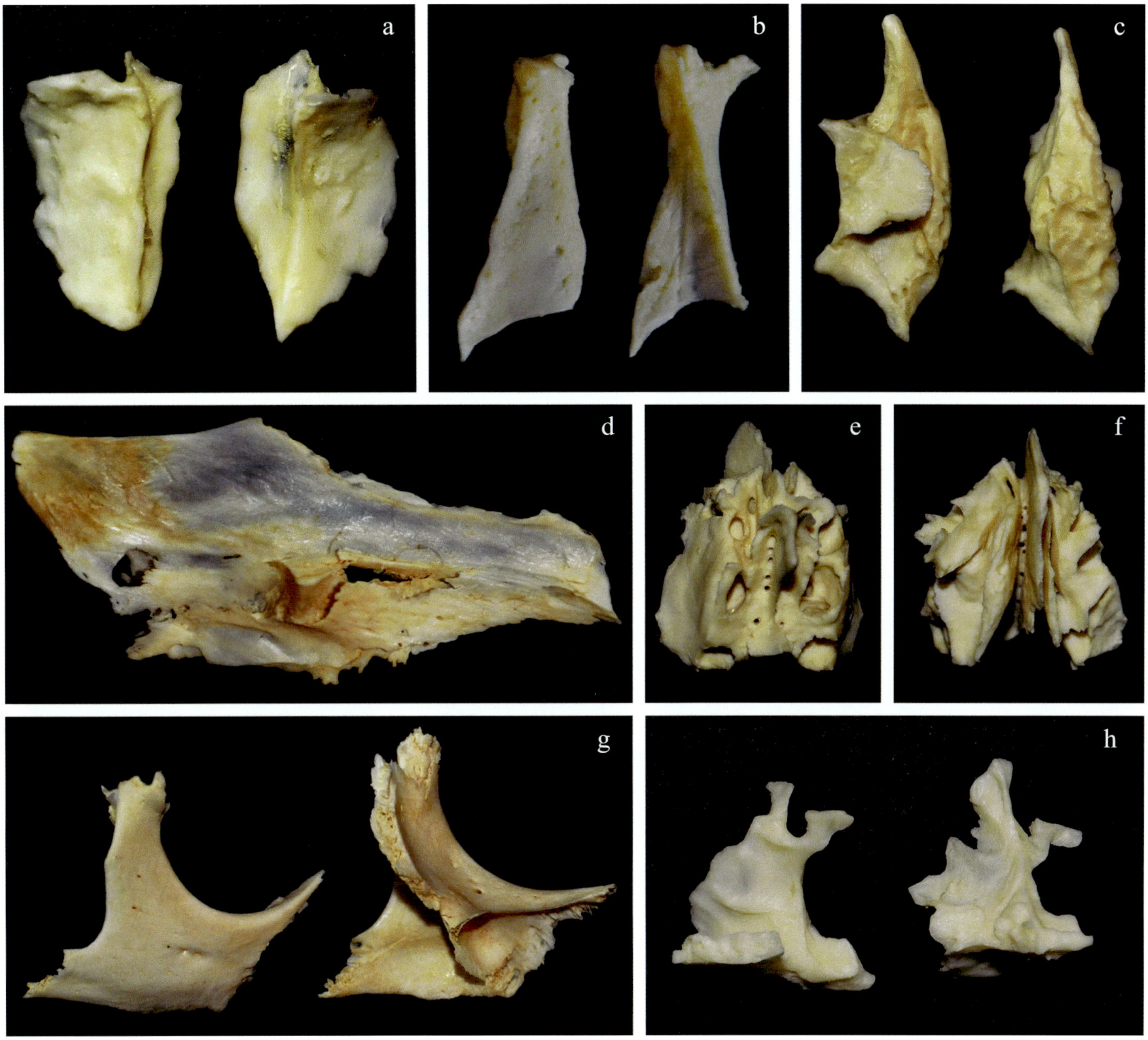

Figure 1.13 The small bones of the face. (a) Lacrimal bones. (b) Nasal bones. (c) Inferior nasal conchae. (d) Vomer. (e) Ethmoid bone, superior view. (f) Ethmoid, anterior view. (g) Zygomatic bone, anterior view (left) and posterior view (right). (h) Palatine bone, lateral view (left) and medial view (right).

The mandible The mandible is an unpaired bone also known as the jaw (Figure 1.14). It **articulates** with the temporal bone at the temporomandibular joint (TMJ). The mandible contains the lower teeth. Once skeletonized, the mandible will be completely disarticulated from the cranium.

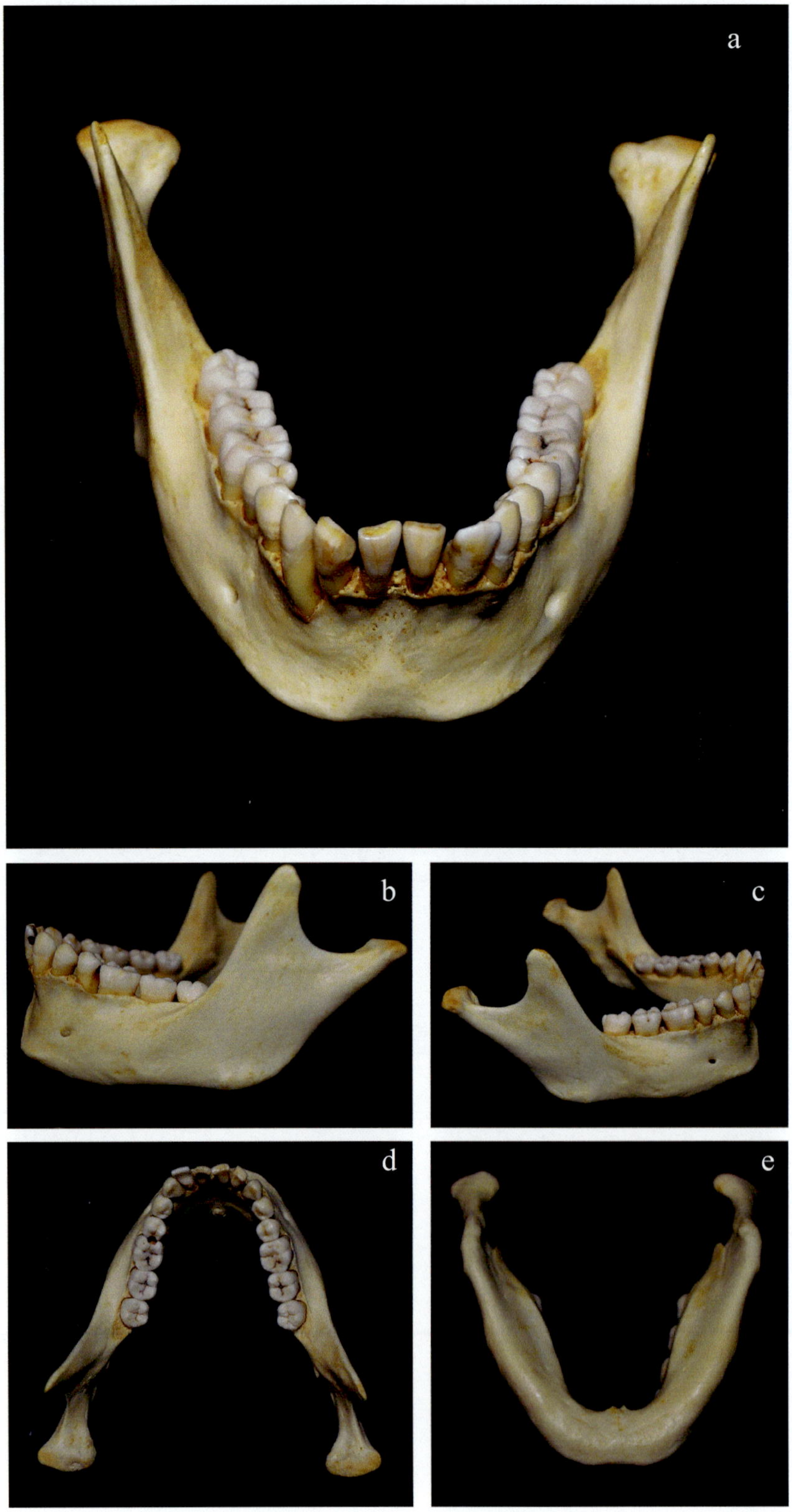

Figure 1.14 The mandible. (a) Anterosuperior view. (b) Left lateral view. (c) Right lateral view. (d) Superior view. (e) Inferior view.

Postcranial bones

The hyoid bone

The hyoid is a U-shaped bone located in the neck (Figure 1.15). It does not articulate with another bone but rather provides an attachment point for several muscles. The hyoid consists of five bones that fuse together to form the complete bone. The central portion is called the body, and the paired side portions are called the horns (lesser and greater).

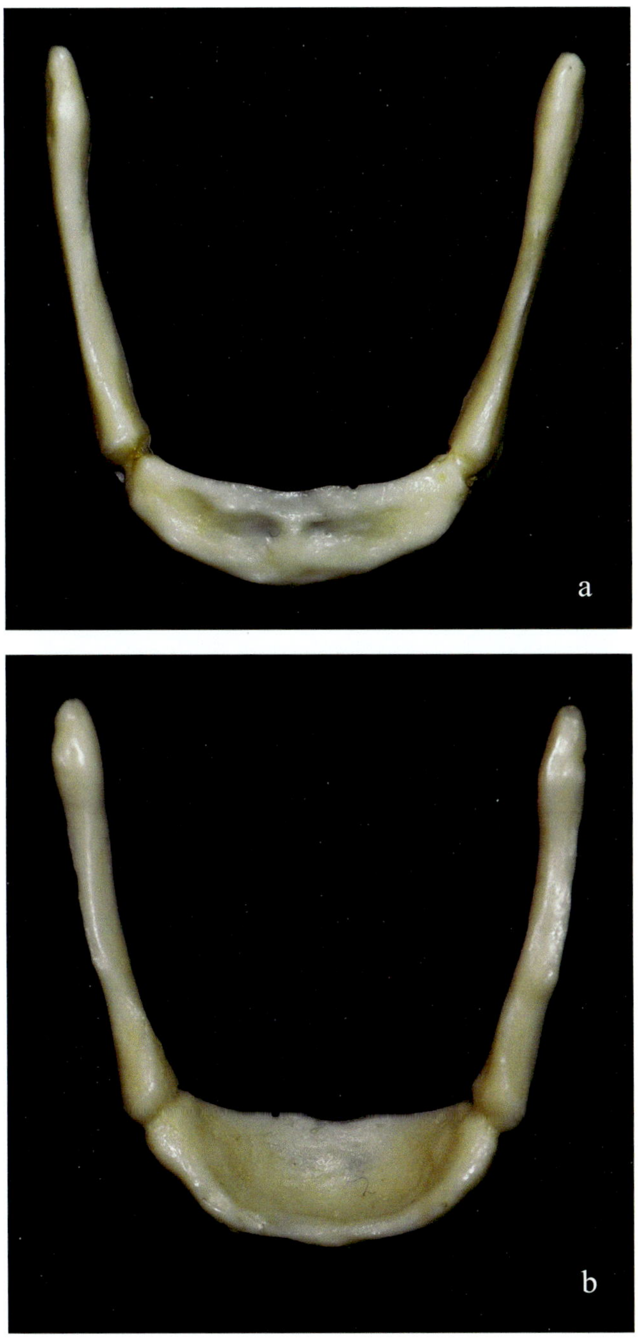

Figure 1.15 The hyoid. (a) Superior view. (b) Inferior view.

However, the hyoid does not always fuse. In adults, the hyoid can be represented by one fused U-shaped bone, separate unfused bones, or one horn fused to the body while the other remains unfused. All types of fusion are considered normal variations.

A fractured hyoid can be a result of compression to the neck region and is often implicated in cause and/or manner of death determinations. Trauma interpretation by a forensic anthropologist is needed to determine if the bones have been fractured or if they are naturally unfused.

Due to its small size and the potential for it to be represented by many even smaller pieces, this bone is not always recovered.

The sternum The sternum, also known as the breastbone, is a flat bone unpaired that provides an anchor point for the cartilage that attaches to the ribs and connects to the shoulder girdle (Figure 1.16). There are typically two portions of the bone: a triangular-shaped bone called the manubrium, and a narrow portion called the body. These bones typically fuse but are sometimes naturally unfused. A third portion called the xiphoid process is not always present. The xiphoid process is a bony extension on the inferior end of the sternal body.

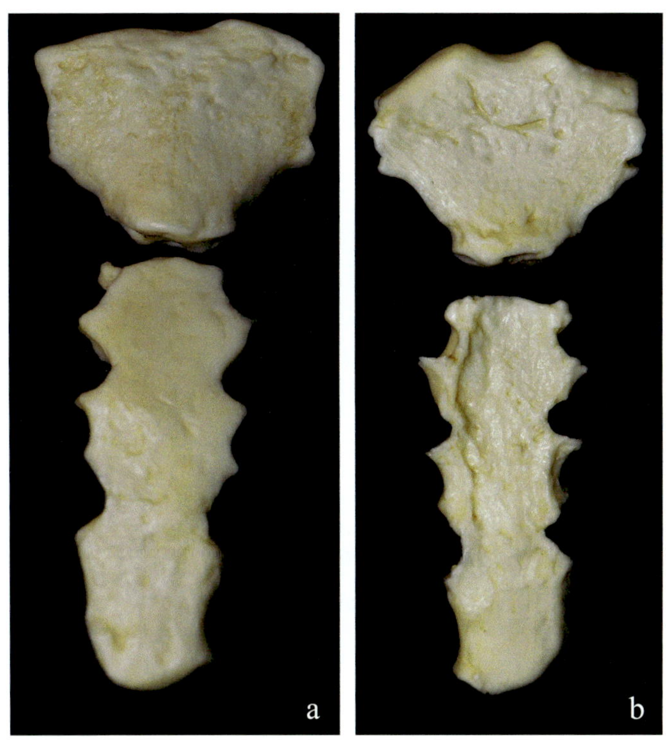

Figure 1.16 The sternum: the manubrium (top) and body (bottom). (a) Anterior view. (b) Posterior view.

The ribs

The ribs consist of 12 pairs of crescent-shaped bones in the thorax. There are 24 ribs in total (Figure 1.17). All ribs articulate posteriorly with the thoracic vertebrae. Ribs numbered one through ten articulate anteriorly to the cartilage that connects either directly or indirectly to the sternum. Ribs 11 and 12 do not connect to cartilage anteriorly and are called “floating ribs.” There is significant variation in the size and curvature of the ribs. Notably, rib number one is small, acutely curved, and flat, while ribs 11 and 12 lack significant curvature.

The vertebrae The vertebral column typically consists of 24 unpaired vertebrae and five segments of the sacrum. There are 7 cervical vertebrae (bones of the neck), 12 thoracic vertebrae (bones of the midback or thoracic region), and 5 lumbar vertebrae (bones of the lower back) (Figures 1.18 and 1.19). Each vertebra has a large hole called the vertebral foramen in the center of the bone. This hole is for the spinal cord. Each type of vertebrae has distinctive characteristics that can be used to identify them. All vertebrae except cervical vertebra number one (C1) have a **body**, which is the bulky portion of bone.

The cervical vertebrae (C1–C7) are generally smaller in size than the thoracic and lumbar vertebrae. Additionally, they possess a small hole (**transverse foramen**) on the laterally positioned projections of bones (**transverse processes**). These foramina are for the passage of veins, arteries, and nerves. Cervical vertebra number one (C1 or atlas) and cervical vertebra number two (C2 or axis) have slightly different features from cervical vertebrae numbered three through seven and can be seen in Figure 1.21a. Cervical vertebra number seven (C7) is a transitional vertebra and

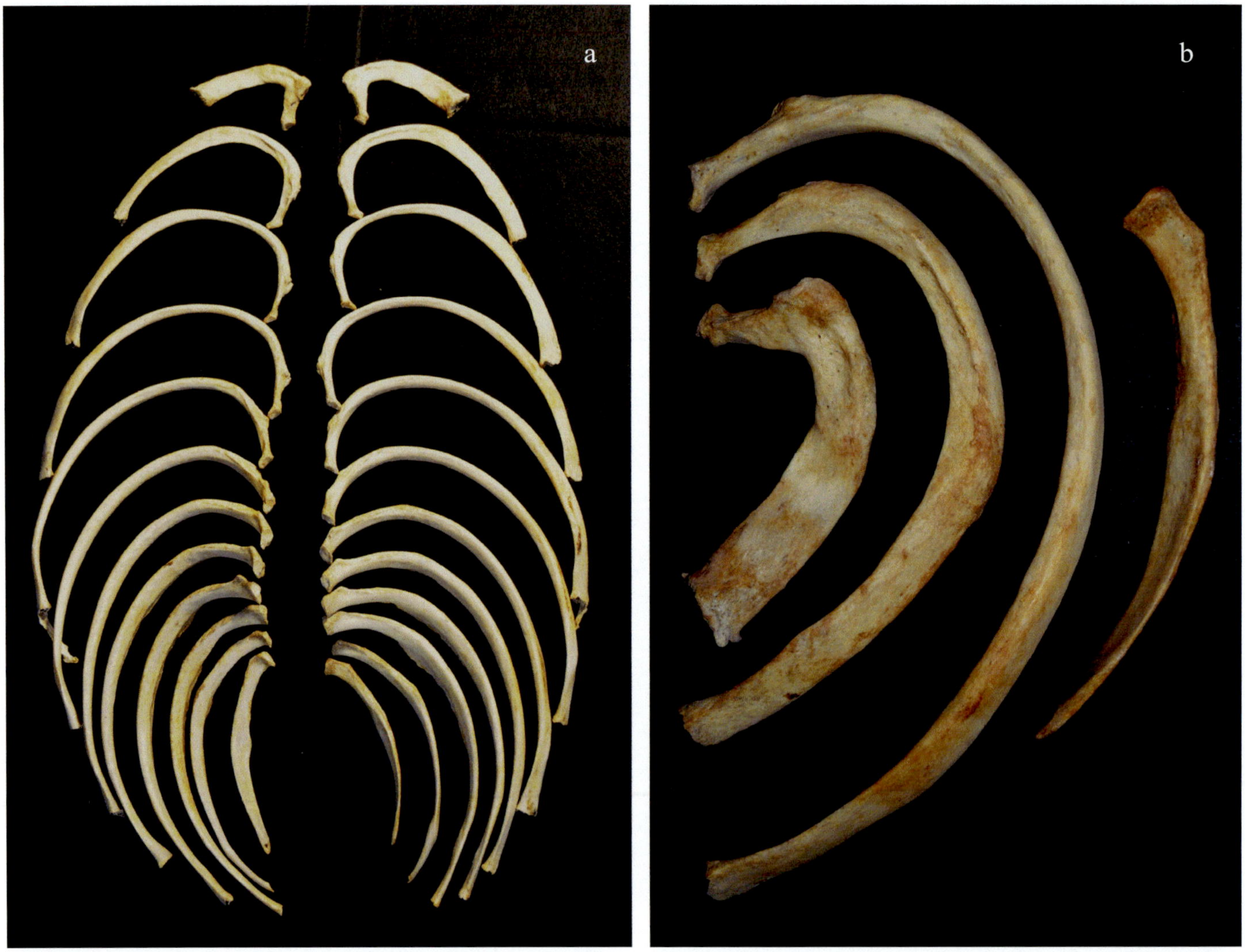

Figure 1.17 The ribs. (a) The complete set of left and right ribs. (b) From left to right: the variation of the shapes and sizes of the first rib, second rib, fourth rib, and twelfth rib.

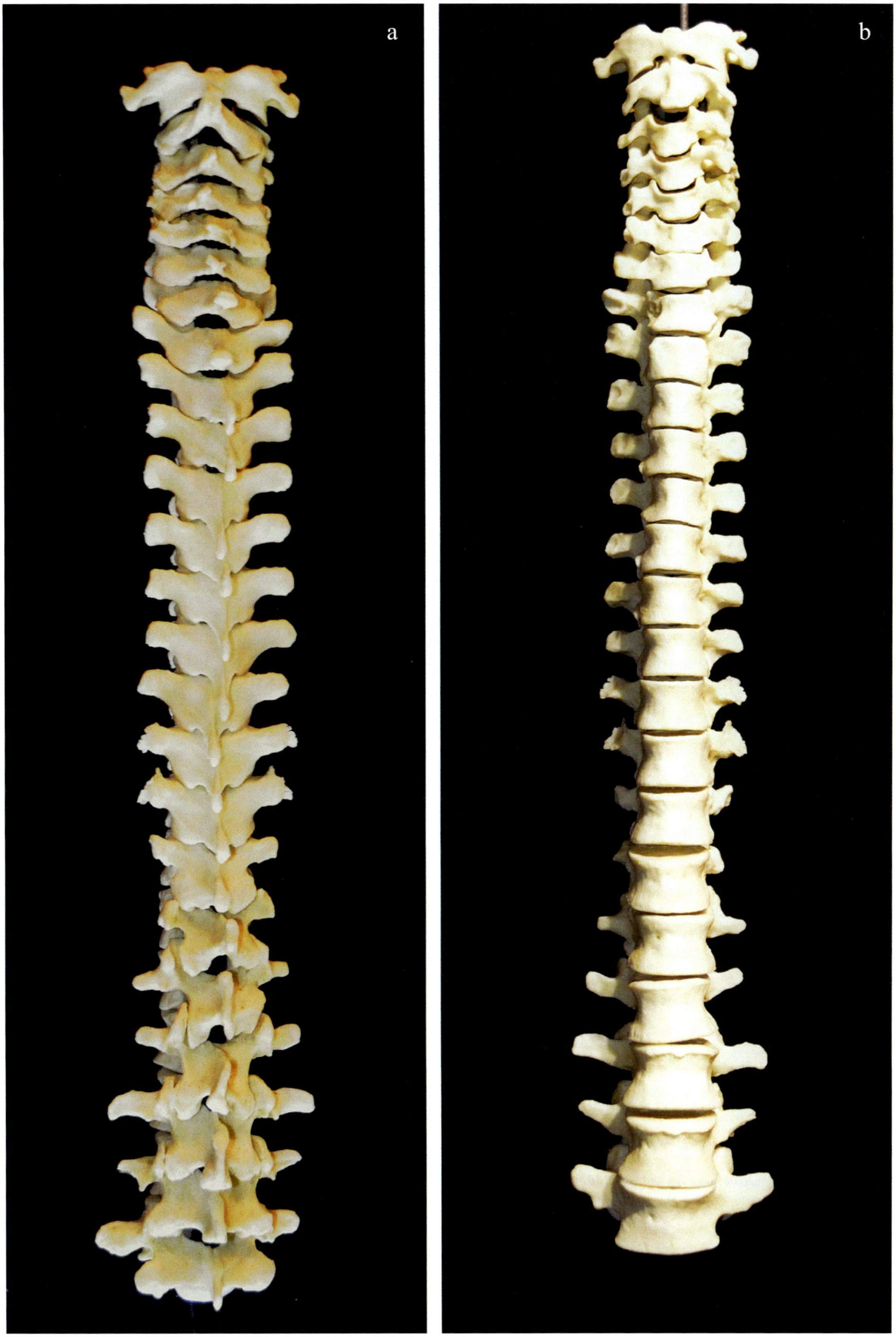

Figure 1.18 The articulated vertebral column without the sacrum. (a) Anterior view. (b) Posterior view.

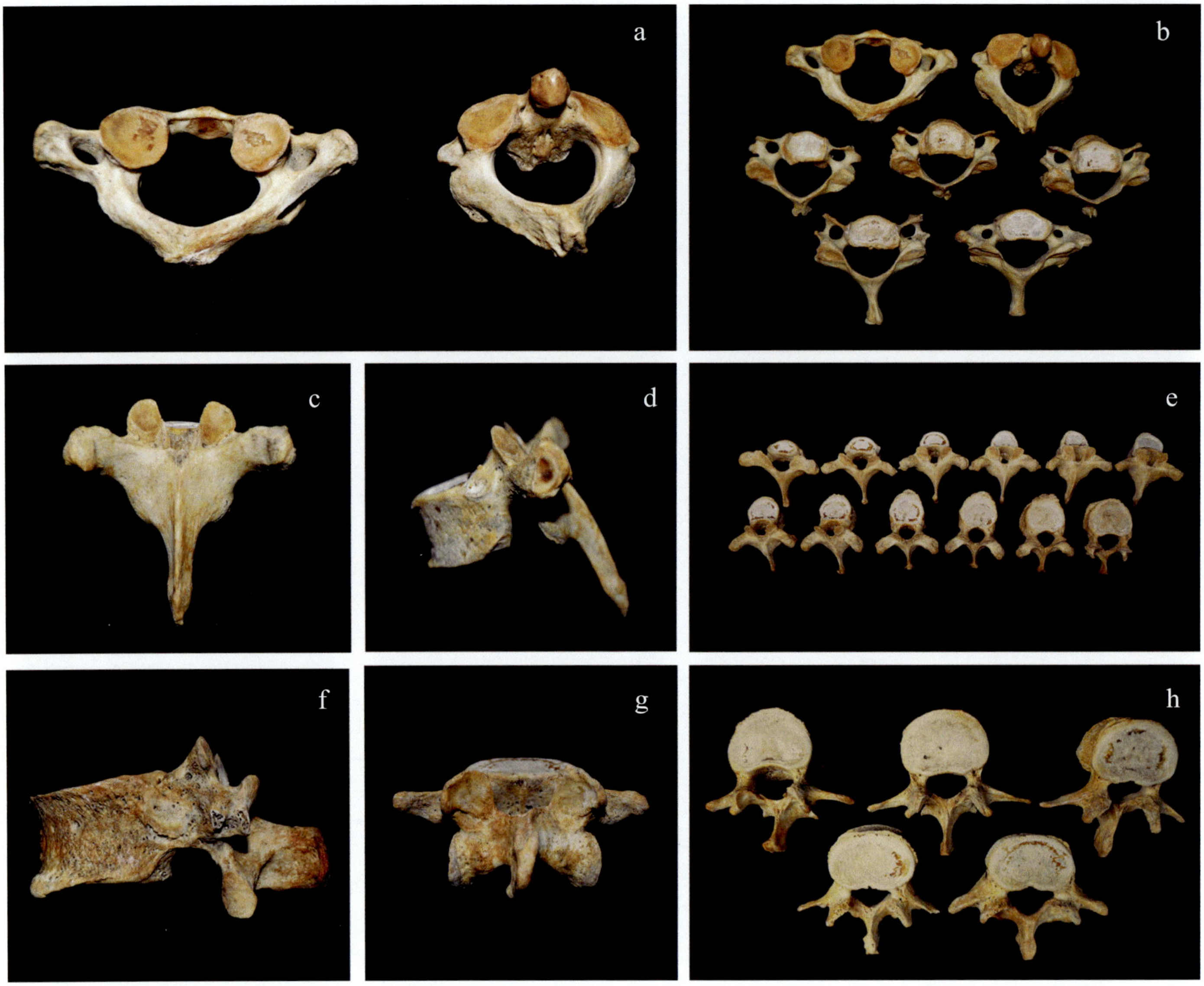

Figure 1.19 Variation among the vertebrae. (a) Superior view of cervical vertebrae number one/atlas (left) and cervical vertebra number 2/axis (right). (b) All seven cervical vertebrae. (c) Thoracic vertebra, posterior view. (d) Thoracic vertebra, lateral view. (e) All 12 thoracic vertebrae. (f) Lumbar vertebra, lateral view. (g) Lumbar vertebra, posterior view. (h) All five lumbar vertebrae.

has the appearance of a thoracic vertebra but retains the transverse foramen.

The thoracic vertebrae (T1–T12) are overall consistent in shape, although they increase in size further down the spinal column. Thoracic vertebrae articulate with the ribs and have small **facets** on each side of the body of the vertebra for that articulation. Thoracic vertebrae number 12 is transitional and takes on the appearance of a lumbar vertebra but retains the facets for the ribs.

Lumbar vertebrae (L1–L5) are large and bulky and do not have facets for rib articulations. Lumbar vertebra number five (L5) articulates with the sacrum.

The clavicle The clavicle, also known as the collarbone, is an S-shaped paired bone forming the anterior portion of the shoulder girdle (Figure 1.20).

The scapula The scapula, also known as the shoulder blade, is a triangular-shaped paired flat bone forming the posterior portion of the shoulder girdle (Figure 1.21).

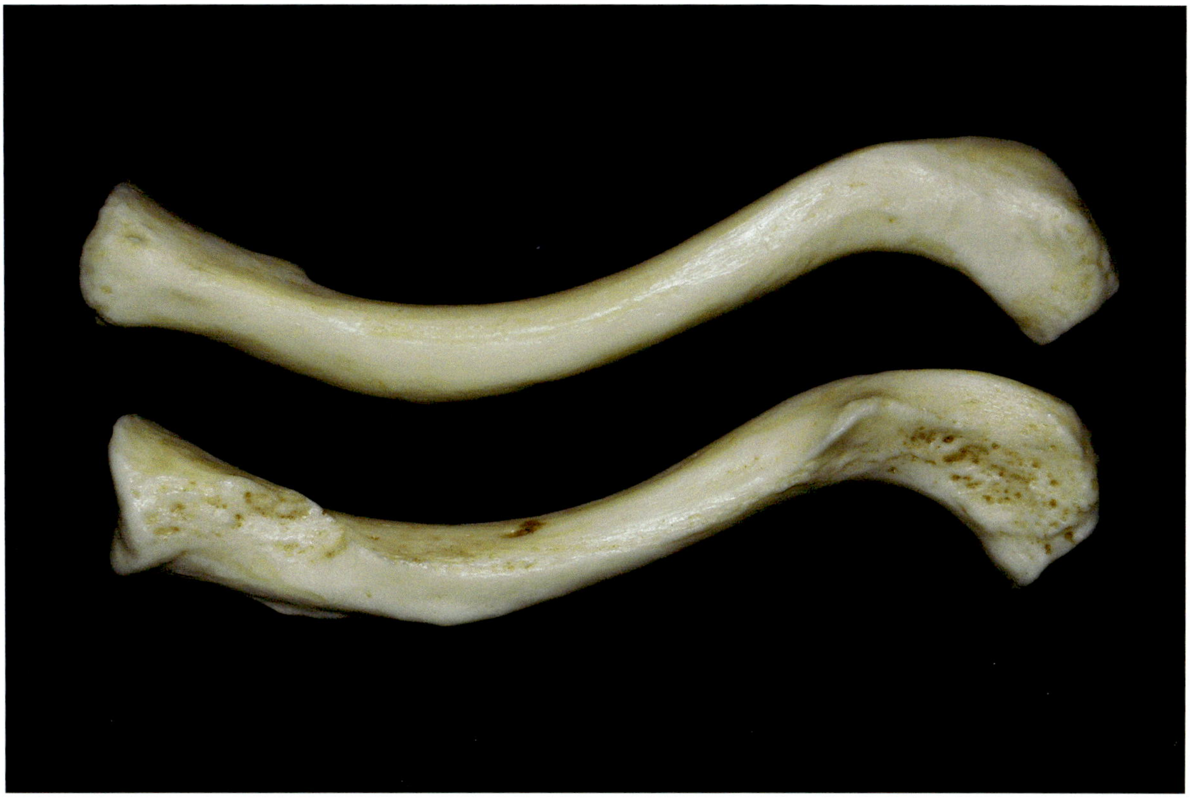

Figure 1.20 The clavicle. Inferior view of the right clavicle (bottom) and superior view of the left clavicle (top).

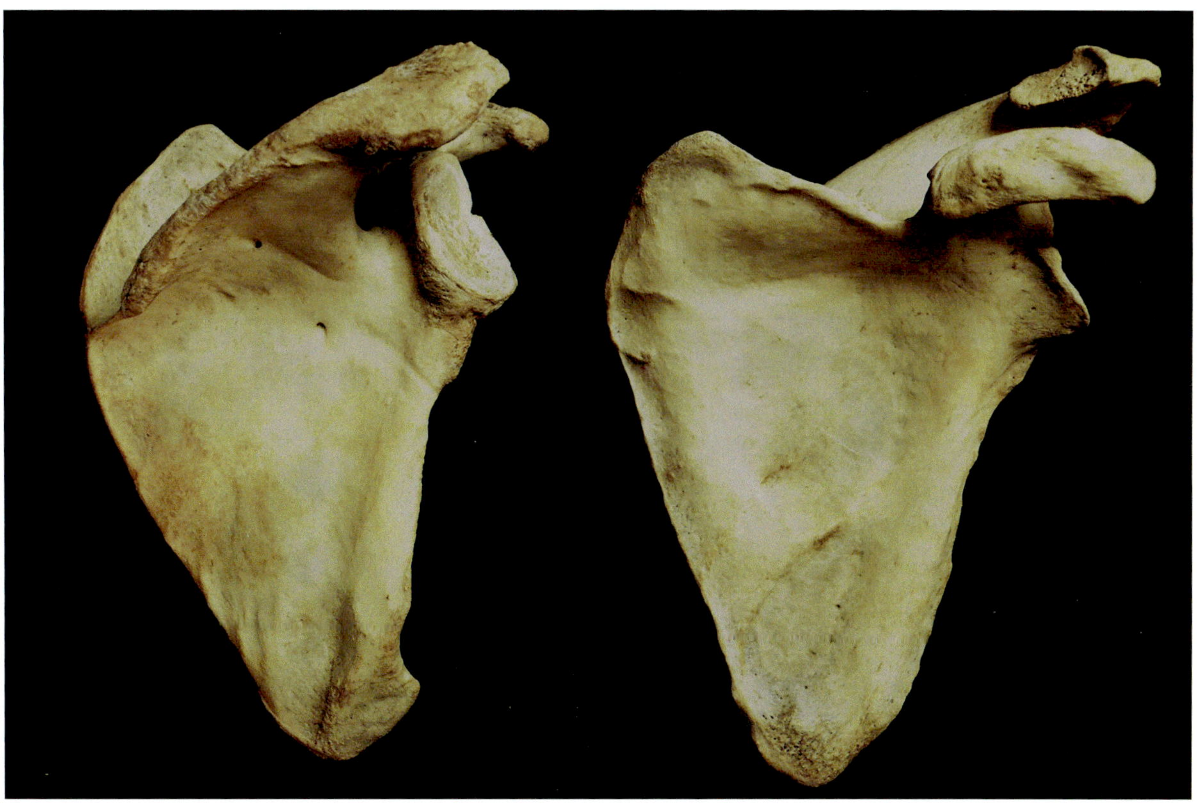

Figure 1.21 The scapula. Posterior view of the right scapula (left) and anterior view of the left scapula (right).

The humerus (bone of the arm) articulates with the scapula creating a loose ball-and-socket joint primarily held together by ligaments and tendons.

The humerus The humerus is the bone of the arm (Figure 1.22). It is a paired long bone consisting of a head (proximal end) that articulates with the scapula to form

Figure 1.22 The humerus. Anterior view of a left humerus (left) and the posterior view of a right humerus (right).

the shoulder joint, a **diaphysis** or shaft, which is the long narrow portion of the bone, and a distal end that articulates with the ulna to form the elbow joint.

The forearm The forearm is made up of two bones: the ulna and the radius (Figure 1.23). The ulna is a paired bone and positioned medially in the forearm. It has a distinctive

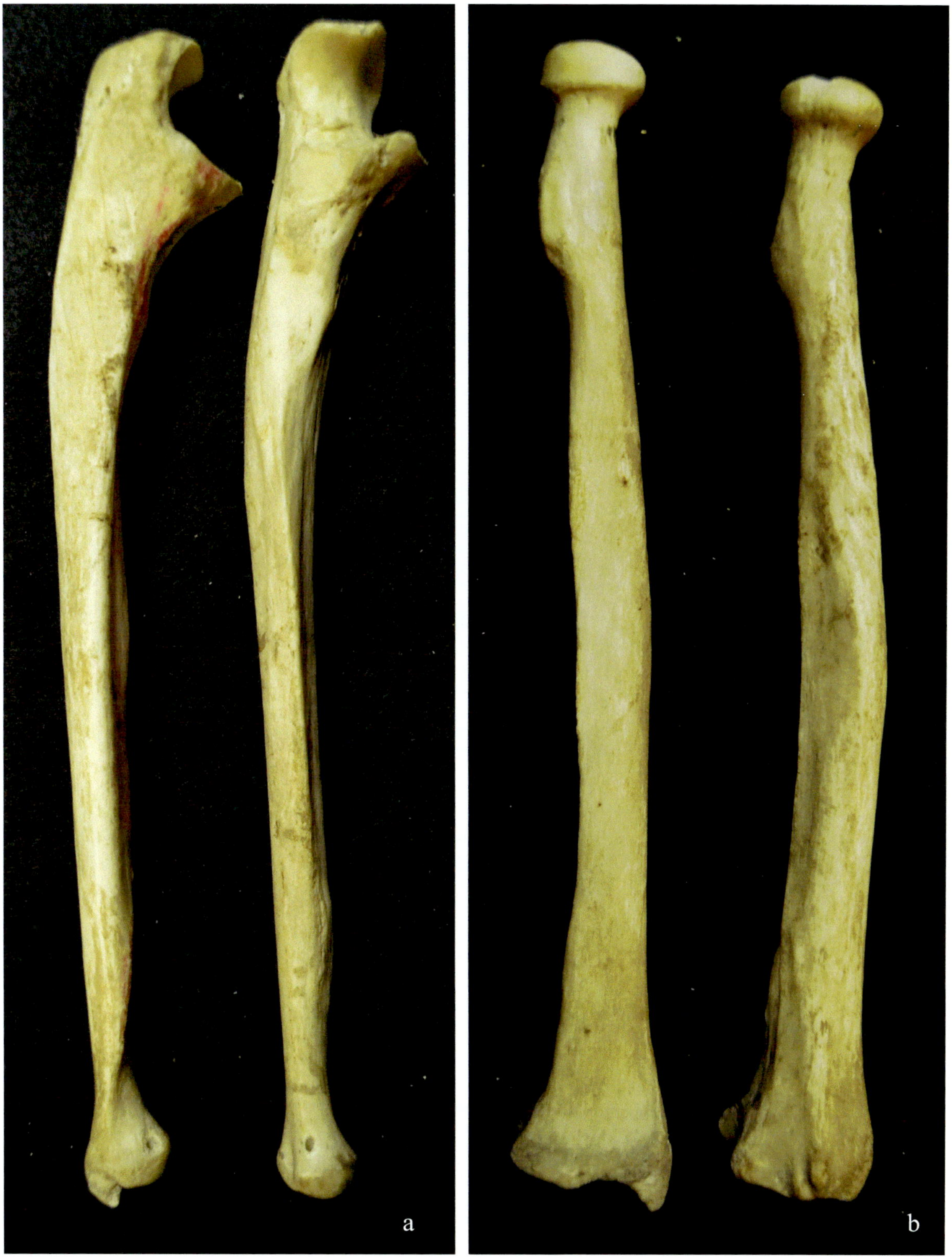

Figure 1.23 The forearm. (a) Medial view of a left ulna (left) and lateral view of a right ulna (right). (b) Anterior view of the right radius (left) and posterior view of the right radius (right).

scoop-shaped proximal end for articulation with the humerus at the elbow joint. The radius is a paired bone and positioned laterally in the forearm. Its proximal end is circular in shape allowing for rotation around the ulna. This rotation allows the forearm to **pronate** and **supinate**. Figure 1.24 shows the anterior and posterior views of the radius and ulna together. When the palm of the hand is facing forward, in the correct anatomical position, the

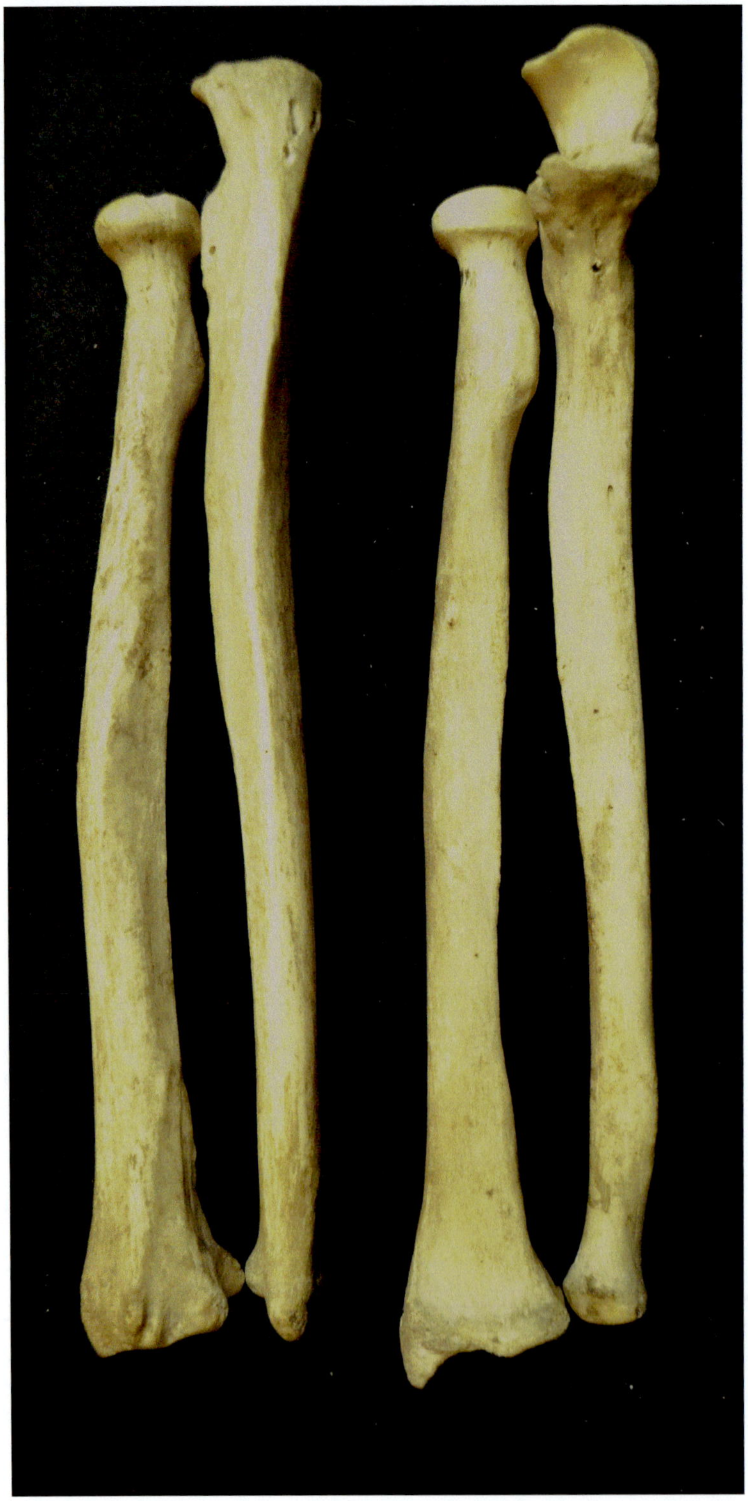

Figure 1.24 The radius and ulna together. Left: posterior view of the right radius and ulna. Right: anterior view of the right radius and ulna.

radius is positioned laterally, and its shaft is not crossed over the shaft of the ulna. When the palm of the hand is positioned posteriorly (not in anatomical position), the shaft of the radius is crossed over the shaft of the ulna.

The hand There are 27 paired bones in the hand, not including small sesamoid bones (Figure 1.25). There are eight carpal bones (bones of the wrist), five metacarpal bones (bones of the palm), and 14 phalanges (finger bones).

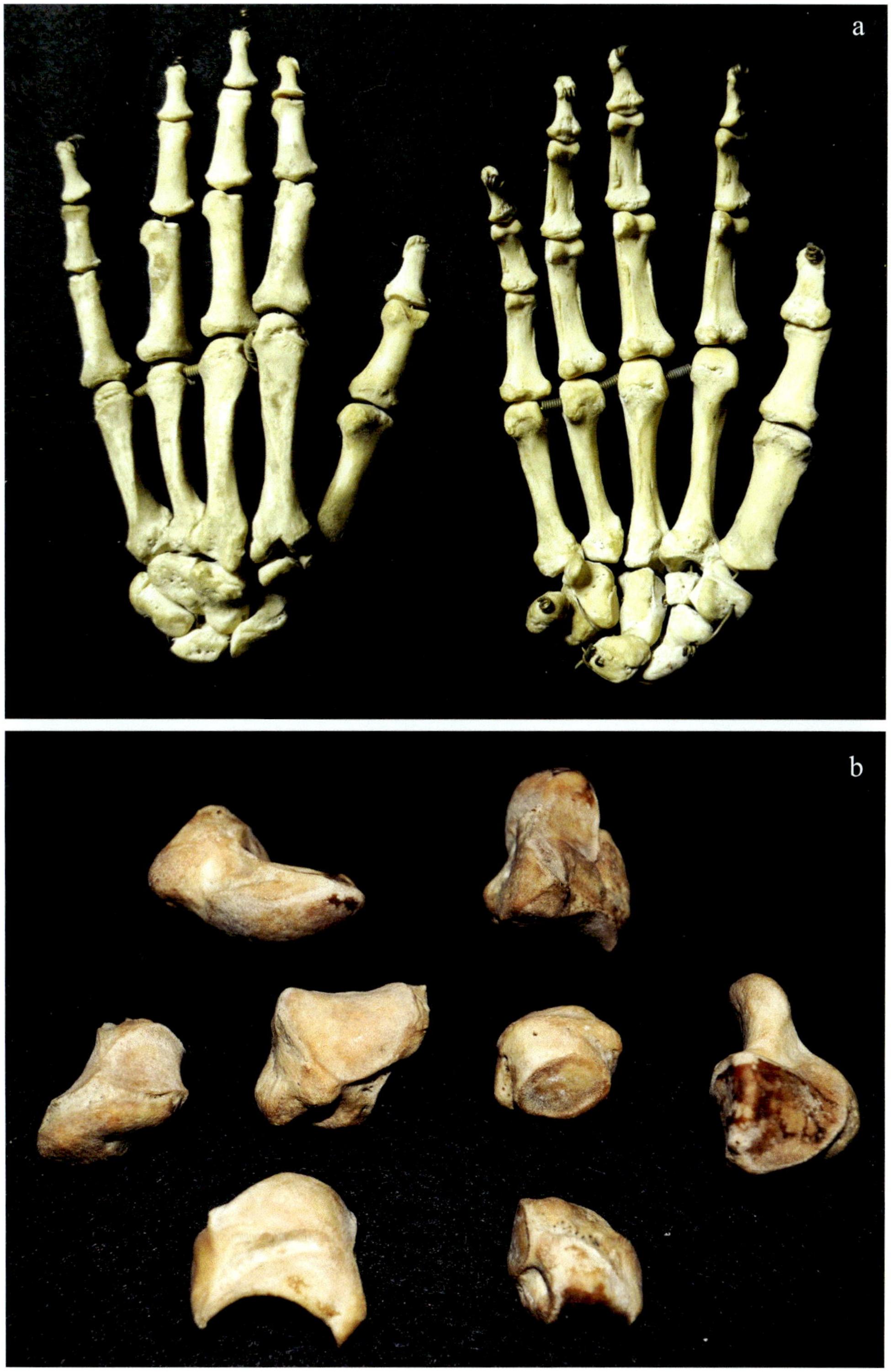

Figure 1.25 The bones of the hand. (a) Posterior (dorsal) view of the left hand (left) and anterior (palmar) view of the right hand (right). (b) All eight carpals. Top row: scaphoid and capitate. Middle row: trapezoid, trapezium, pisiform, and hamate. Bottom row: lunate and triquetral.

The carpals (wrist) consist of the scaphoid, capitate, trapezoid, trapezium, pisiform, hamate, lunate, and triquetral. Of the phalanges, there are five proximal hand phalanges (segment where rings sit), four intermediate hand phalanges (middle segment, note the thumb does not have an intermediate phalange), and five distal hand phalanges (fingertips). The bones of the hand can often be hard to recover from a scene as they are small, mimicking rocks and sticks, and prone to animal scavenging.

The pelvis The pelvis contains the paired os coxae (or innominate bones), the unpaired sacrum, and the unpaired coccyx bone (Figure 1.26). The os coxae are made up of three separate bones that fuse during growth

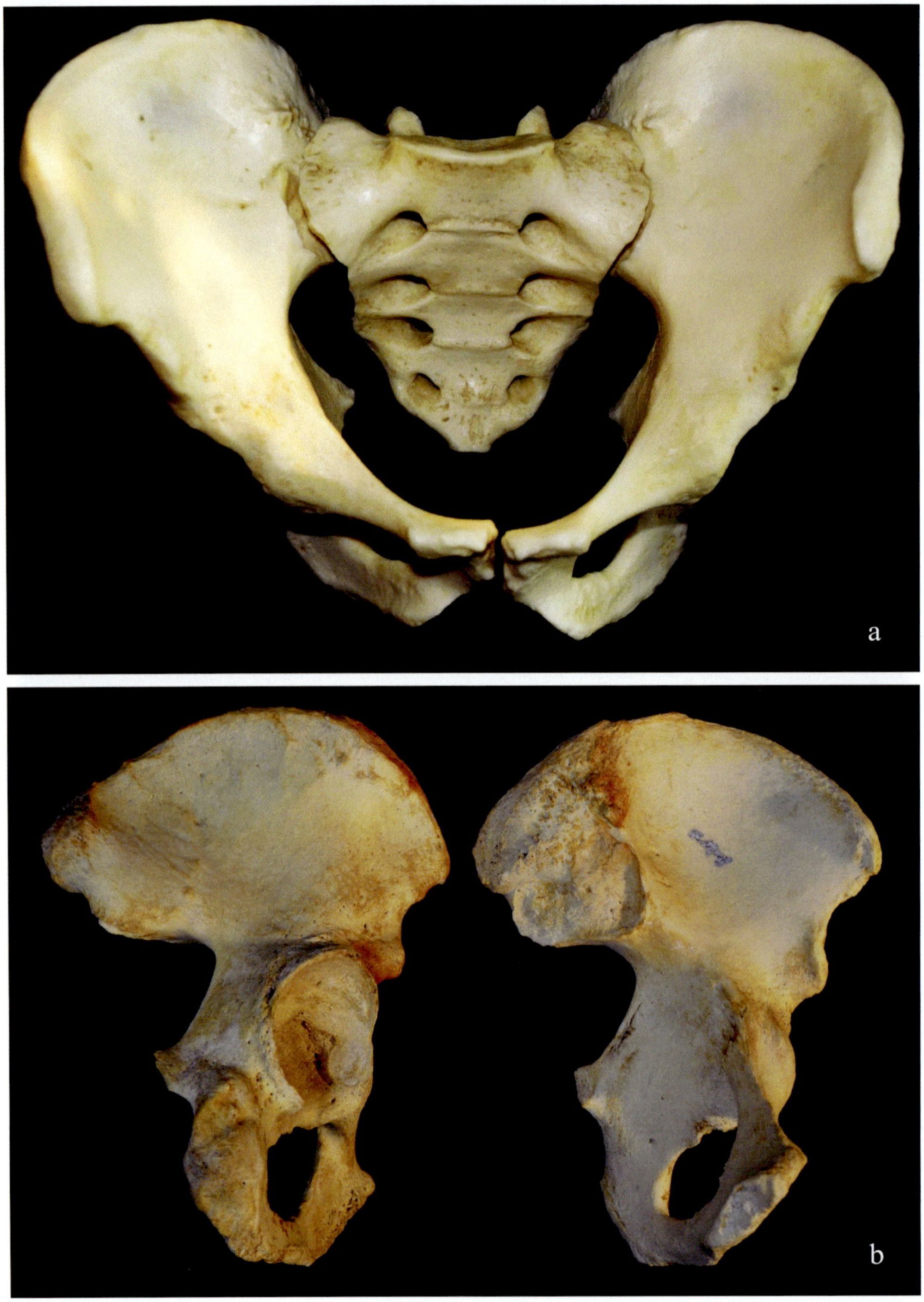

Figure 1.26 The pelvis. (a) The pelvis in anatomical position (anterosuperior view) without the coccyx. (b) Lateral view of the right ox coxa (right) and medial view of the left os coxa (right).

and development (ilium, ischium, pubis). The point where all three bones fuse together is called the **acetabulum**, which is the articulation point for the femur (bone of the thigh). This articulation is called a ball-and-socket joint, as the ball head of the femur fits into the socket that is the acetabulum.

The sacrum forms the base of the spinal cord and the posterior portion of the pelvis (Figure 1.27). It is typically

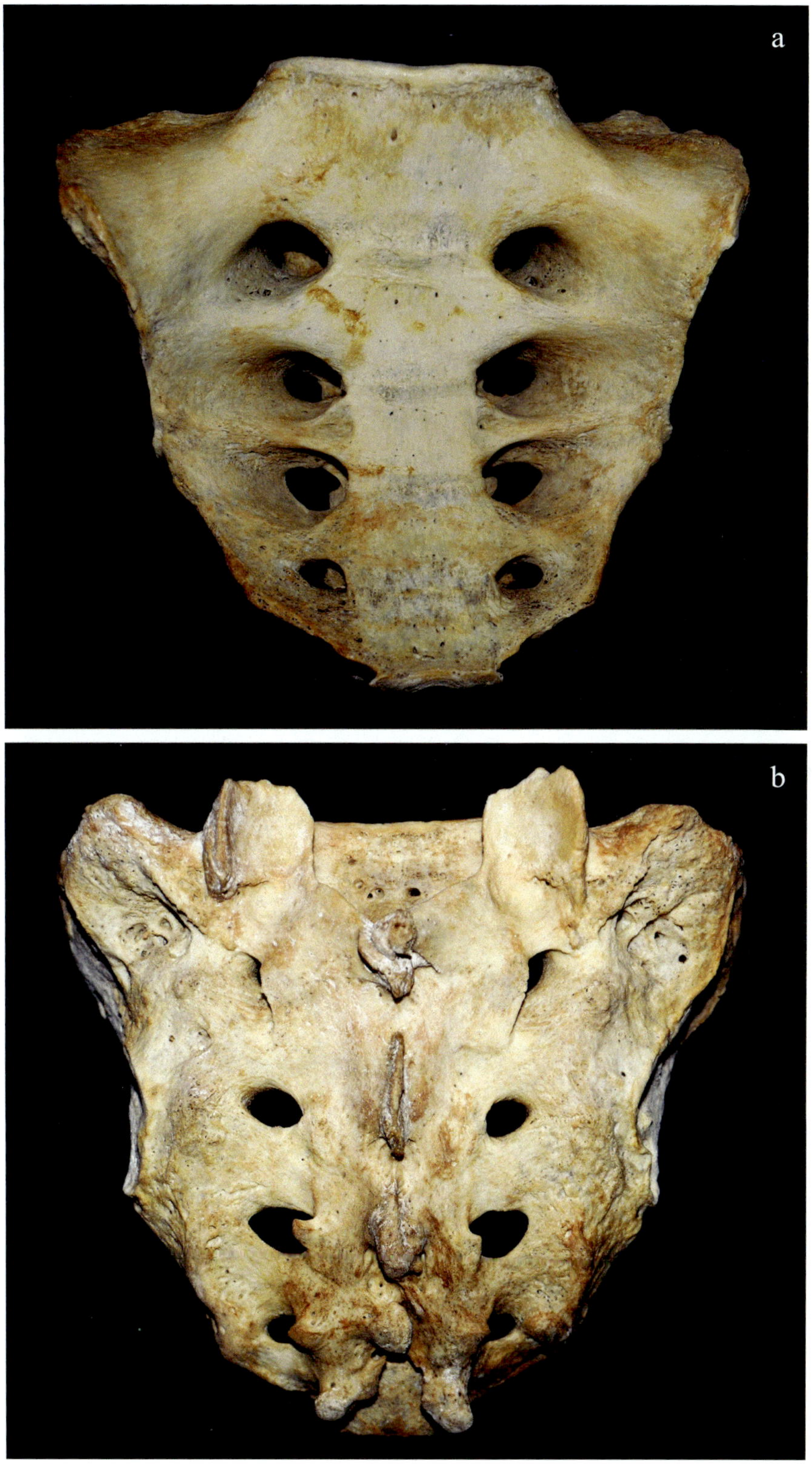

Figure 1.27 The sacrum. (a) Anterior view. (b) Posterior view.

composed of five segments (although four to six may be present), which fuse together during growth and development. The coccyx (also called the tailbone) is the remnant of the vestigial tail (Figure 1.28). The coccyx contains multiple fused segments and articulates with the distal portion of the sacrum.

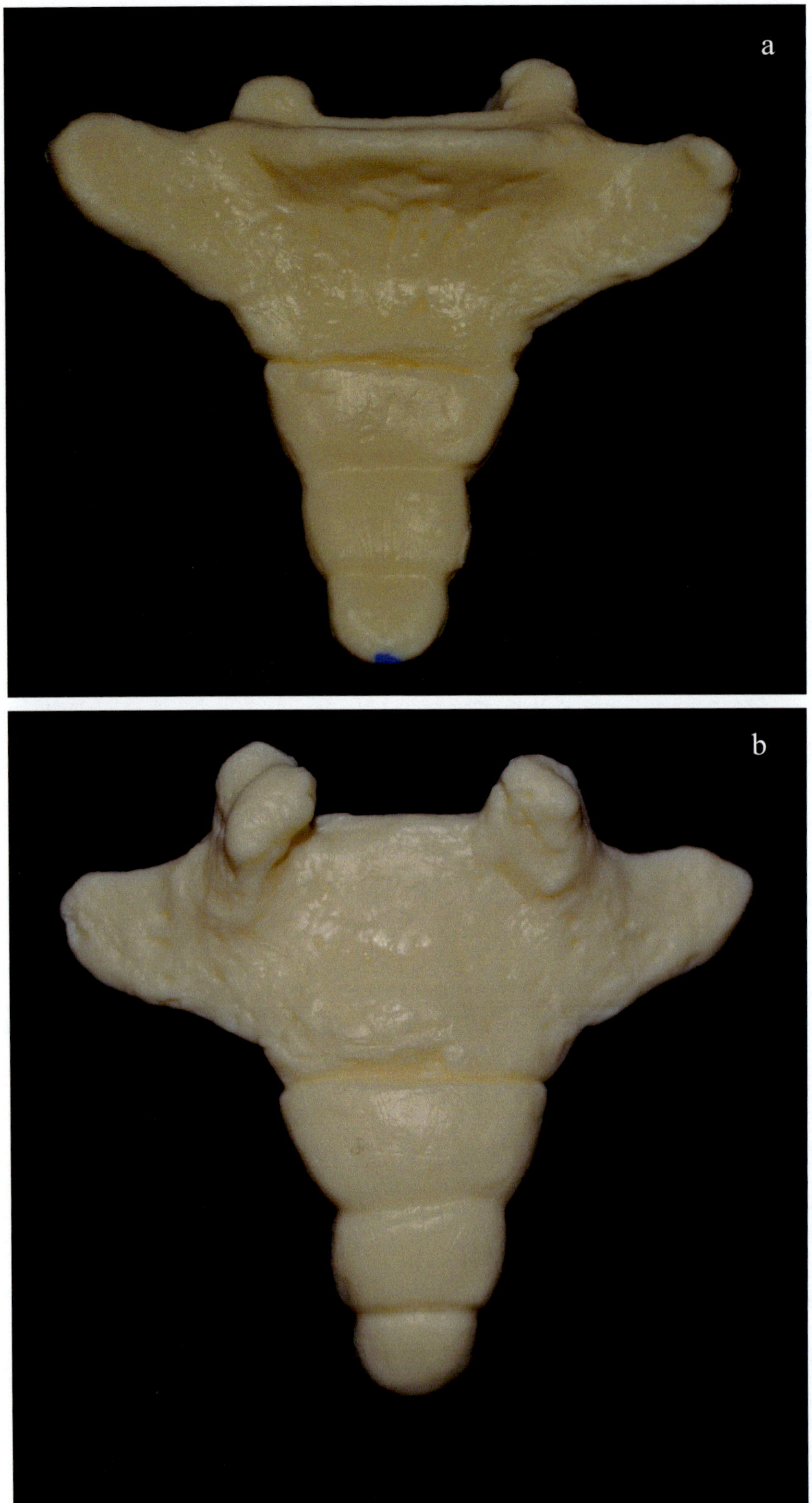

Figure 1.28 The coccyx. (a) Posterior view. (b) Anterior view.

The femur The femur is the paired bone of the thigh (Figure 1.29). It is the largest and longest of the long bones and articulates proximally with the os coxa and distally with the patella and tibia. The proximal end contains the distinctive round femoral head.

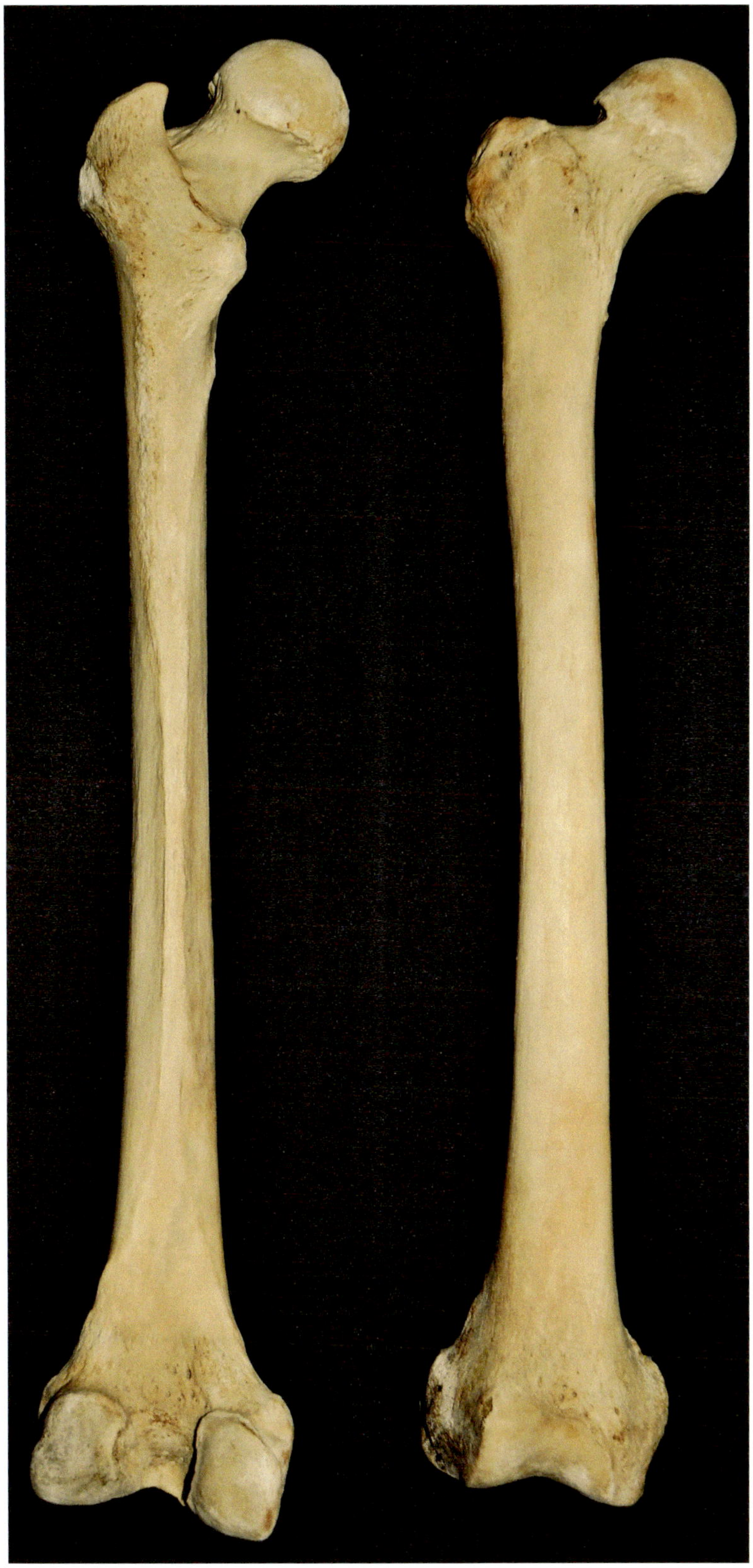

Figure 1.29 The femur. Posterior view of the left femur (left) and anterior view of the right femur.

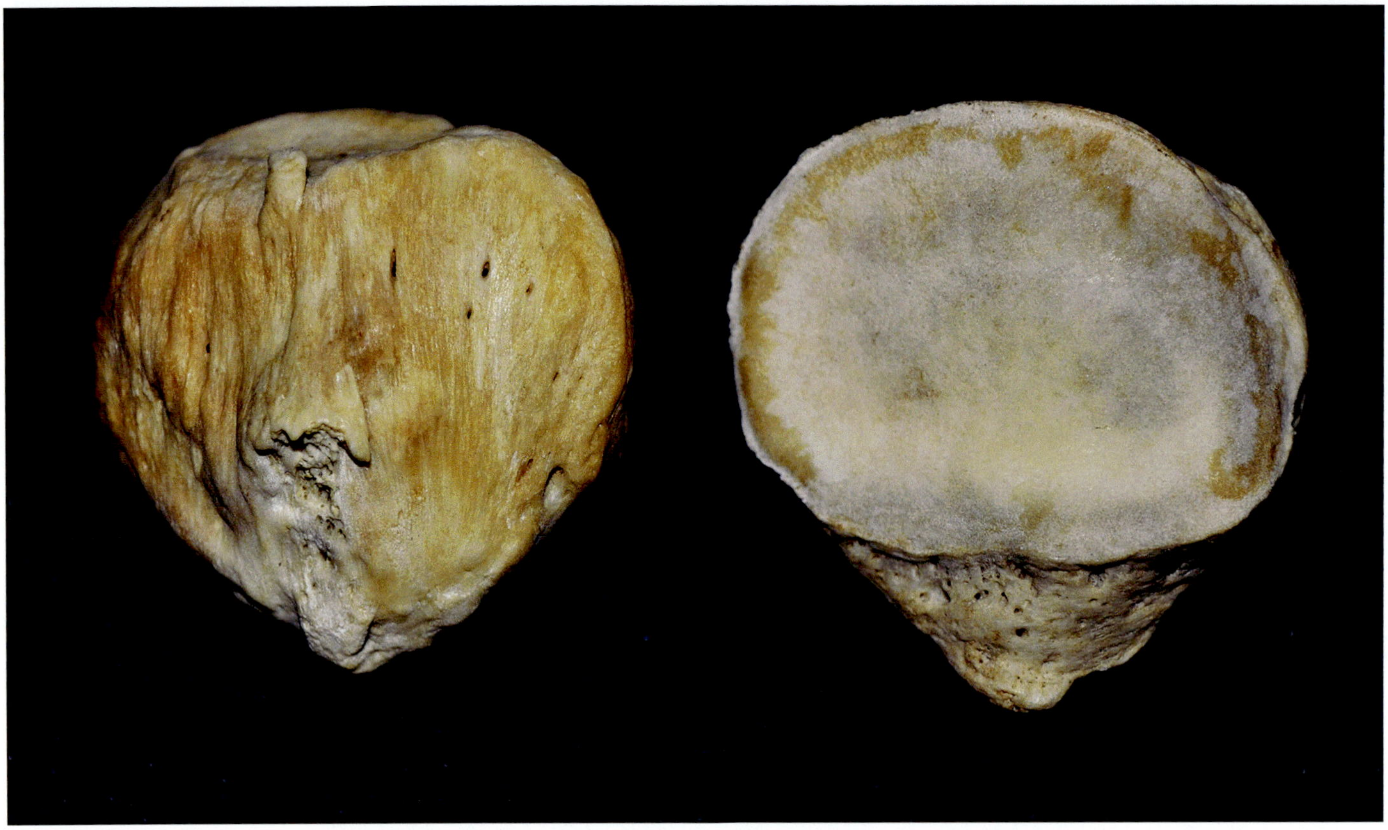

Figure 1.30 The patella. Anterior view of the left patella (left) and posterior view of the right patella (right).

The patella The patella is a paired bone and is best known as the kneecap (Figure 1.30). It is the largest of the sesamoid bones in the body. It articulates with the anterior portion of the distal end of the femur. It is not a true articulation in that the bone is held in place by a tendon and glides along the surface of the distal femur.

The leg The leg (shin) contains two paired bones: the tibia and the fibula (Figure 1.31). The tibia is the larger of the two bones and is positioned medially in the leg. The anterior tibia can be felt by touching the front of the shin. The proximal end of the tibia articulates with the femur and the distal end articulates with the talus bone of the foot. The fibula is the laterally positioned bone of the leg. Figure 1.32 shows the tibia and fibula in anatomical position.

The foot There are 26 paired bones in the foot, not including small sesamoid bones (Figure 1.33). There are 7 tarsal bones, 5 metacarpal bones, and 14 foot phalanges (toe bones).

The tarsals consist of the calcaneus (heel bone), talus, cuboid, navicular, medial cuneiform, intermediate cuneiform, and lateral cuneiform. There are five metatarsal bones. Similar to the hand, there are five proximal foot phalanges, four intermediate foot phalanges (note the big toe does not have an intermediate phalange), and five distal foot phalanges. The bones of the foot can often be hard to recover from a scene as they are small, mimicking rocks and sticks, and prone to animal scavenging.

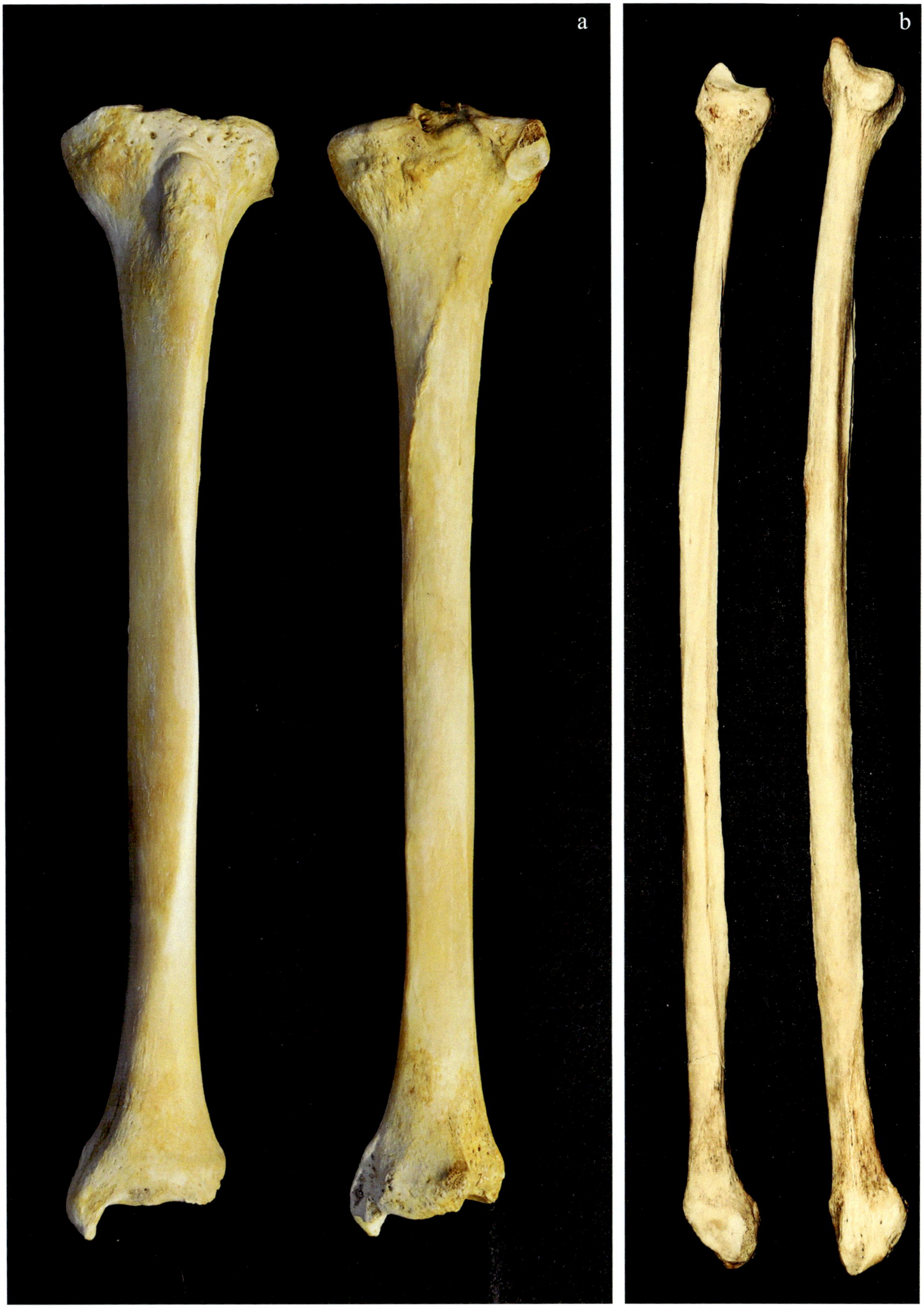

Figure 1.31 The leg. (a) Anterior view of the left tibia (left) and posterior view of the right tibia (right). (b) Lateral view of the left fibula (left) and medial view of the right fibula (right).

Figure 1.32 The tibia and fibula together. Anterior view of the right fibula and tibia (left) and the posterior view of a left fibula and tibia (right).

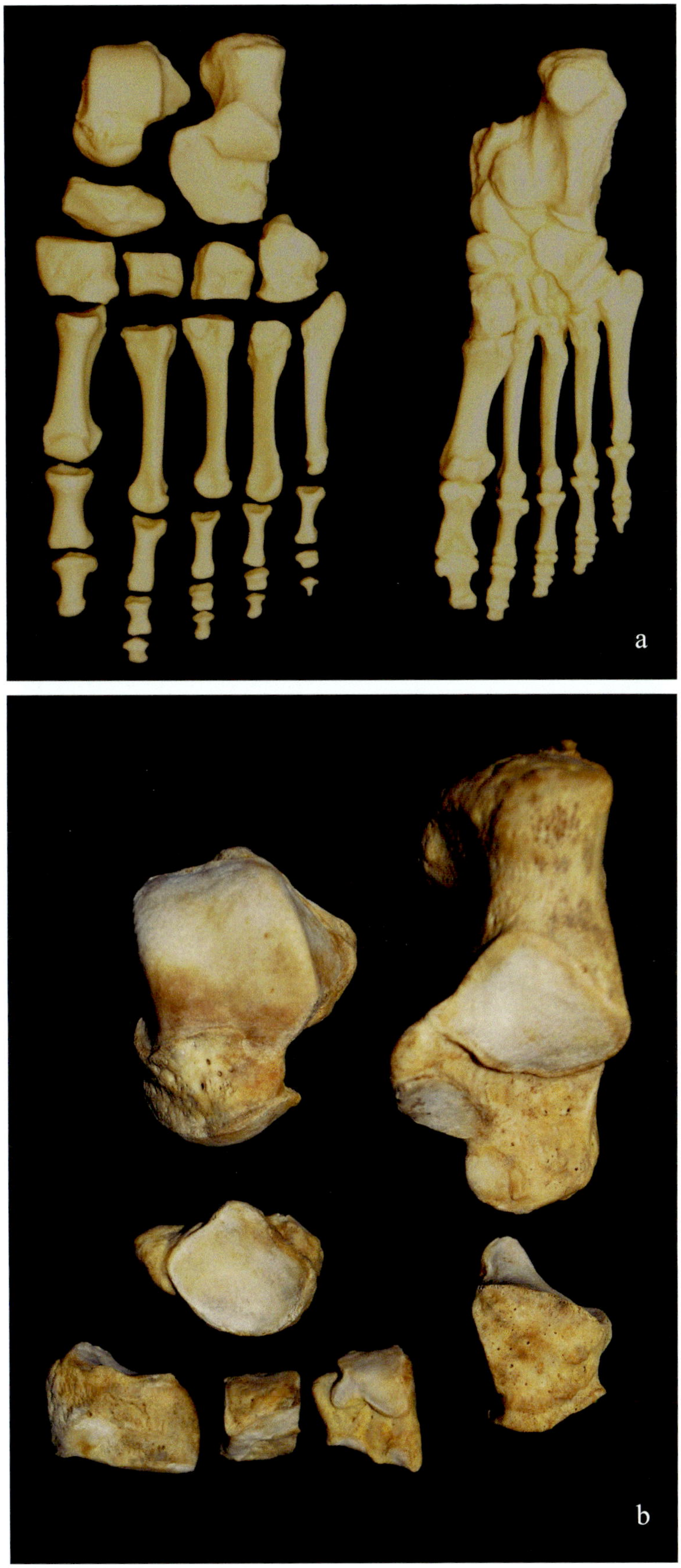

Figure 1.33 The bones of the foot. (a) Dorsal view of the left foot (left) and plantar view of the right foot (right). (b) All seven tarsals: talus, calcaneus, navicular, medial cuneiform, intermediate cuneiform, lateral cuneiform, and cuboid.

Subadult human osteology

Introduction

The medicolegal investigator may encounter juvenile (**subadult**) skeletal remains, but how would they know? Are subadult bones the same shape as their adult counterparts but smaller? The short answer is no. Most subadult bones are not small versions of adult bones and vary dramatically in appearance and size depending on the age of the individual. For example, a 4-in.-long fully formed femur bone is not that of a young child, rather it is from an adult nonhuman animal. Subadult human bones grow and develop in multiple portions and do not always look like adult bones.

This section briefly introduces subadult osteology and the growth and development processes involved in bone formation. The purpose of this section is to provide a resource to identify subadult osseous materials in order to properly recover them. This summary is by no means a comprehensive explanation of how subadult bones form and develop into adult forms, rather it serves as a simplified descriptive and visual demonstration of the differences between the subadult and adult forms. A complete examination of bone formation, growth, and development can be found in Louise Scheuer and Sue Black's *Developmental Juvenile Osteology* published in 2000.

Growth and development in the subadult individual occur in predictable intervals. However, individual variation exists due to factors such as nutritional status, pathological conditions, and environmental conditions. These factors can influence growth rates and other developmental milestones (Scheuer and Black, 2000). Despite these challenges, the forensic anthropologist is tasked to provide investigators with an approximate age of recovered skeletal remains. The more skeletal elements present for analysis, the more accurate the age range can be. That is why it is so important to identify and recover as many subadult bones as possible.

Bone growth and development

The adult human skeleton contains an average of 206 fully developed bones. Subadult individuals contain many more. There is no exact number of bones in juveniles, as the number of bones changes throughout the course of development. To explain simply, bones go through the process of **ossification** and form in pieces within **ossification centers**. Ossification centers are located throughout the body, and there are multiple ossification centers per bone. Bone cells within ossification centers create small bones that are indistinct until further developed (Scheuer and Black, 2000). For example, a bone from an ossification center of the leg cannot be distinguished from a bone from an ossification center of the arm. Ossification centers are surrounded by soft tissues including cartilage. Cartilage is the basis for the growth plate. Over time, bone cells replace the growth plate allowing the bone to grow and develop. For a long bone such as the femur, ossification centers form the diaphysis (shaft) and multiple points on the proximal and distal ends of the bone. These small bones at the proximal and distal ends of long bones are called **epiphyses**. Eventually, the epiphyses replace all the cartilage surrounding them and the process of **bone fusion** occurs. The bone stops developing when fusion is complete.

Bone fusion varies across the human skeleton; in other words, it occurs at different rates (Scheuer and Black, 2000). The differential rates of fusion allow the forensic anthropologist to provide a reliable age range for subadult individuals. Once all the bones in the body are fused, age estimations provided by anthropologists are based on degenerative processes. Degeneration is highly variable among adult individuals, resulting in age estimations with larger ranges.

The remaining pages of this section contain figures illustrating bones in multiple stages of development, from infant to adult. The photos serve as a good reference to compare the **morphology** (shape) and size of bones within various stages of development.

Comparisons of subadult and adult human bones

The skull

The subadult human skull contains multiple bones that fuse together to form the individual bones of the adult human skull (Figure 1.34). Figures 1.35 and 1.36 show infant cranial bones with their adult equivalents. Of note is the overall size and shape of the elements as well as the number of bones representing the infant elements as compared to the adult elements.

Figure 1.37 shows the infant mandible with the adult mandible. The infant mandible is unfused at the midline and present in two main portions.

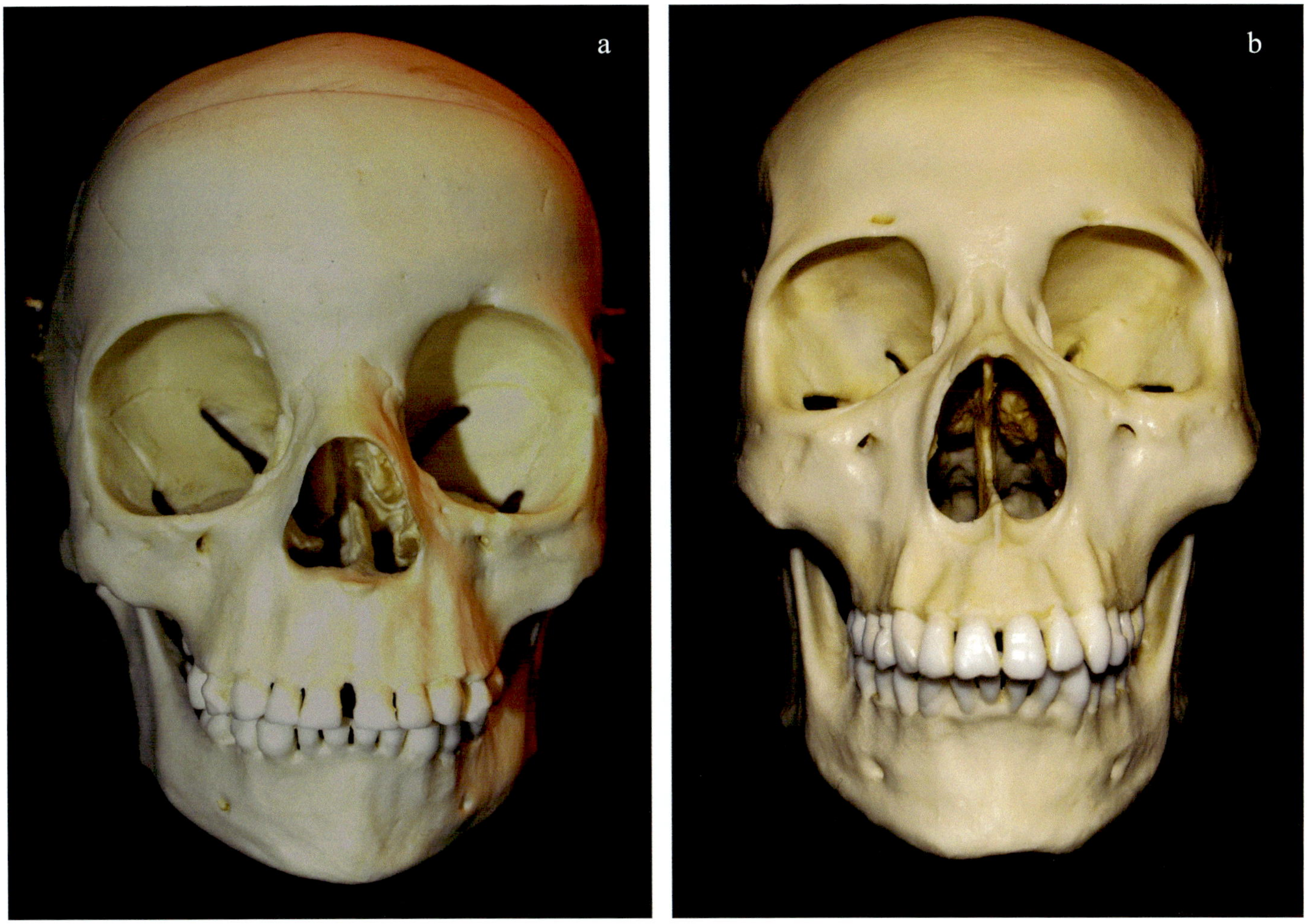

Figure 1.34 The skull. (a) Five-year-old human skull. (b) Adult human skull.

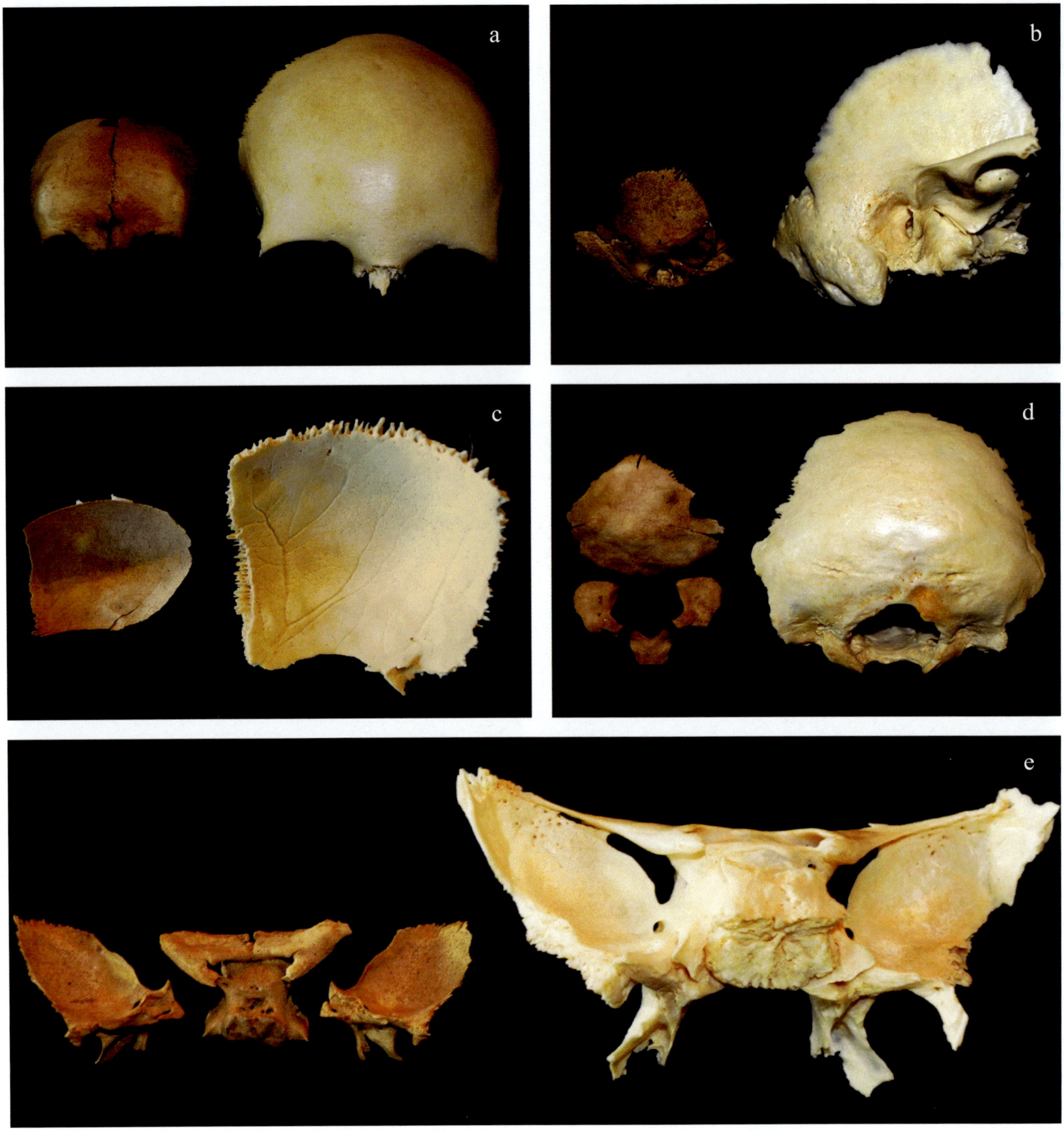

Figure 1.35 Individual cranial bones. (a) Infant frontal bones (left) and the adult frontal bone (right). (b) Infant temporal bone (left) and the adult temporal bone (right). (c) Endocranial view of the infant parietal bone (left) and the adult parietal bone (right). (d) Infant occipital bones (left) and the adult occipital bone (right). (e) Infant sphenoid bones (left) and the adult sphenoid bone (right).

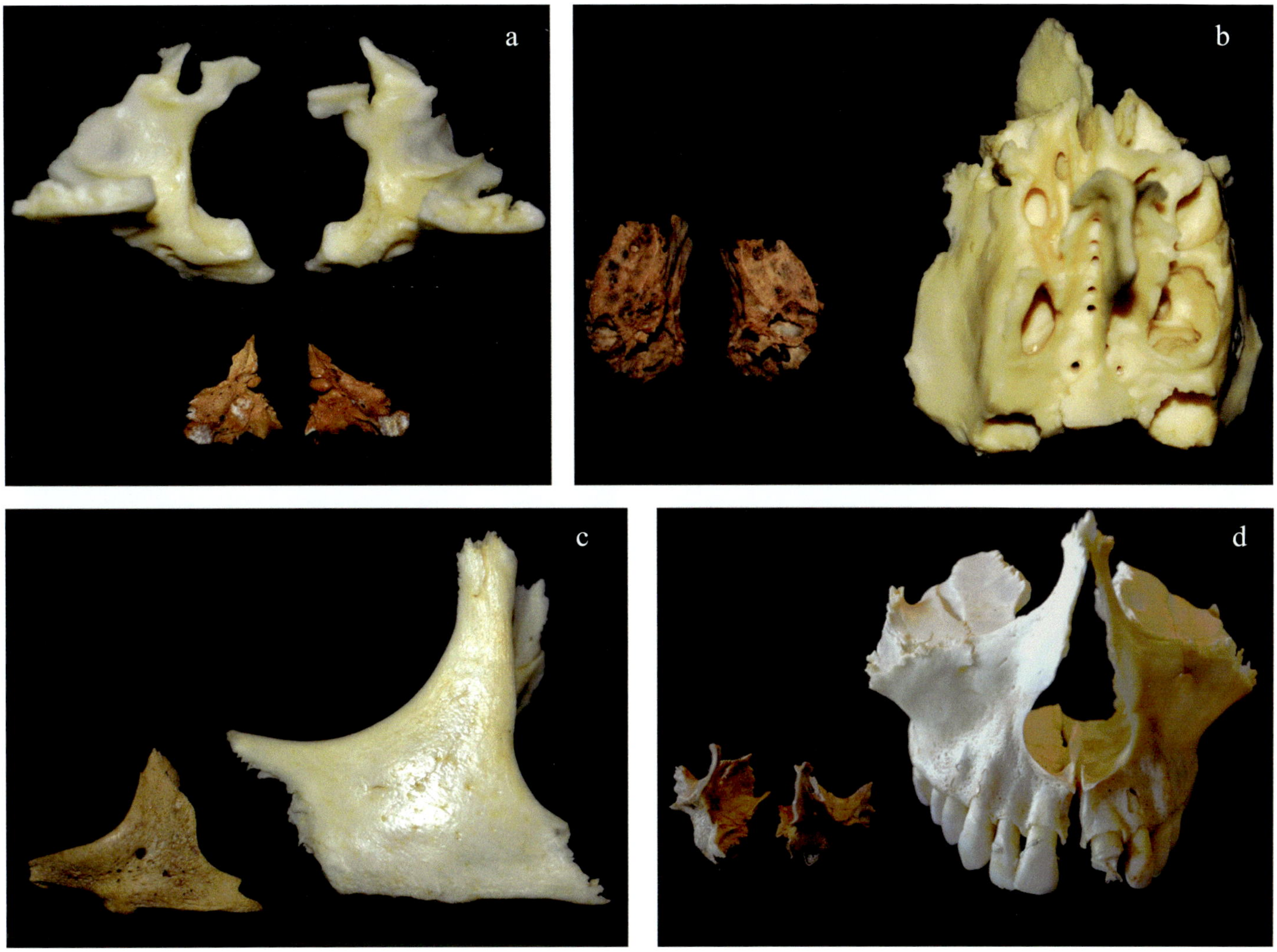

Figure 1.36 Individual facial bones. (a) Adult palatine bones (top) and infant palatine bones (bottom). (b) Infant ethmoid bones (left) and the adult ethmoid bone (right). (c) Infant zygomatic bone (left) and adult zygomatic bone (right). (d) Infant maxillae (left) and adult maxillae (right).

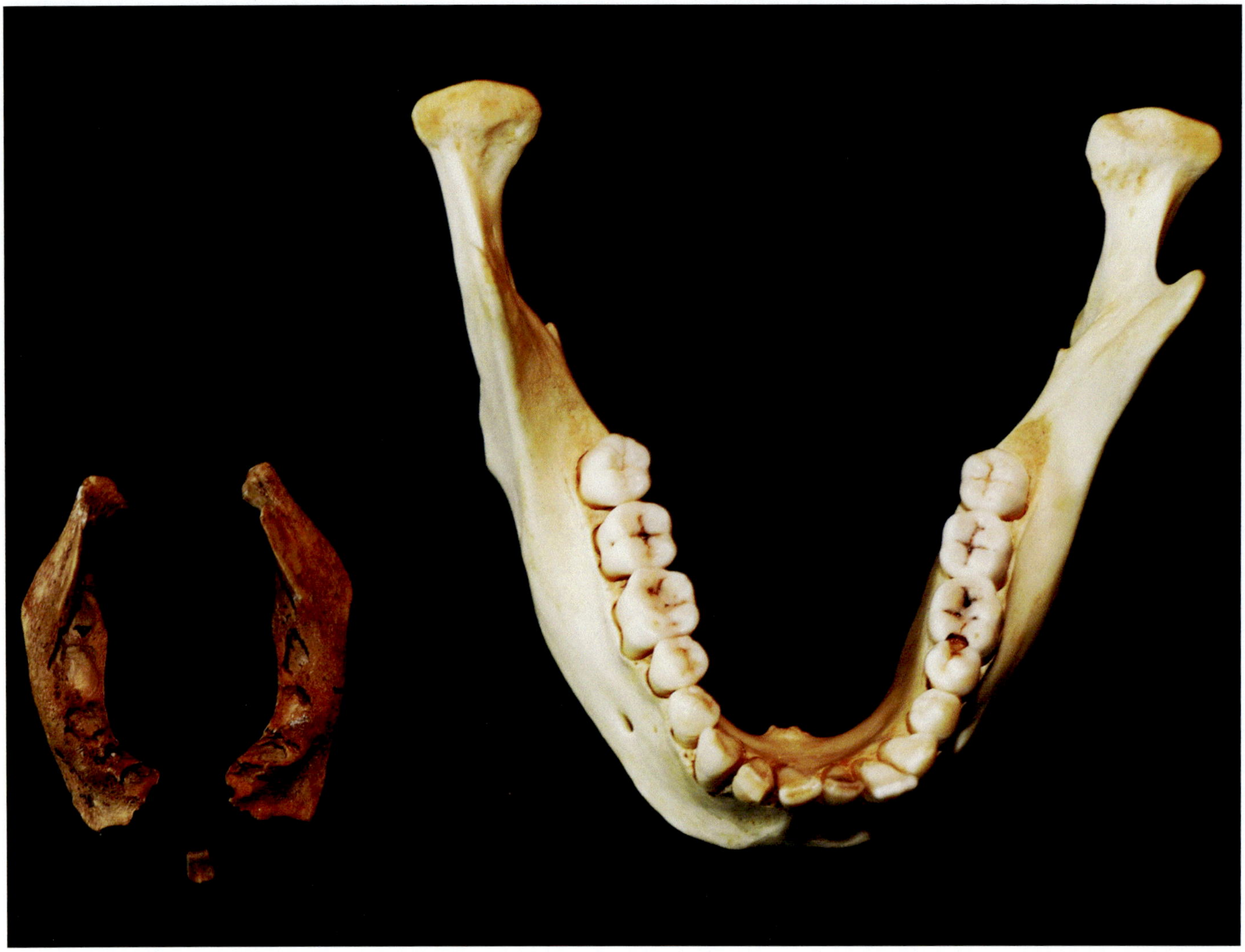

Figure 1.37 The mandible. Infant mandible (left) with tooth crown and adult mandible (right).

Postcranial bones

The hyoid

Figure 1.38 shows the subadult hyoid compared to the adult hyoid. The hyoid typically fuses during development but can remain unfused and retain a similar appearance to the subadult into adulthood.

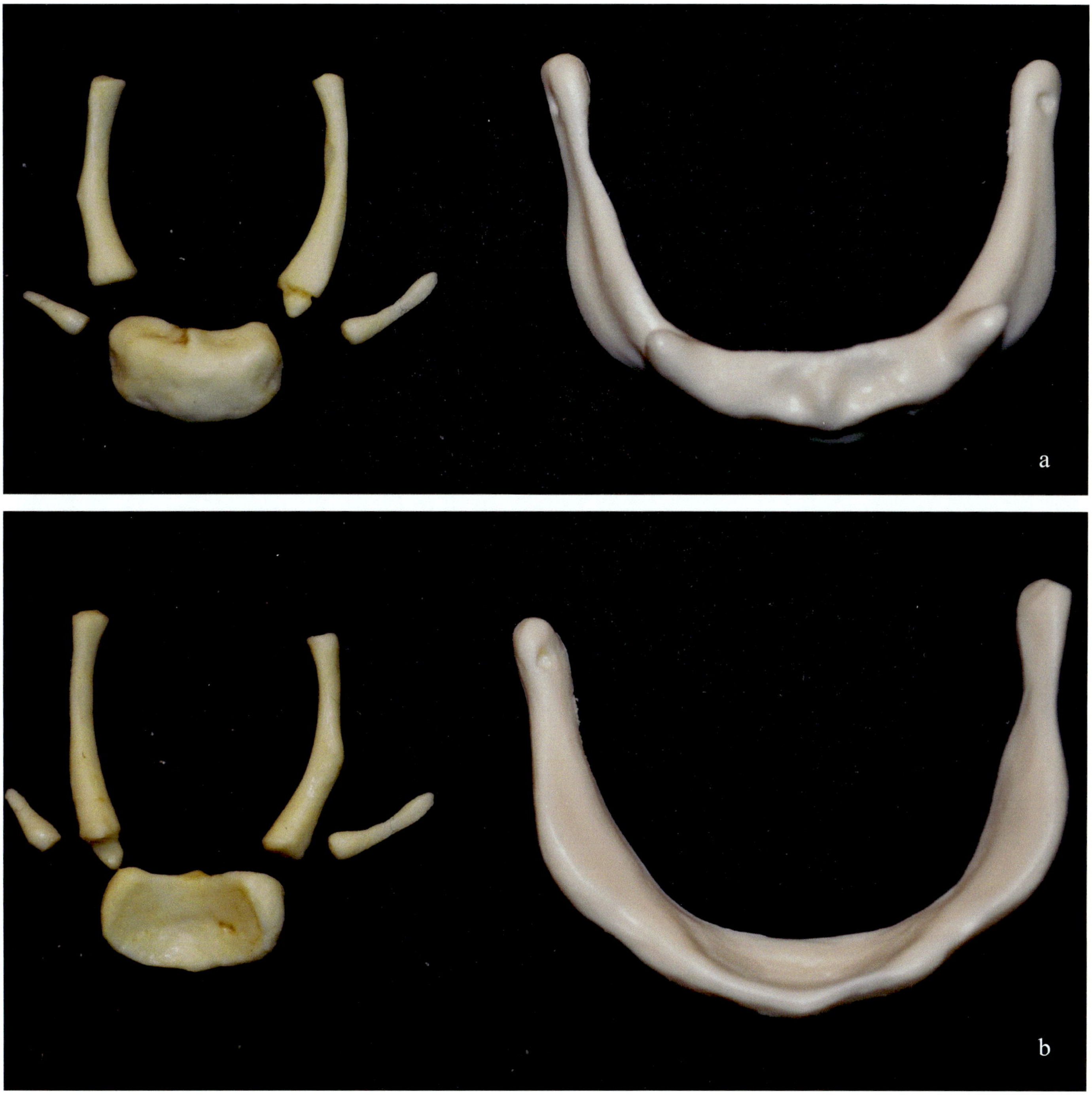

Figure 1.38 The hyoid. (a) Superior view of infant hyoid bones (left) and the adult hyoid bone (right). (b) Inferior view of infant hyoid bones (left) and an adult hyoid bone (right).

The ribs Figure 1.39 shows the ribs of an infant compared to the ribs of an adult. As in the adult, there are 12 pairs of ribs in the infant. Subadult ribs have a similar shape but overall are much smaller. Figure 1.40 shows ribs at different stages of development.

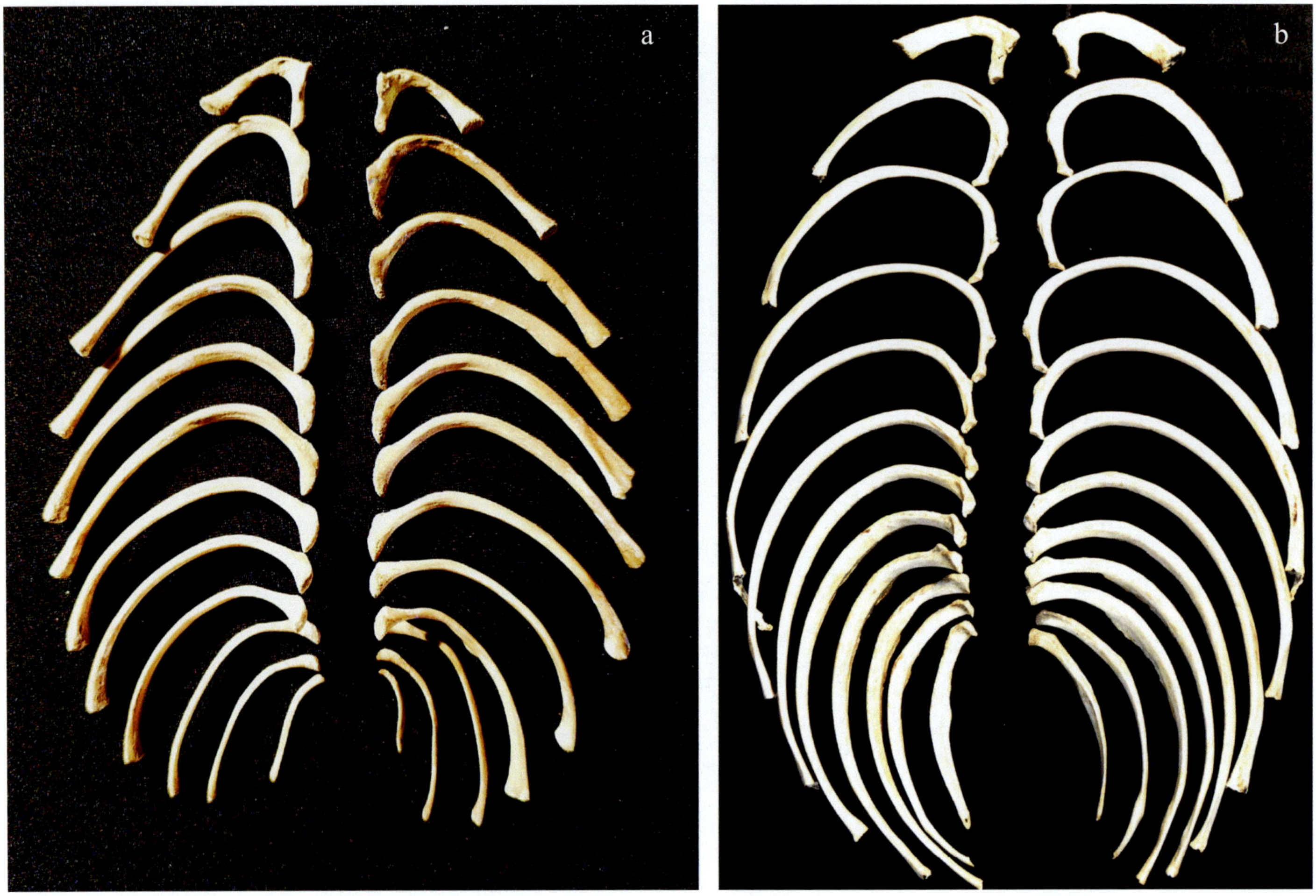

Figure 1.39 The ribs. (a) Infant ribs. (b) Adult ribs.

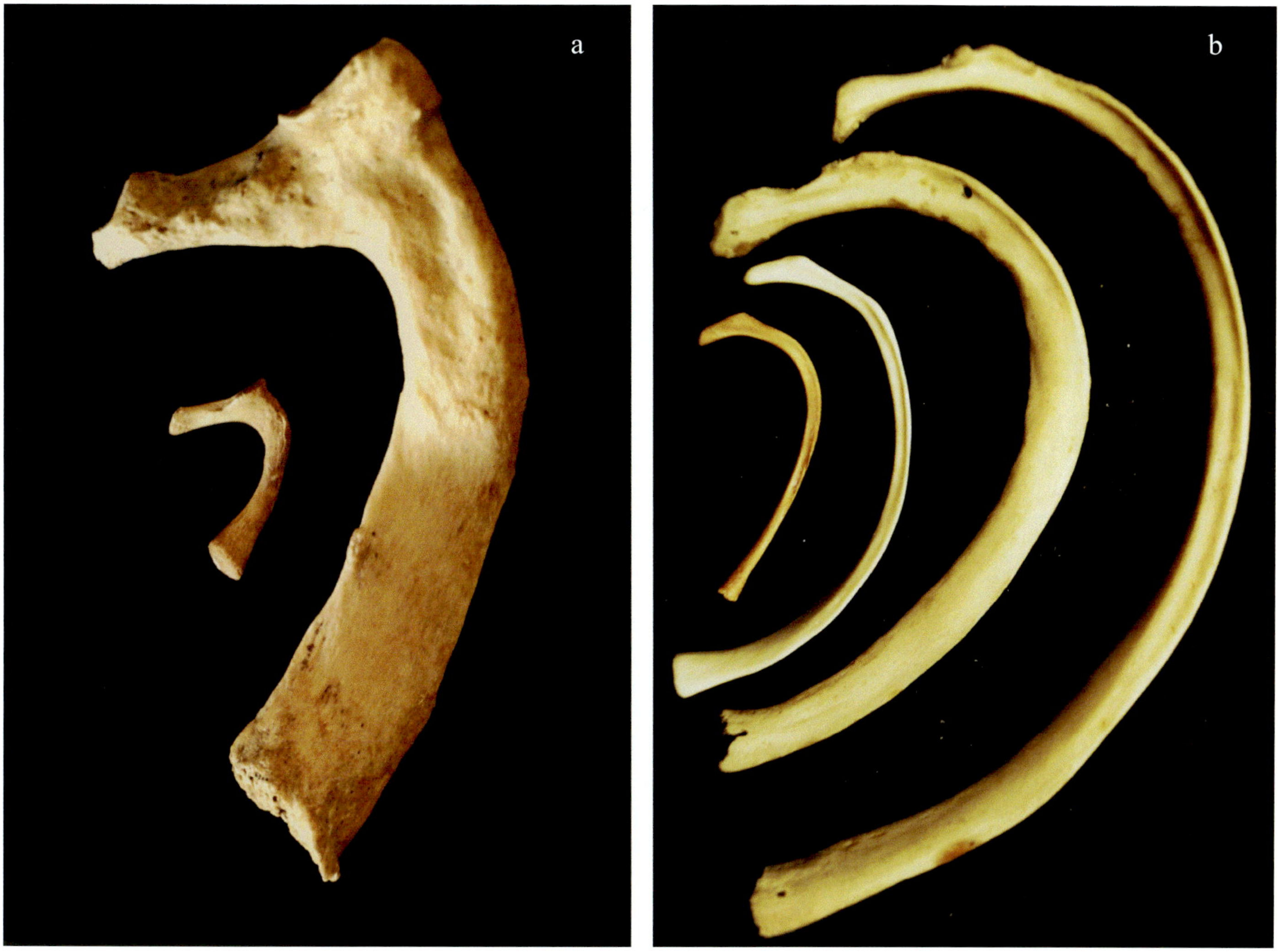

Figure 1.40 (a) Infant first rib (left) and adult first rib (right). (b) From left to right: infant, 5-year-old, and two adult rib bones.

The vertebrae As in adults, subadults have 24 vertebrae including seven cervical vertebrae, 12 thoracic vertebrae, and 5 lumbar vertebrae. Figure 1.41 shows the differences between each of these types of vertebrae at various stages of development.

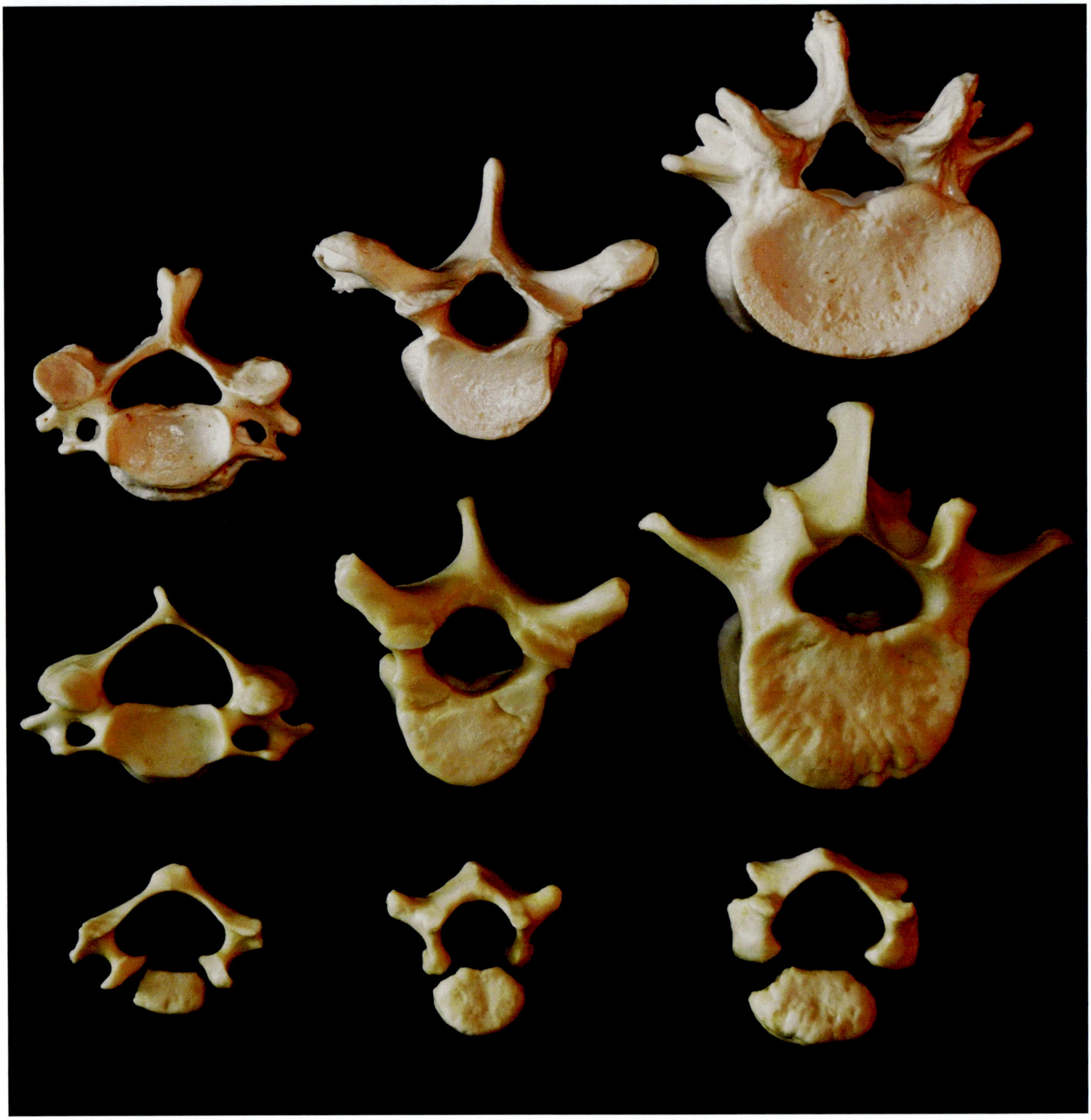

Figure 1.41 Vertebrae. Top row, left to right: adult cervical, thoracic, and lumbar vertebrae. Middle row, left to right: 13-year-old cervical, thoracic, and lumbar vertebrae. Bottom row, left to right: 14–16-month-old cervical, thoracic, and lumbar vertebrae.

The clavicle The subadult clavicle is similar in morphology to the adult clavicle but differs in size, gradually increasing in size throughout development (Figure 1.42). The epiphysis located at the medial end of the clavicle (also called the sternal end) is the last epiphysis to fuse in the body.

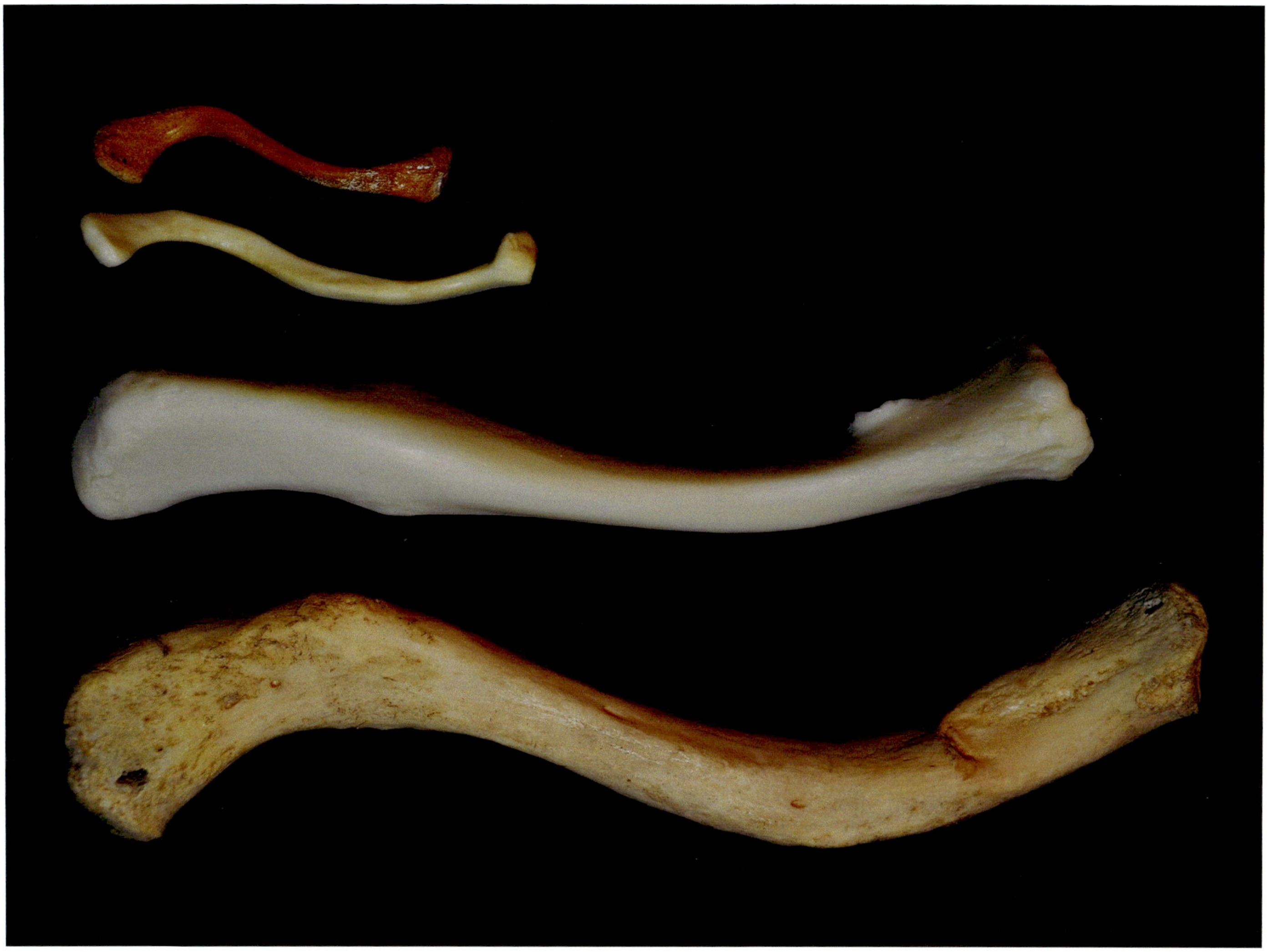

Figure 1.42 The clavicle. From top to bottom: infant, 14–16-month-old, 13-year-old, and adult.

The scapula The subadult scapula is similar in morphology to the adult (Figure 1.43). Notice the small epiphysis in the 5-year-old specimen. It remains unfused in the 13-year-old specimen and is fully fused in adulthood.

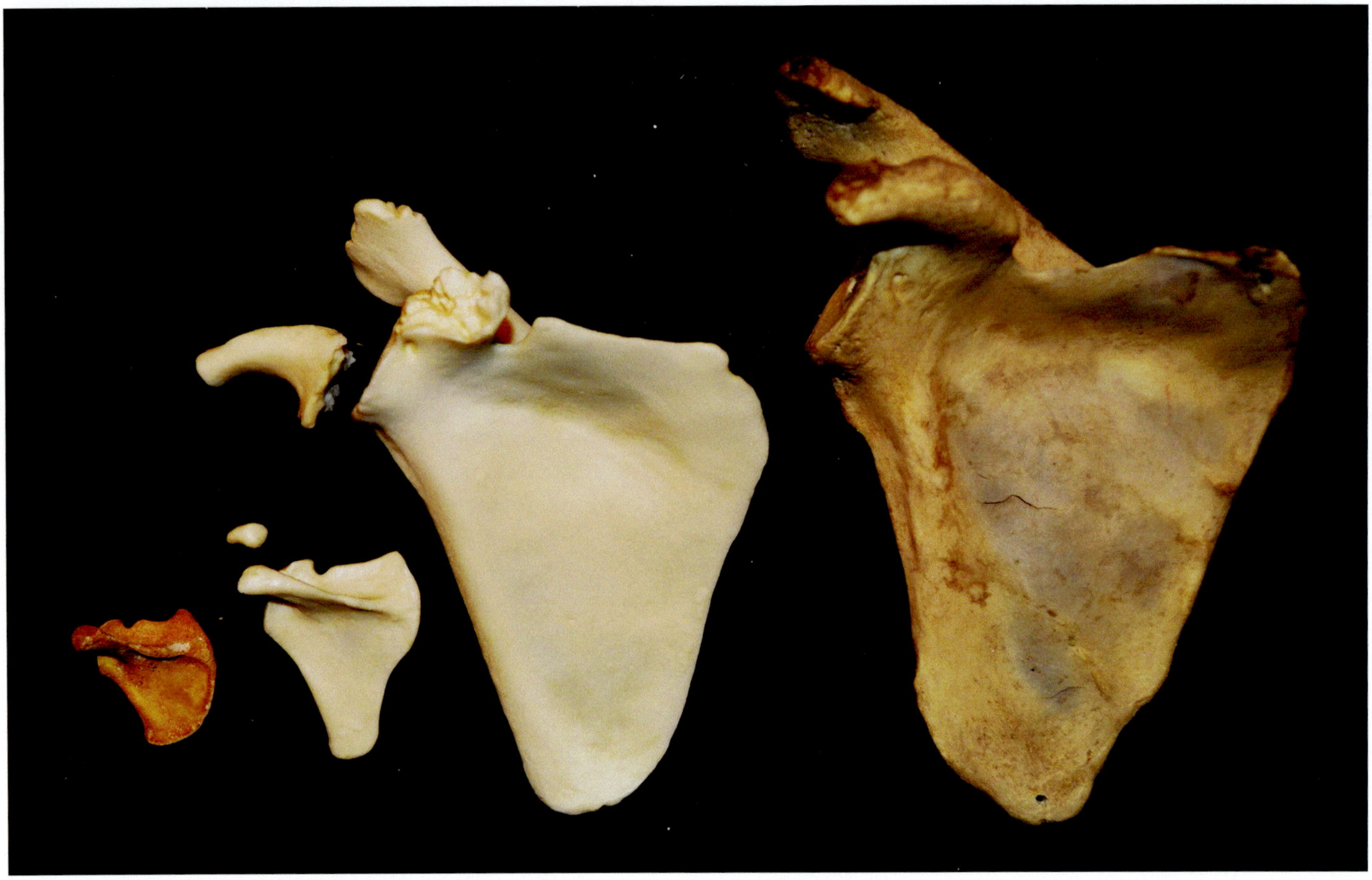

Figure 1.43 The scapula. From left to right: infant, 5-year-old, 13-year-old, and adult scapulae.

The humerus The humerus is the bone of the arm. Figure 1.44 shows the humerus in various stages of development.

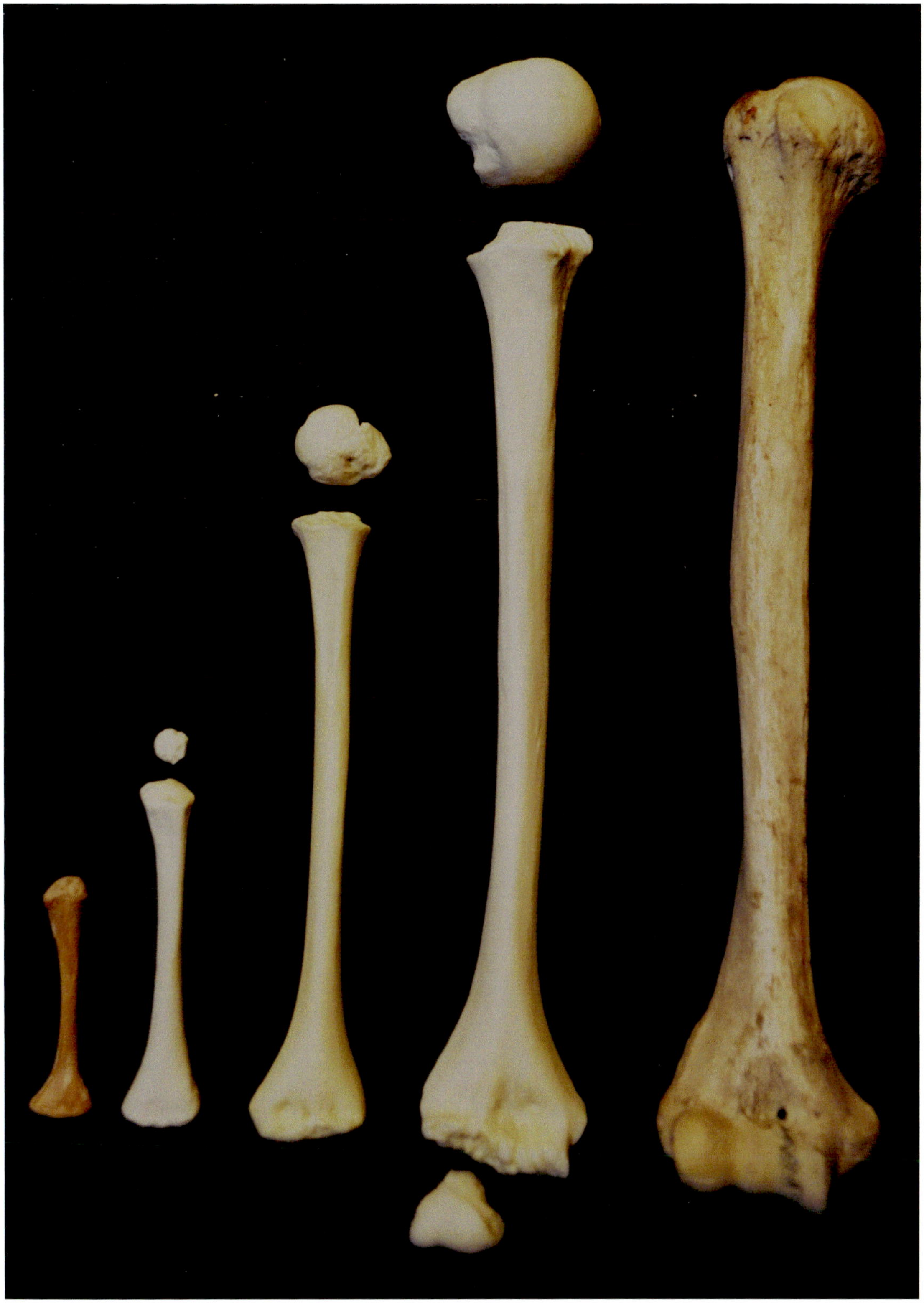

Figure 1.44 The humerus. From left to right: infant, 13–16-month-old, 5-year-old, 13-year-old, and adult humeri.

The forearm The forearm contains the radius and the ulna. Figure 1.45 shows the radius and ulna together at various stages of development.

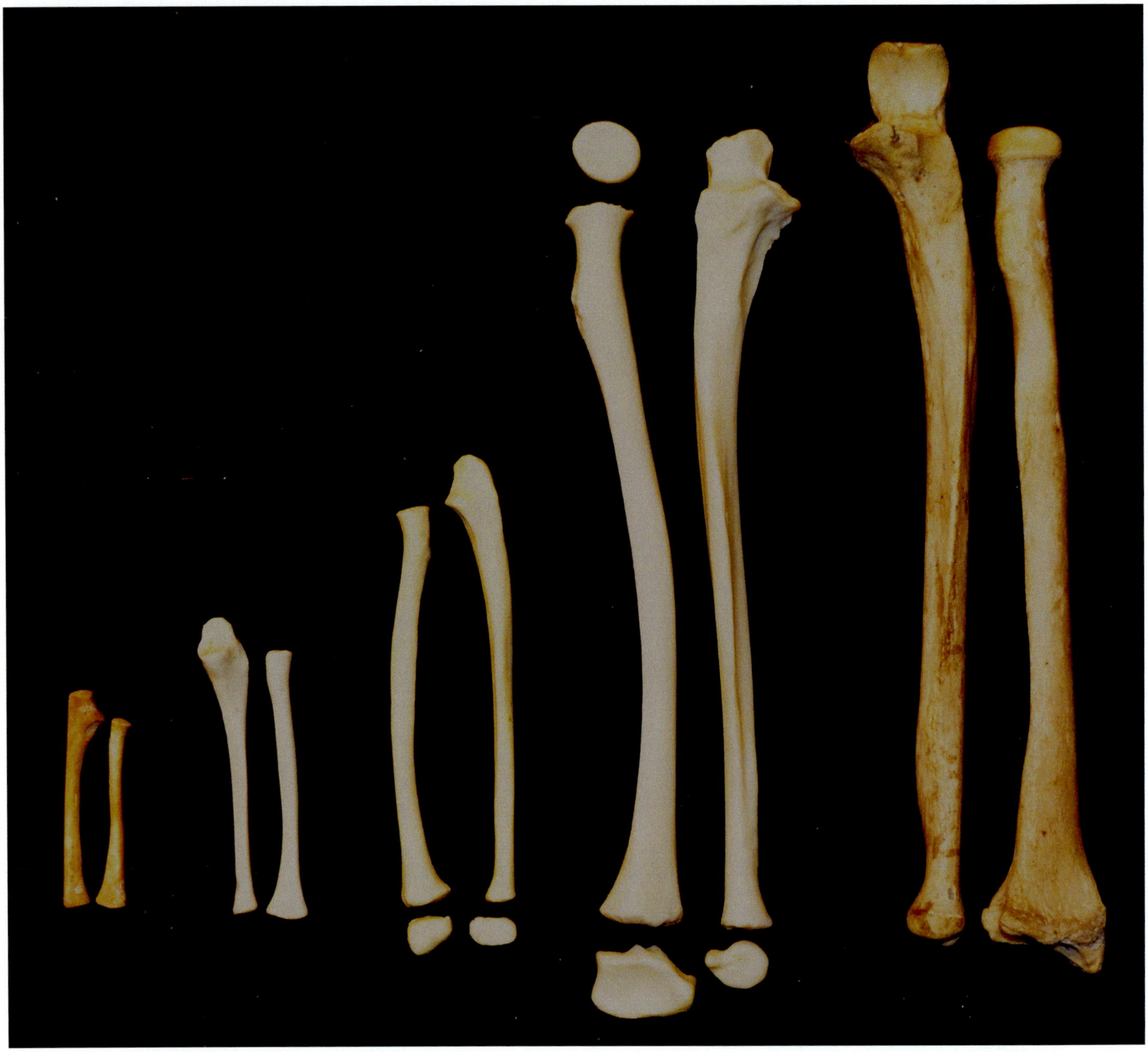

Figure 1.45 The forearm (ulna and radius). From left to right: infant, 13–16-month-old, 5-year-old, 13-year-old, and adult.

The hand The bones of the hand are extremely small in subadult individuals. Figure 1.46 shows a selection of infant hand bones compared to adult hand bones.

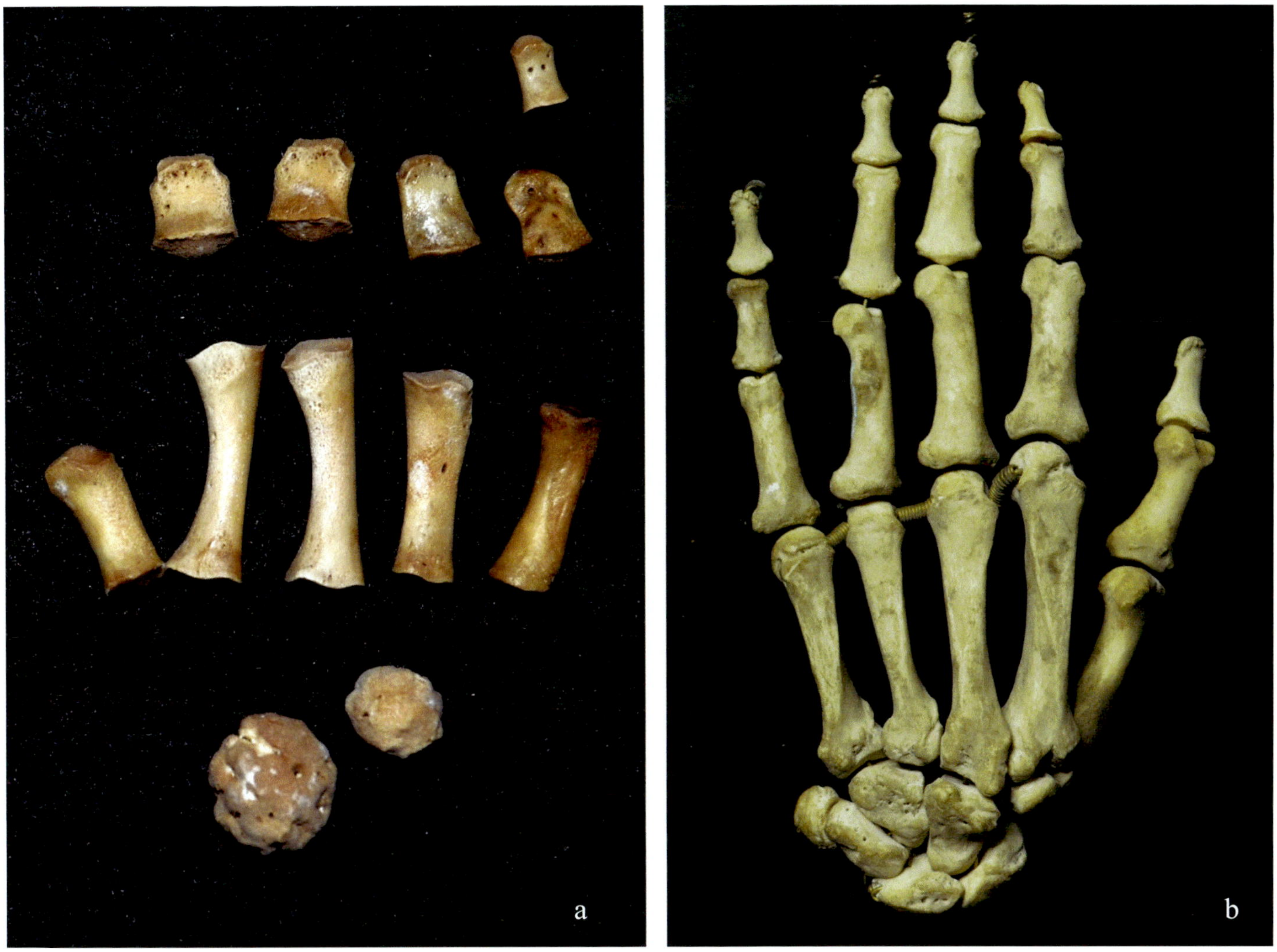

Figure 1.46 The hand. (a) Infant hand. (b) Adult hand.

The pelvis The pelvis contains the paired os coxae, the sacrum, and the coccyx. Figure 1.47 shows the pelvic girdles of a 5-year-old and an adult from the anterior and posterior views. Notice how the unfused portions of the os coxae and the sacrum in the 5-year-old specimen are visible in the articulated pelvic girdle in Figure 1.47. Recall from the Adult Osteology section of this manual that the os coxae consists of three separate bones: the ilium, the ischium, and the pubis. Figure 1.48 shows in detail the fusion of these three bones at various stages of development. Figure 1.49 shows the growth and development of the segments of the sacrum.

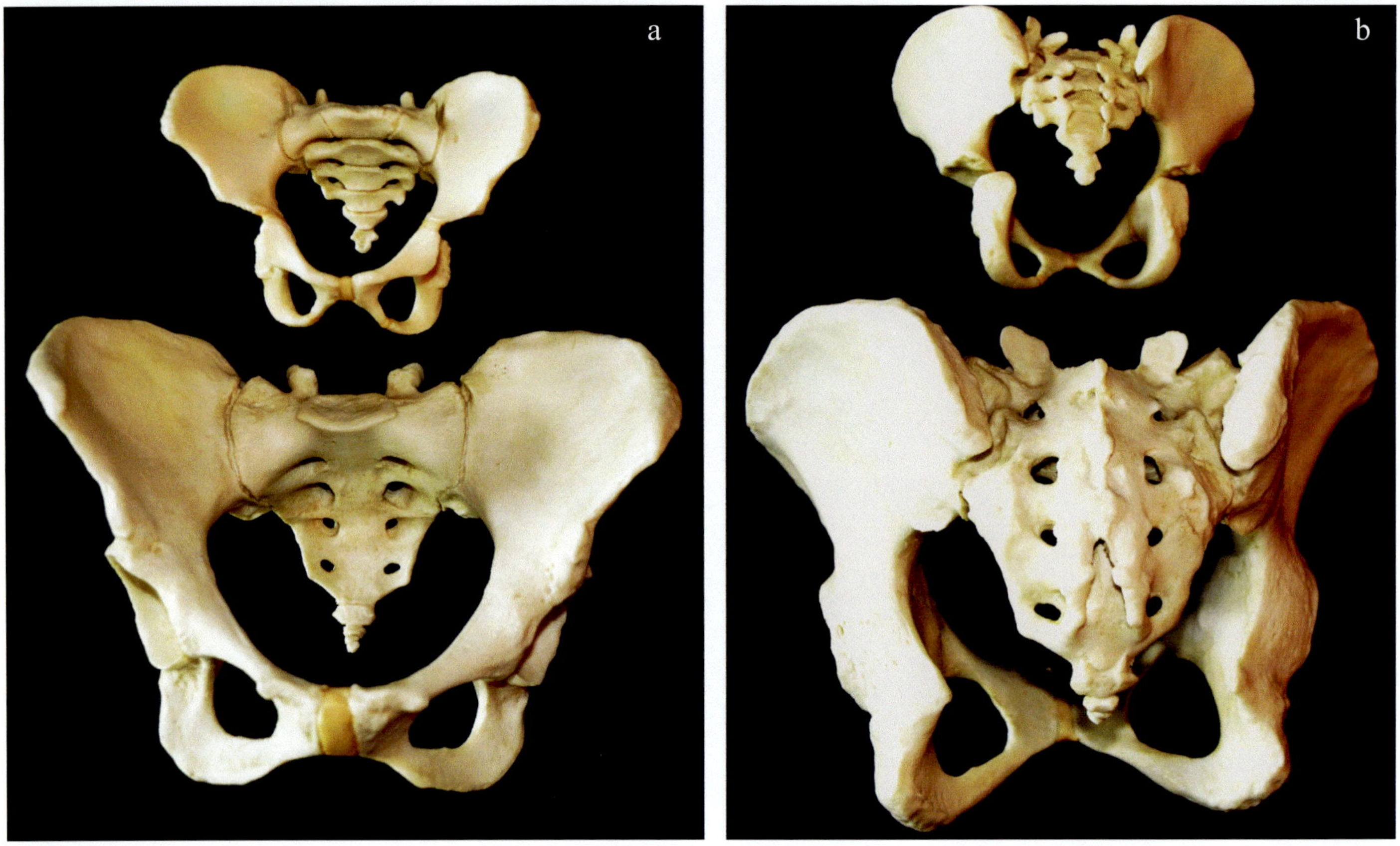

Figure 1.47 The pelvic girdle. (a) Anterior view of the 5-year-old (top) and adult (bottom) pelvis. (b) Posterior view of the 5-year-old (top) and adult (bottom) pelvis.

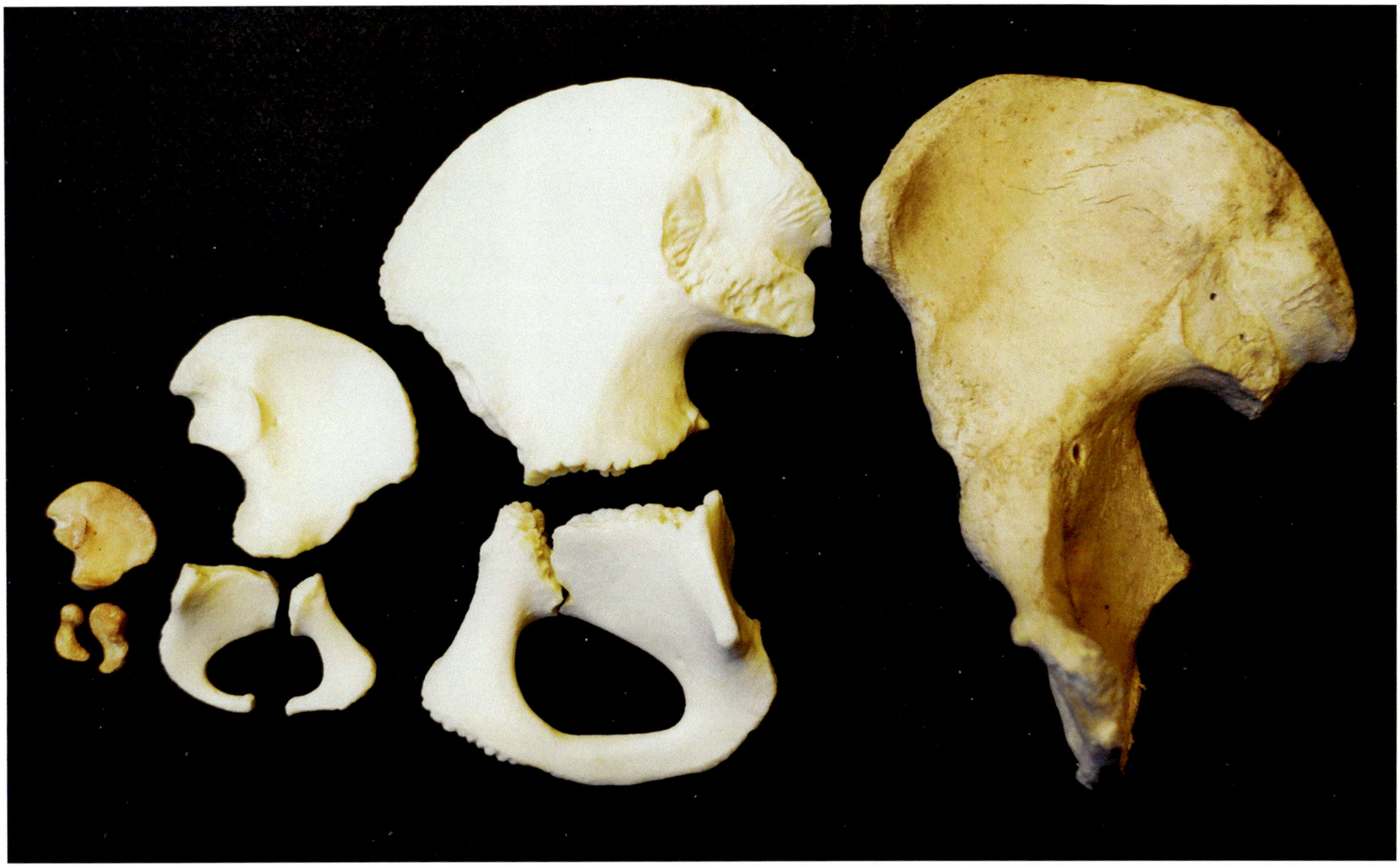

Figure 1.48 The os coxa. From left to right: infant, 5-year-old, 13-year-old, and adult os coxae.

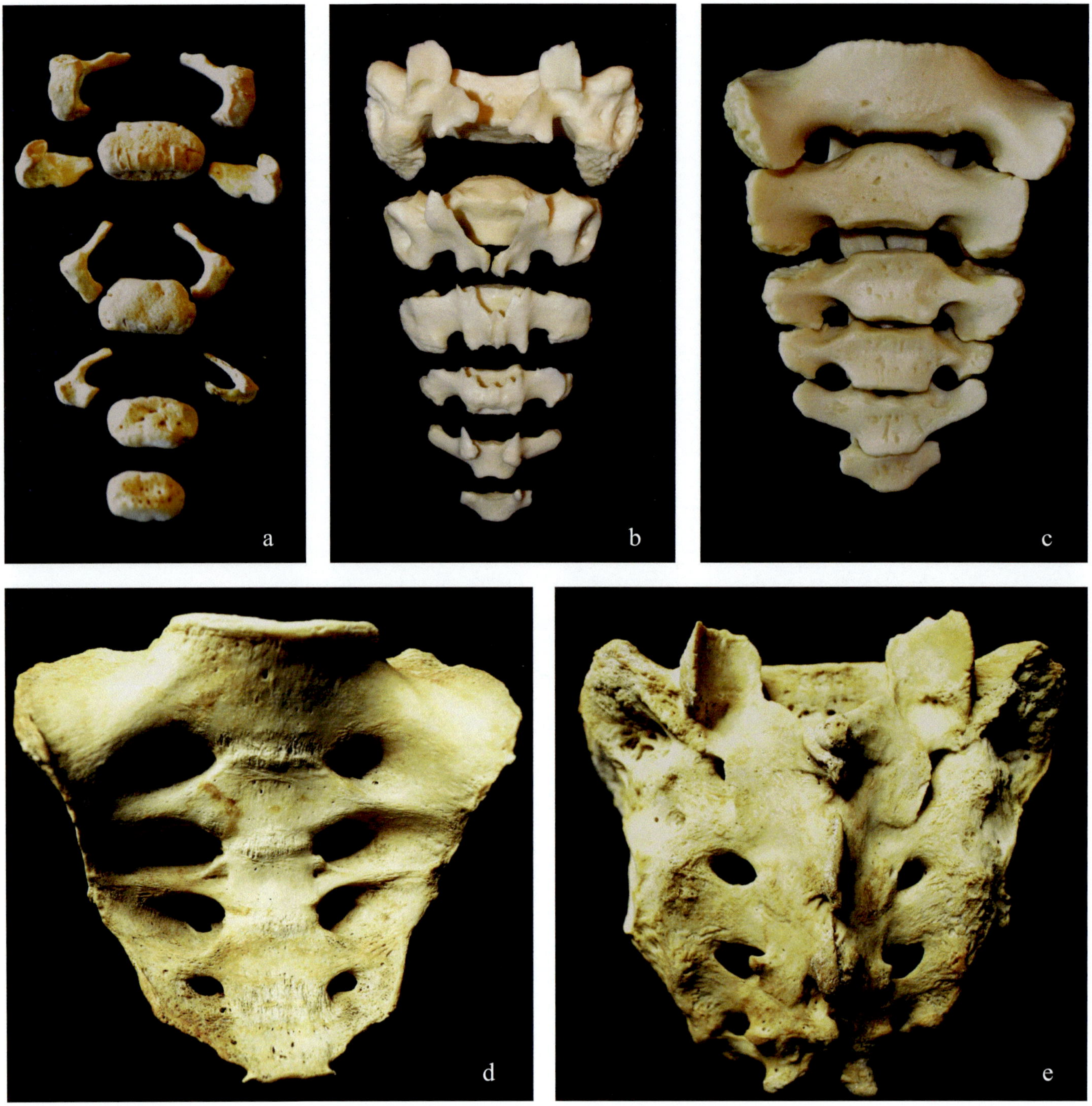

Figure 1.49 The sacrum. (a) Infant. (b) Posterior view of the 13-year-old human sacrum. (c) Anterior view of the 13-year-old sacrum. (d) Anterior view of the adult sacrum. (e) Posterior view of the adult sacrum.

The femur Figure 1.50 shows the growth and development of the femur (bone of the thigh) from infant to adult. The proximal and distal epiphyses grow larger until they eventually fuse to form the adult femur.

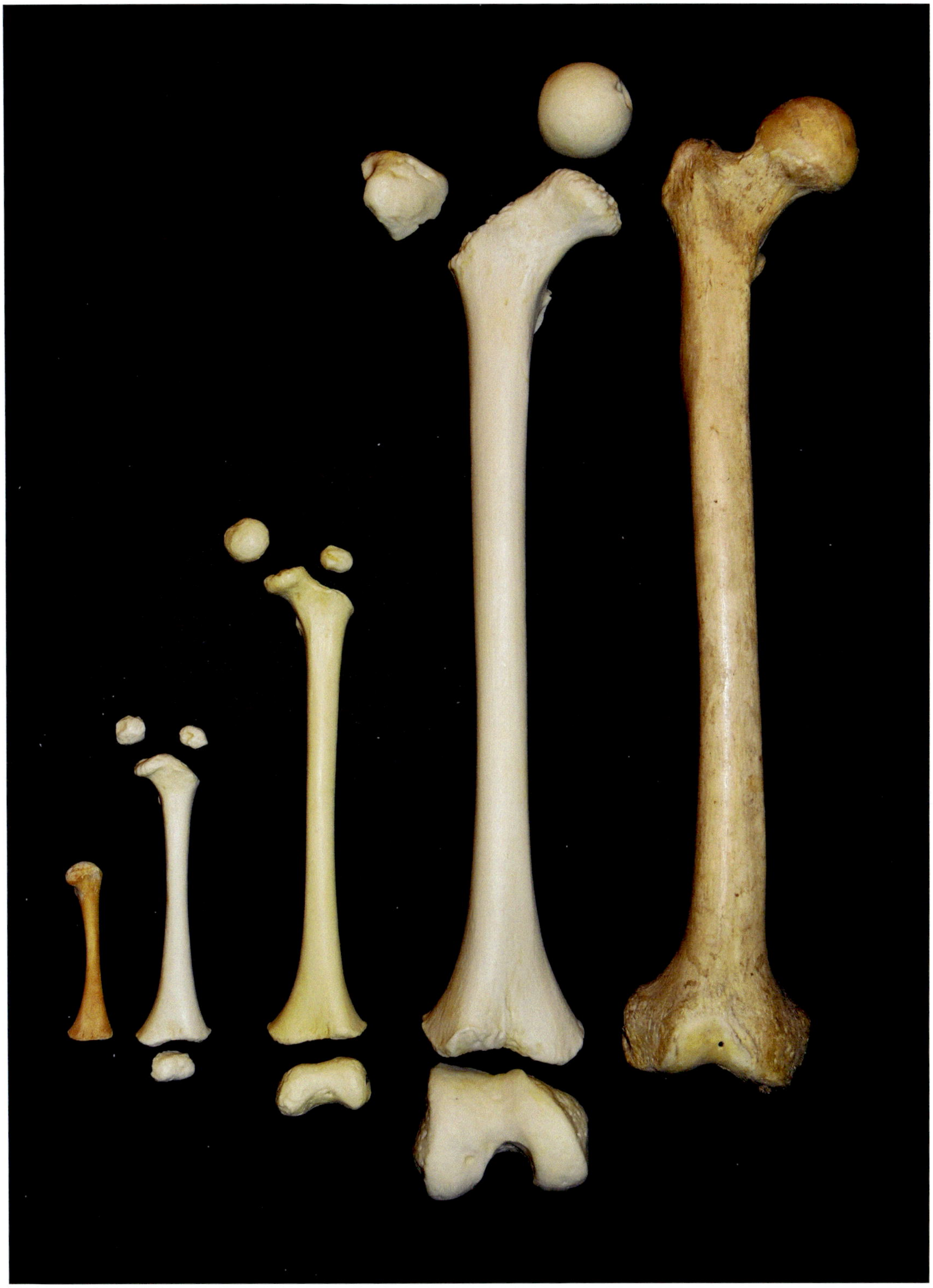

Figure 1.50 The femur. From left to right: infant, 14–16-month-old, 5-year-old, 13-year-old, and adult femora.

The patella The subadult patella (kneecap) is similar in morphology to the adult patella. Figure 1.51 shows that the size is the biggest observable difference between the adult and subadult patella.

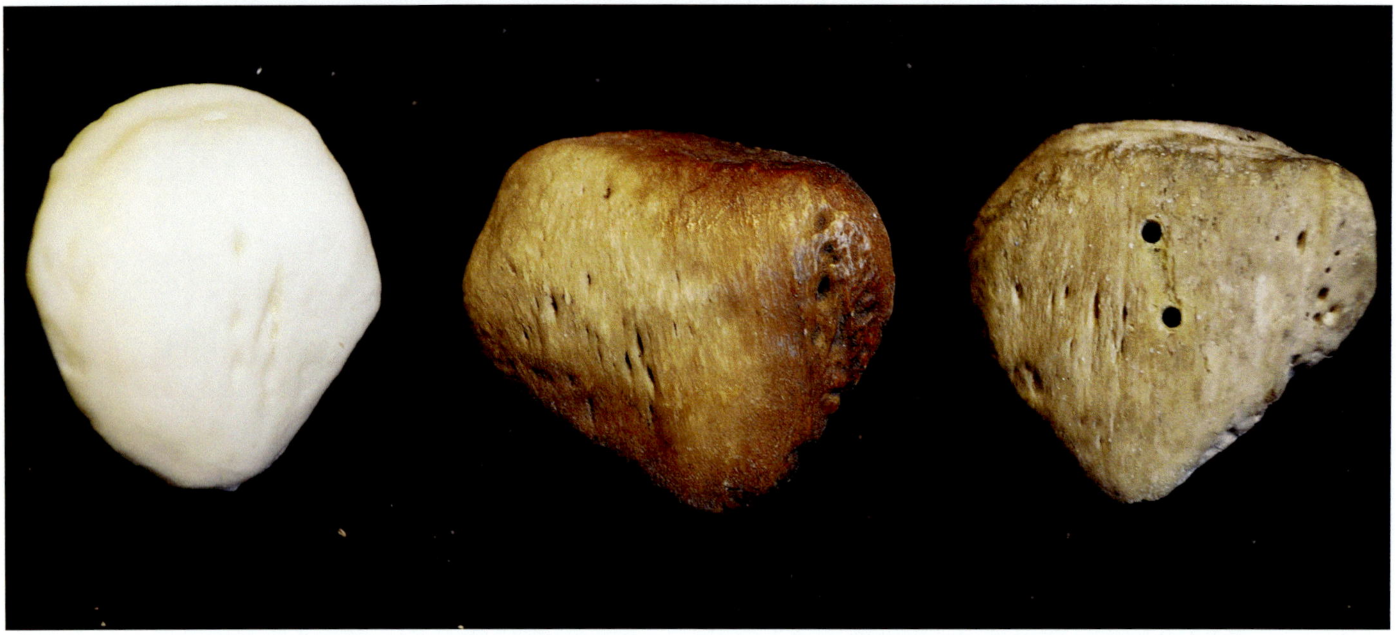

Figure 1.51 The patella. 13-year-old (left) and two adult patellae (middle and right).

The Tibia The tibia is one of the two bones of the leg. Figure 1.52 shows the progression of growth and development from infant to adult.

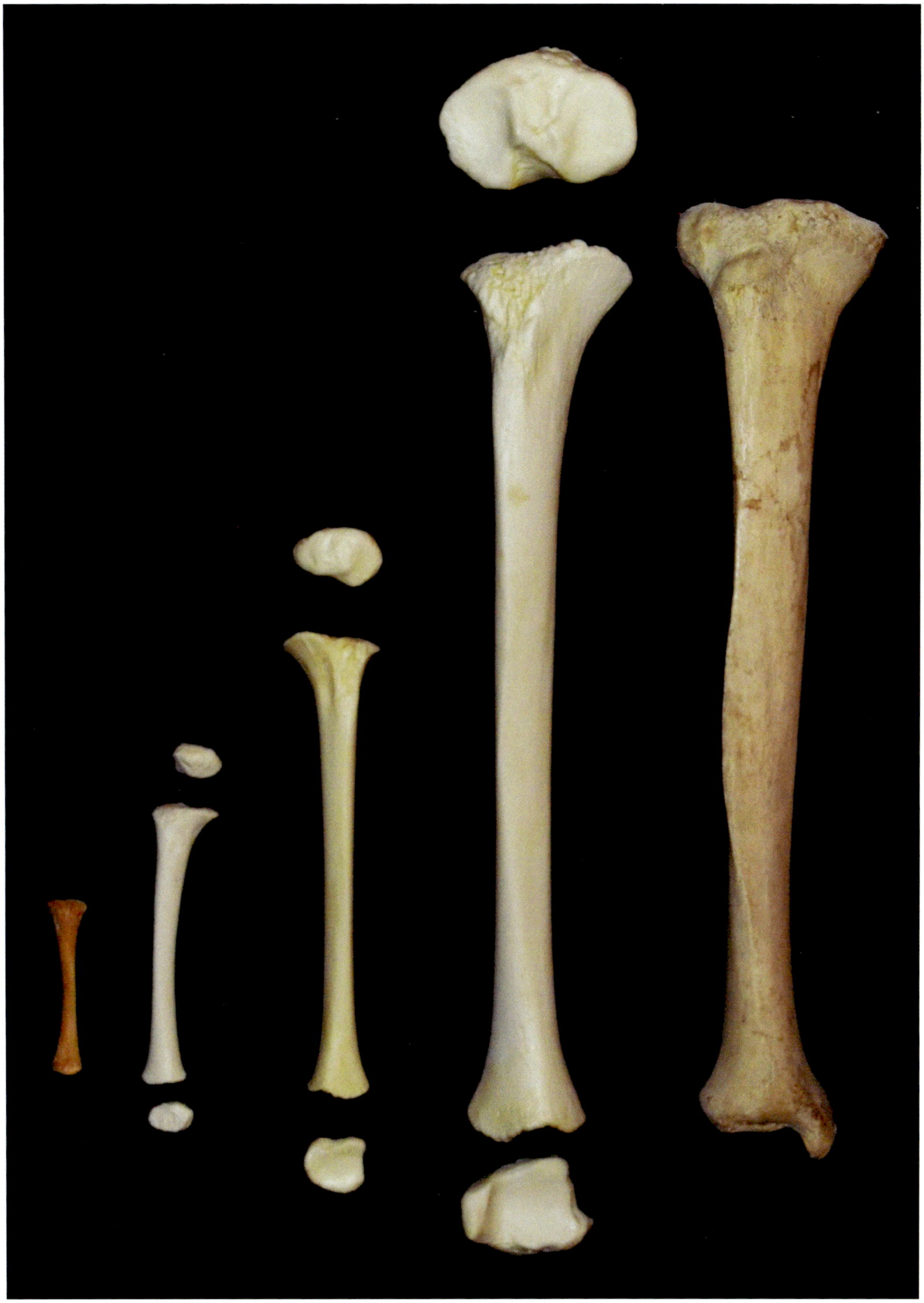

Figure 1.52 The tibia. From left to right: infant, 14–16-month-old, 5-year-old, 13-year-old, and adult tibiae.

The bones of the leg together: the tibia and fibula The bones of the leg contain the tibia and the fibula. Figure 1.53 illustrates the growth and development of the tibia and fibula together from infant to adult.

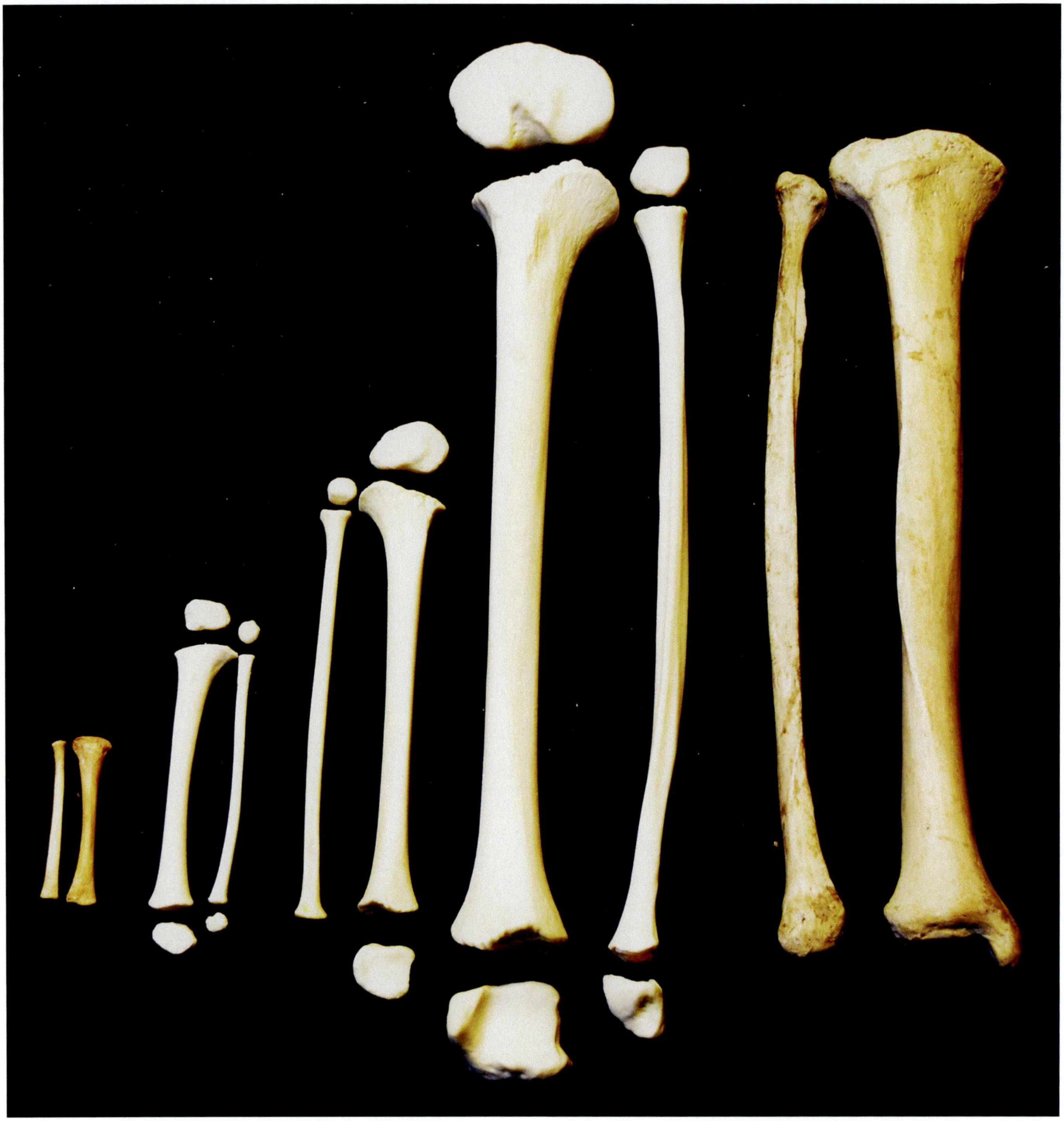

Figure 1.53 The bones of the leg (fibula and tibia). From left to right: infant, 14–16-month-old, 5-year-old, 13-year-old, and adult tibiae and fibulae.

The foot Similar to the bones of the hands, the bones of subadult feet are extremely small. Figure 1.54 shows the difference in morphology and size between the foot bones of an infant and an adult.

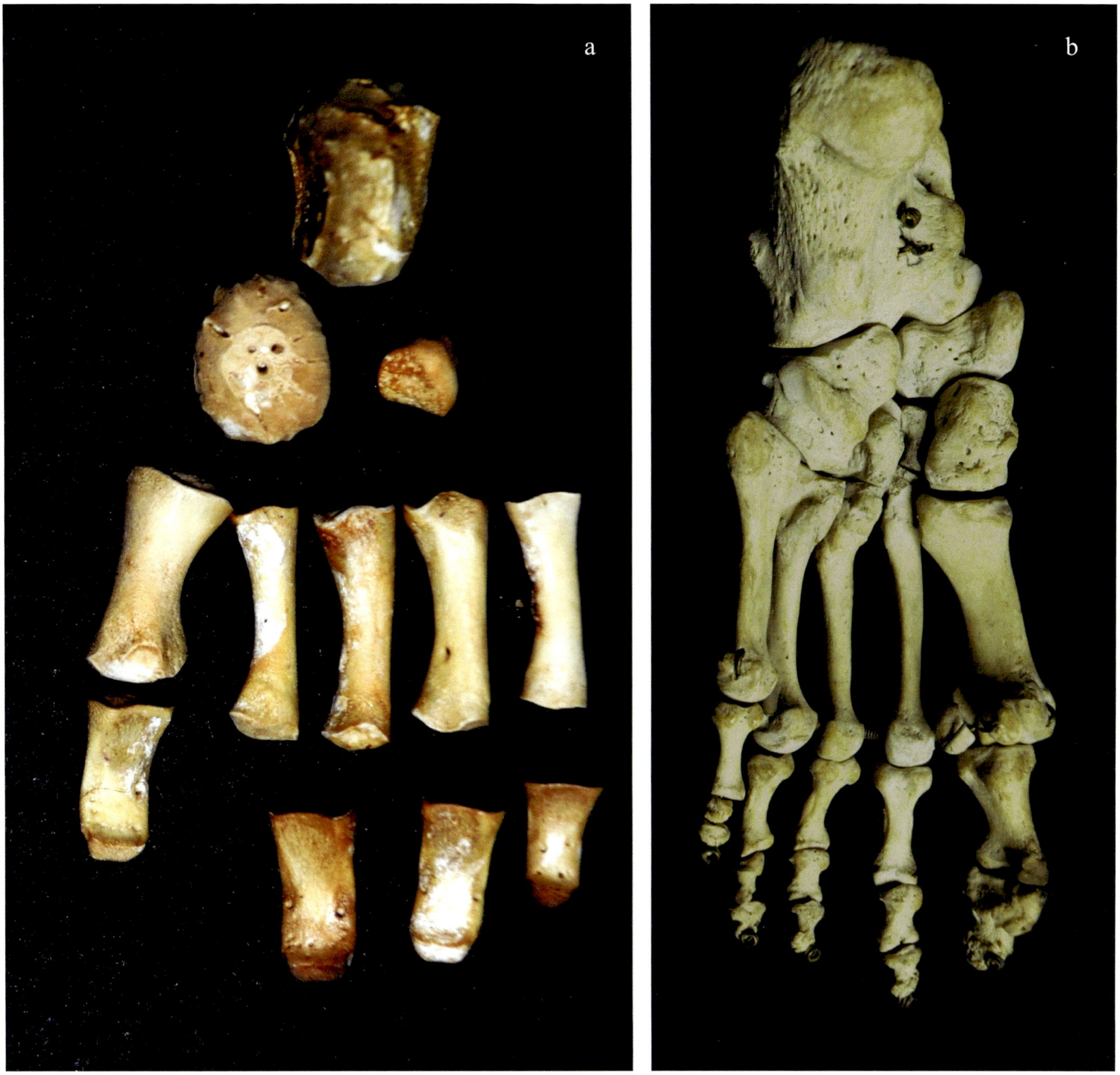

Figure 1.54 The foot. (a) Infant foot bones. (b) Adult foot bones.

Human versus nonhuman osteology

Introduction

Most law enforcement personnel and other investigators will likely encounter possible bones over the course of their careers. It is important to have a basic understanding of what constitutes non-osseous (non-bony) material from **osseous** (bony) material, and human bone from nonhuman bone. For instance, can a stick look like one of the subadult bones shown in the previous section? Can a weathered coconut husk look like a part of a human skull? Can rocks or pieces of coral resemble human carpal or tarsal bones? The answer to all those questions is yes! But how will the investigator tell them apart?

Bone morphology

First, it is important to understand basic human bone growth and development, which was discussed in the previous section. Second, it is necessary to understand bone morphology or shape (i.e., long, short, flat, irregular, and sesamoid), type (cortical or spongy), and function. The shape of bones, as described previously, plays a significant role in differentiating human from nonhuman remains. When nonhuman bones are approximately the same size as adult human bones, we can look at morphological (shape) differences. If the skull is available, it is easy to differentiate human from nonhuman. Postcranial bones are often difficult to differentiate because the function of these bones tends to be similar, so the bone shape is the same. Form follows function and vice versa. Last, subadult human bones will have unfused or missing epiphyses, while mature, nonhuman bones, approximately the same size, will display fused epiphyses.

Bone types

There are two types of bones: **cortical bone** (also referred to as hard or **compact bone**) and **trabecular bone** (also referred to as **spongy** or **cancellous bone**). Most bones contain both cortical and trabecular bone, but the distribution and concentration vary based on the bone's overall function. Trabecular bone is lightweight and porous and is found in the vertebral bodies, the ends of long bones, short bones, and sandwiched between flat bones. Cortical bone is harder and has a tighter weave than trabecular bone. It is located on the external surface of bones and found within the walls of bone shafts. If those two types of osseous tissue do not appear on a suspected bone, it is possible the object is not bone. In addition, bone tends to be lighter in weight than rocks of the same size.

Bone functions

Bones have specific functions. They provide stability, support, leverage, protection, and attachment points for muscles and tendons. If human bones function differently than nonhuman bones, their morphology will normally differ.

Developing a skill set

The figures in this section will show similarities and differences between several human and nonhuman bones. It is not meant to portray an exhaustive list, rather it is meant to show a sample of bones and the variations that exist. The authors recommend several comparative osteology books, especially those contrasting human to nonhuman skeletal remains. Diane L. France's, *Human and Nonhuman Bone Identification: A Color Atlas* and *Human and Nonhuman Bone Identification: A Concise Field Guide* are two of those books.

Finally, law enforcement personnel and/or scene investigators commonly identify bones **macroscopically**. This is usually done on scene and without the aid of a microscope. This is why it is a good idea to use different tools, books, or comparative osteological collections to develop a skill set for more accurate identifications. To hone that skill set, the authors recommend: (1) purchasing comparative osteology books and studying them, (2) purchasing a full-sized disarticulated human skeleton model and an articulated one, if funds are available, (3) collecting **faunal** remains from the area for a comparative collection, with permission from appropriate authorities, and finally (4) attending short-courses like those offered by the authors. The human and nonhuman craniums (skull minus the mandible) have many of the same bones, but the morphology (shape) is different as shown in Figure 1.55.

Figure 1.55 Nonhuman and human crania. (a) From left to right: anterior view of mountain lion, adult deer, subadult deer, subadult human, and adult human. (b) From left to right: superior view of mountain lion, adult deer, subadult deer, subadult human, and adult human. (c) From left to right: mountain lion 2-piece mandible and cranium, adult deer cranium and mandible, subadult deer cranium, subadult human mandible and cranium, and adult human mandible and cranium.

Figure 1.56 displays the base of a deer and a human cranium. One of the easiest ways to differentiate the two is in the maxillae (upper jawbone). The human maxilla does not extend outward like the deer maxilla. In addition, the foramen magnum (large oval-shaped hole on the human and the triangular-shaped hole on the deer), on each skull is in a different location. The position is important because it is an indicator of locomotion, which is the movement of an organism from one place to another. Humans are **bipedal (orthograde)**, meaning walking on two legs with an upright posture. Hence, the foramen magnum on the human cranium is centered and aligned with a more vertical trunk. Deer are **quadrupedal (pronograde)**, meaning walking on four legs with a horizontal posture. Thus, the foramen magnum on the deer cranium is off-center to align with a horizontal trunk that is parallel to the ground.

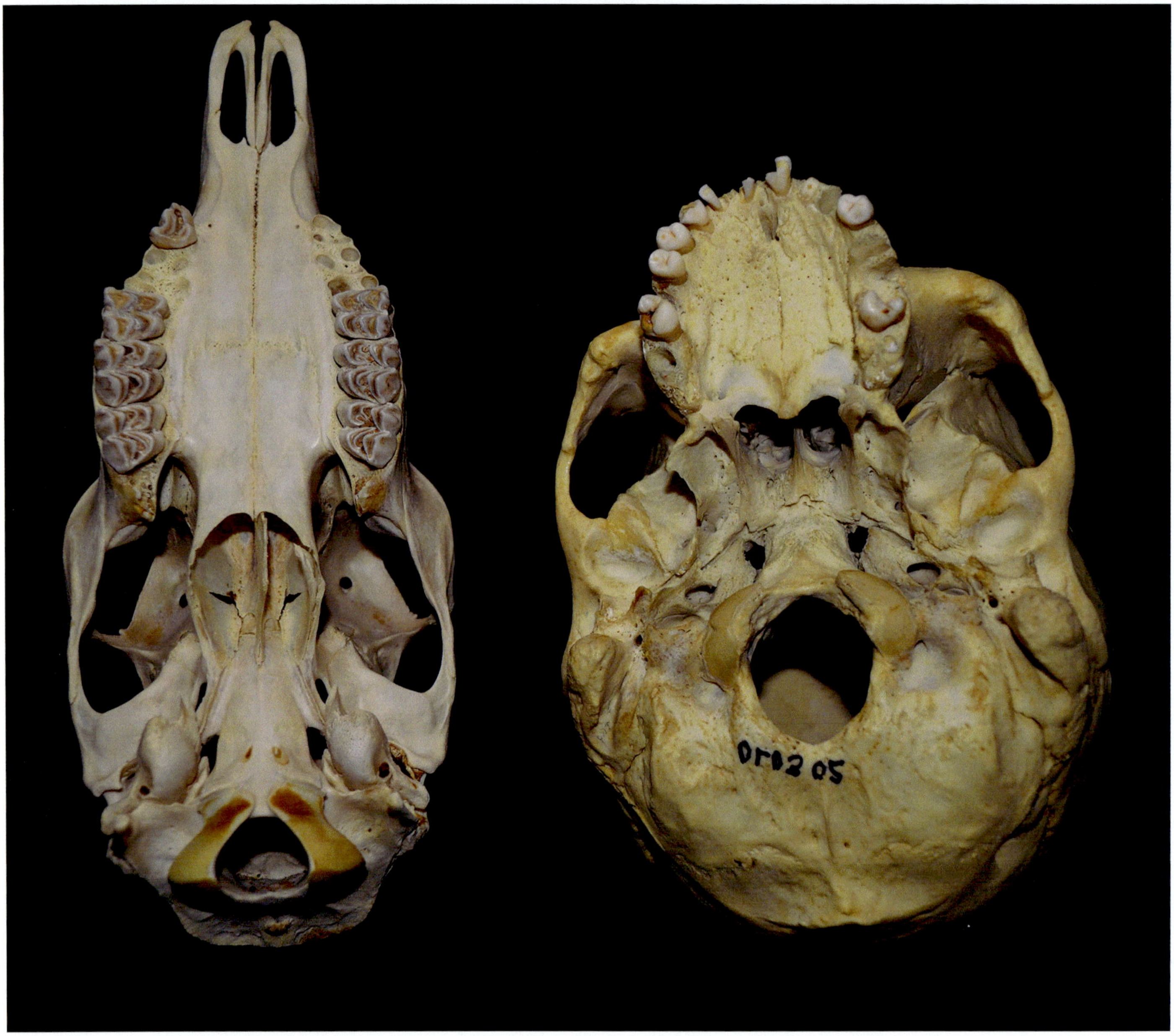

Figure 1.56 Deer and adult human crania. Inferior view of deer (left) and adult human (right).

Figure 1.57 shows the occipital bones of a subadult deer and a human. This bone is located at the back (posterior portion) of the skull. The foramen magnum is depicted toward the bottom of each.

Figure 1.57 Two-piece subadult deer occipital bone (left) and adult human occipital bone (right).

Figure 1.58 illustrates the mandible (lower jawbone) of a deer and a human. Notice that the deer mandible is unfused, resulting in two bones, while the human mandible is fused, resulting in one bone.

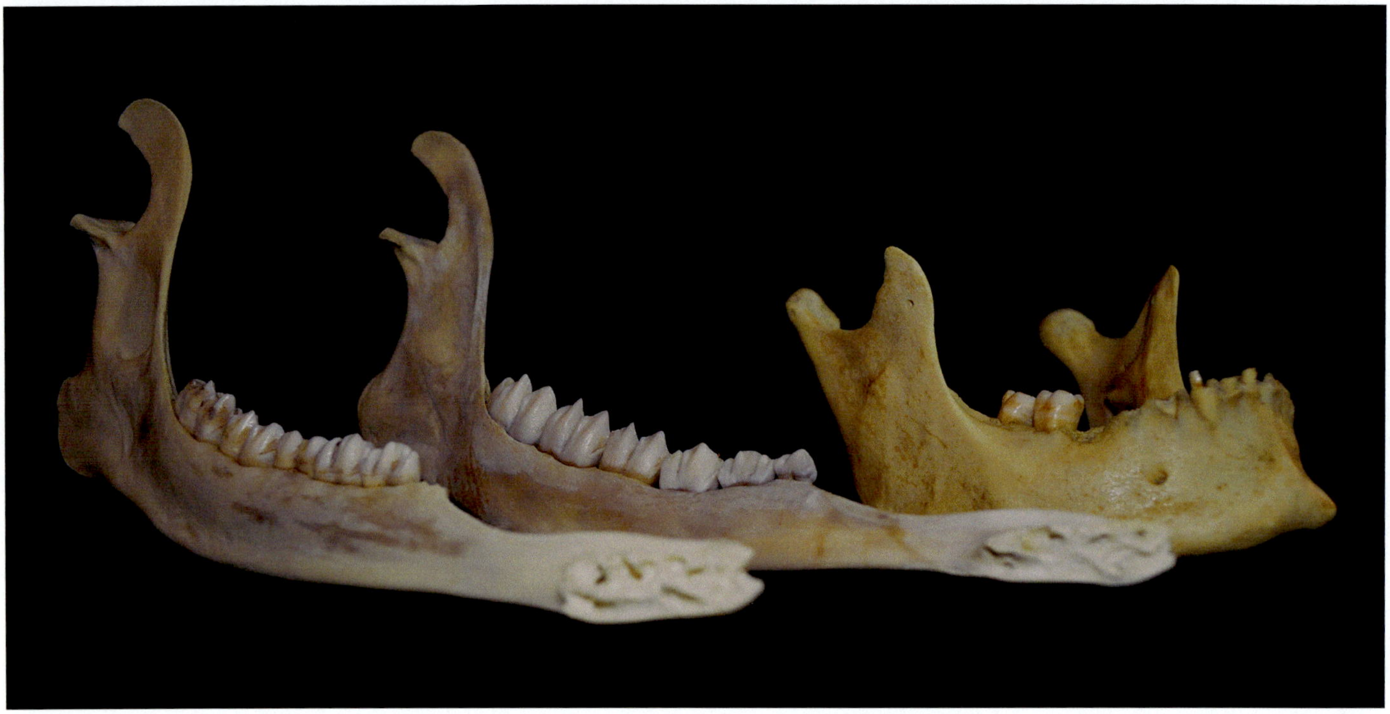

Figure 1.58 Two-piece deer mandible (left and center) and adult human mandible (right).

Figure 1.59a shows four cervical vertebrae. The two bones on the top are called atlases or the first cervical vertebrae, while the two bones on the bottom are called axes or the second cervical vertebrae. If found isolated from the rest of the skeleton, they are easy to differentiate. Figure 1.59b shows various vertebrae both human and other animals.

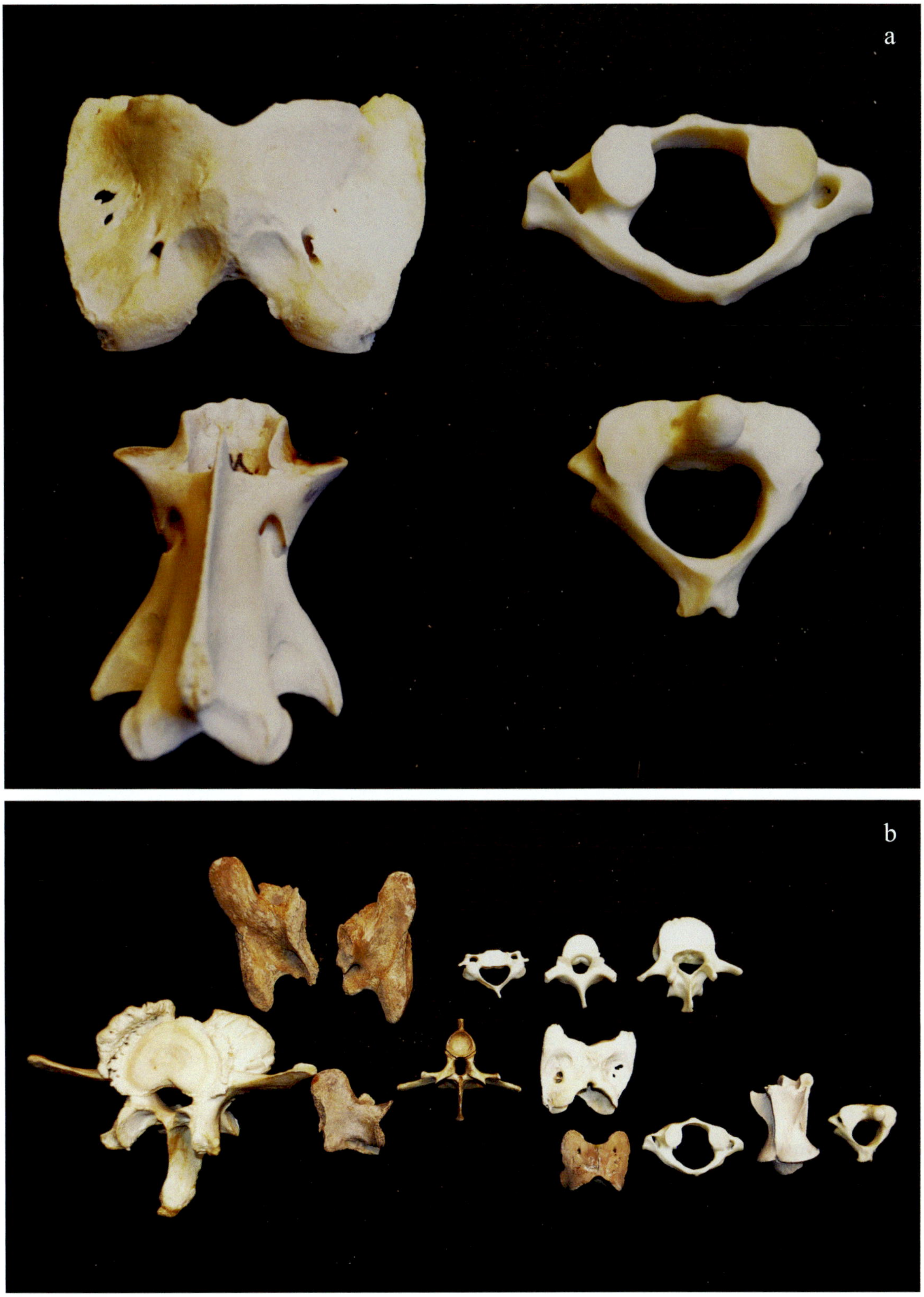

Figure 1.59 Vertebrae. (a) Top row left to right: deer atlas (C1) and human atlas (C1). Bottom row left to right: deer axis (C2) and human axis (C2). (b) Assorted human and nonhuman vertebrae, showing variation.

Figure 1.60 displays a variety of human and nonhuman ribs. The human ribs tend to be more curved than those of deer or other quadrupeds, which is due to the shape of their rib cages.

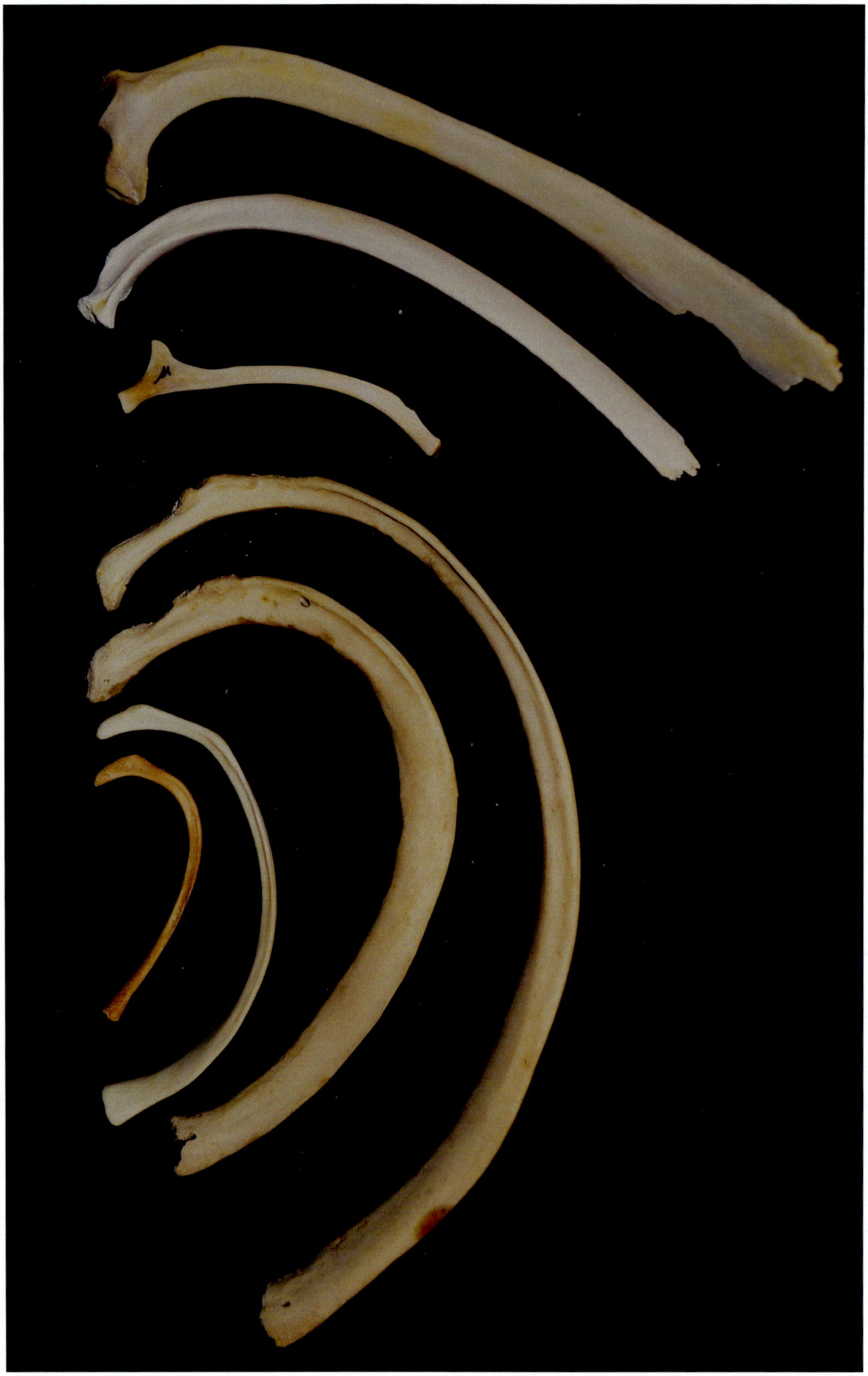

Figure 1.60 Assorted human and nonhuman rib bones.

Figure 1.61a shows a variety of human and nonhuman scapulae, which are also colloquially known as shoulder blades. The scapula connects with the clavicle in humans. Deer (and other animals) do not have clavicles. This allows their scapulas to pivot independently. Figure 1.61b shows the shape of a human scapula on the left and the two deer and bison scapula on the right. Several features (acromion and coracoid processes) on the top of each scapula look quite different because they have different functions. Remember from before, form follows function and vice versa.

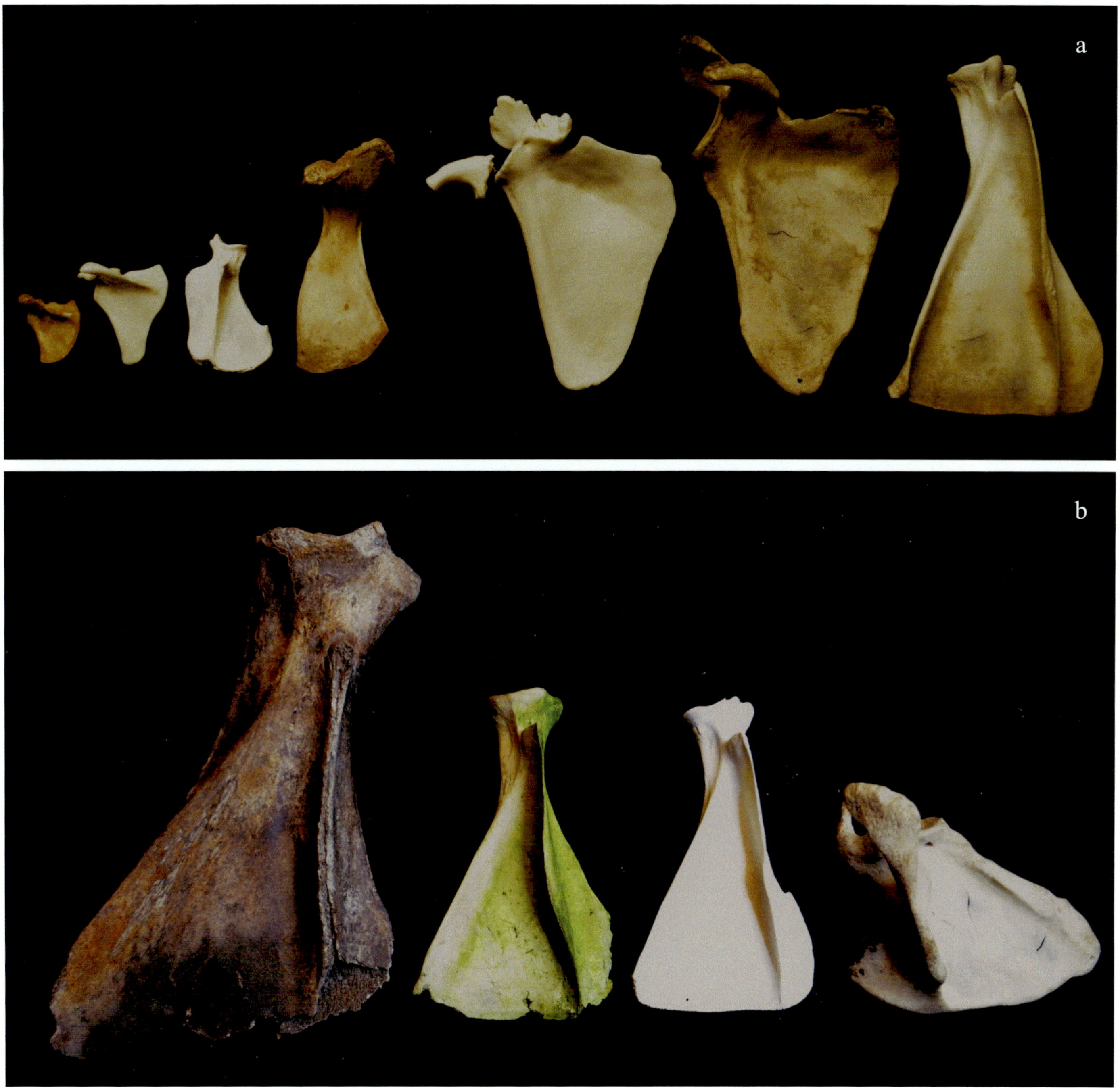

Figure 1.61 Assorted scapulae. (a) From left to right: infant human, 5-year-old human, raccoon, alligator, 13-year-old human, adult human, and deer. (b) From left to right: human, deer, deer, and bison.

Figure 1.62 depicts a variety of human and nonhuman humeri. The extra bones on the third, fifth, sixth, and eighth from the left show the epiphyses that were discussed in the subadult human osteology section of this guide.

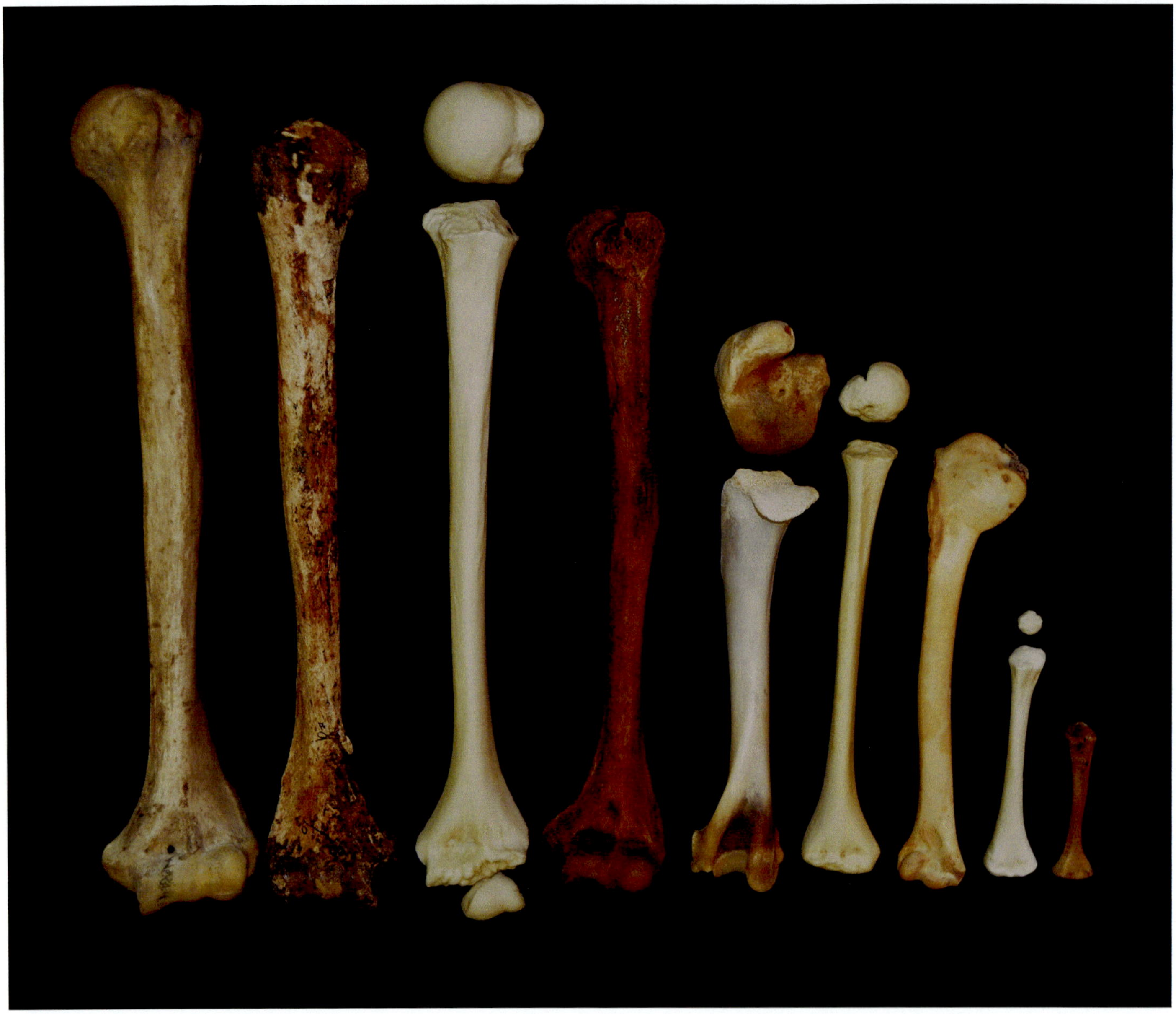

Figure 1.62 Assorted humeri. From left to right: adult human, adult human, 13-year-old human, adult human, deer, 5-year-old human, goose, 13–16-month-old human, and infant human.

Figures 1.63a, b illustrate both human and nonhuman radii. The extra bones on the second and fourth from the left are the epiphyses. It can be difficult to differentiate a human from a nonhuman radius, especially if they are isolated from the rest of the skeleton.

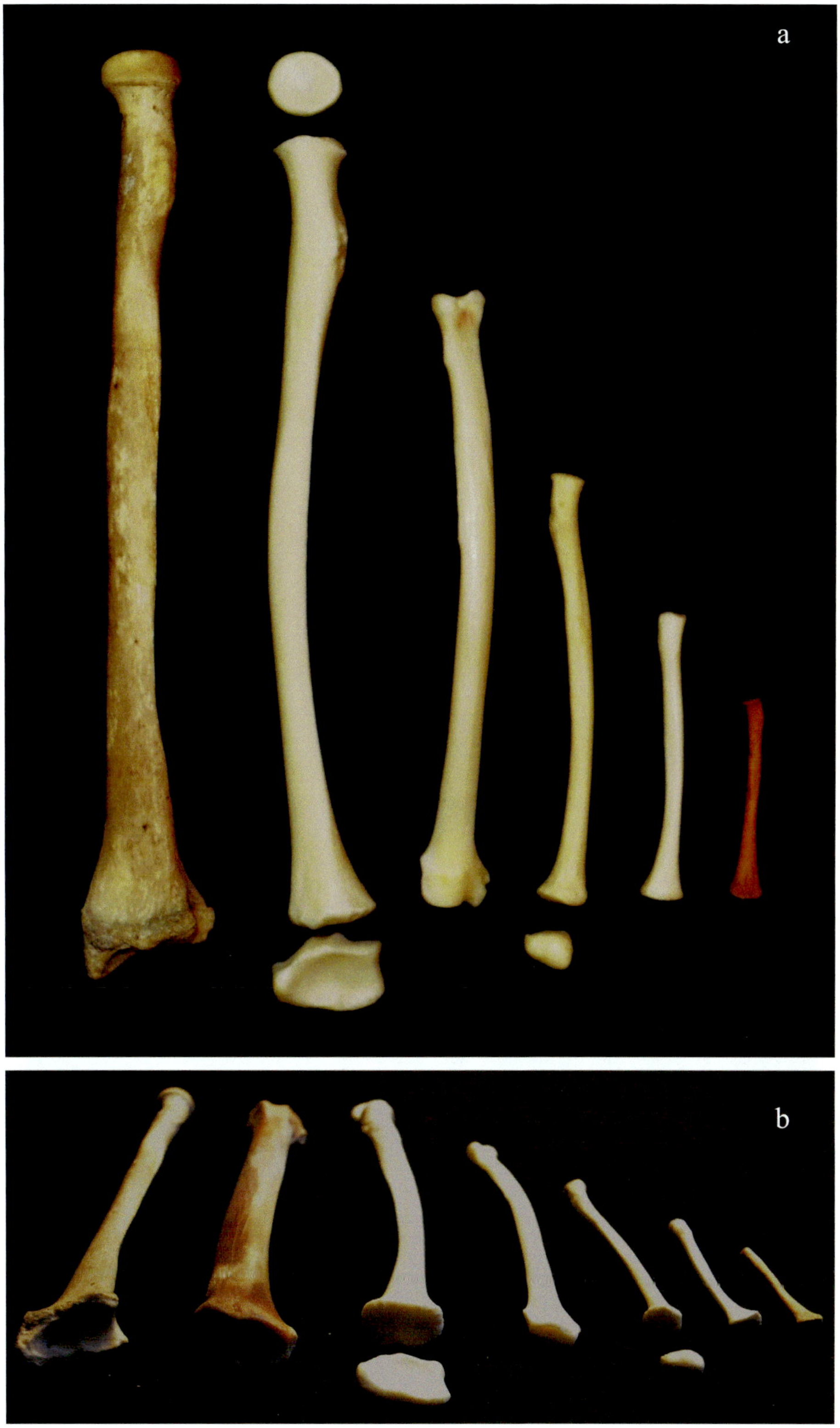

Figure 1.63 Assorted radii. (a) From left to right: adult human, 13-year-old human, coyote, 5-year-old human, 13–16-month-old human, and infant human. (b) Distal view of humeri. From left to right: adult human, deer, 13-year-old human, coyote, 5-year-old human, 13–16-month-old human, and infant human.

Figure 1.64a shows a variety of human and nonhuman ulnas. The additional small bones on the bottom are the epiphyses. Figure 1.64b shows the radii and ulnae of both humans and nonhumans.

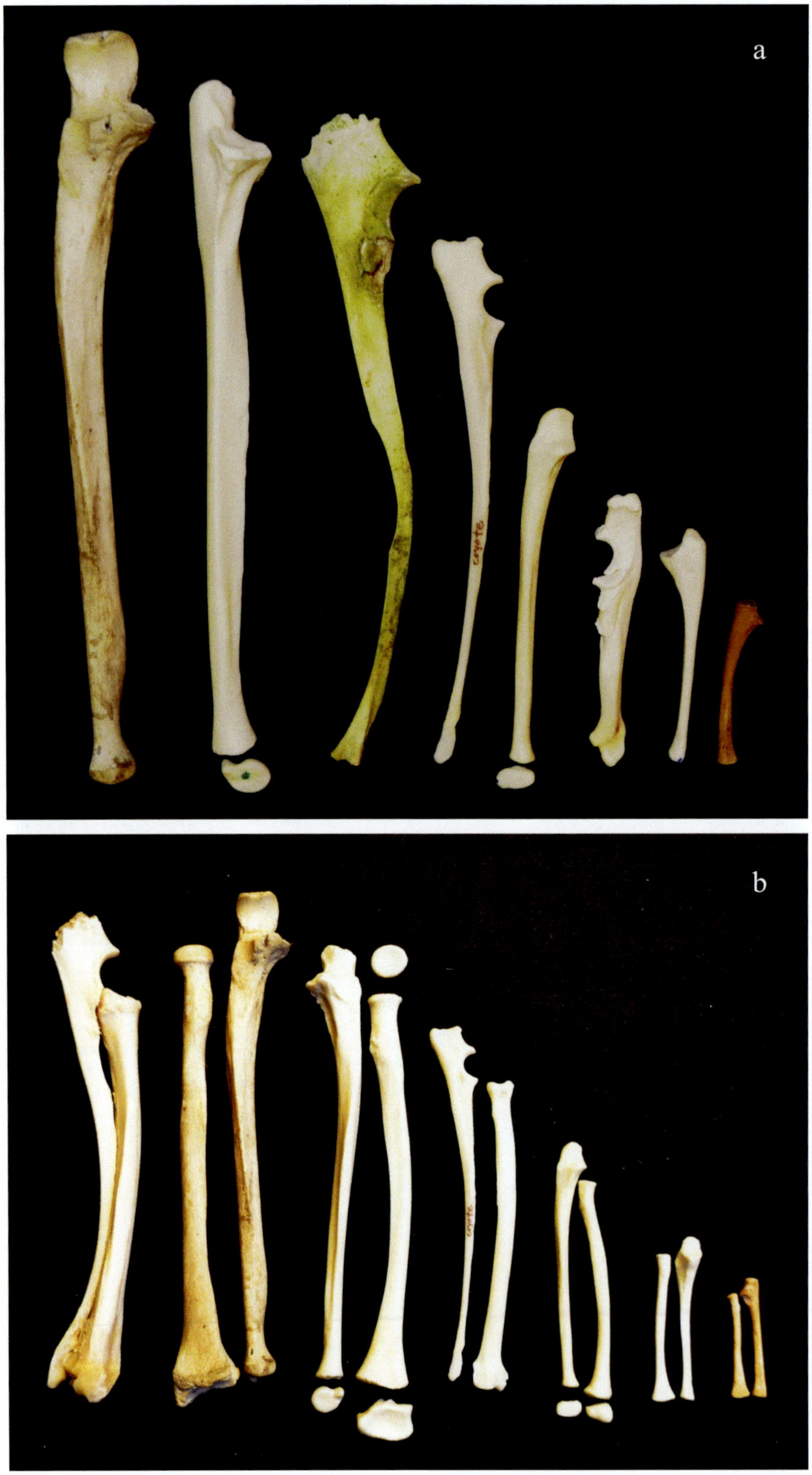

Figure 1.64 Assorted ulnae and radii. (a) From left to right: adult human, 13-year-old human, deer, coyote, 5-year-old human, raccoon, 13–16-month-old human, and infant human. (b) From left to right: deer, adult human, 13-year-old human, coyote, 5-year-old human, 13–16-month-old human, and infant human.

Figures 1.65a–e illustrate human and nonhuman hands/forepaws and metacarpals. One differentiation between human metacarpals and those of bears and other nonhumans is at the distal end of the proximal metacarpal. The distal end of the metacarpals of humans is smooth. Bears and other nonhuman metacarpals have a distinct ridge of bone. Correspondingly, the nonhuman proximal phalanges have a groove that articulates with the metacarpal ridge. The human proximal phalanges do not have this groove.

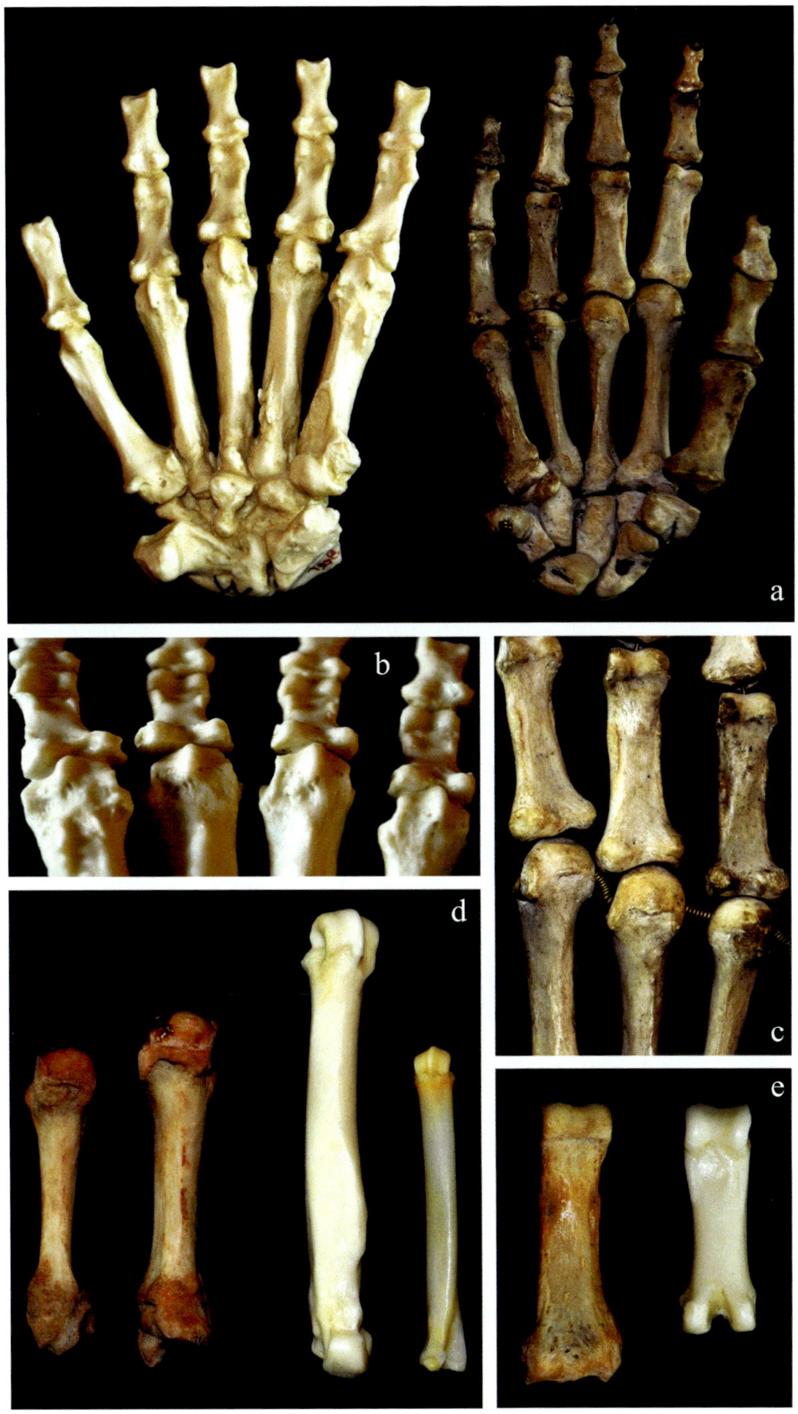

Figure 1.65 Assorted hand and forepaw bones. (a) Bear forepaw (left) and human hand (right). (b) Close-up of bear metacarpals showing ridges on distal ends. (c) Close-up of human metacarpals showing no ridges on distal ends. (d) From left to right: two human metacarpals with no ridges, a dog metacarpal with a ridge, and a raccoon metacarpal with a ridge. (e) Human phalange with no groove on the proximal end (left) and a dog phalange with a groove on the proximal end of the phalange (right). The ridge fits into the groove, where depicted.

Figures 1.66a, b show an assortment of human and nonhuman os coxae. The previous section on subadult human osteology discussed ossification and bone fusion. Several of the os coxae depict unfused bones. As a result, the three parts of the os coxa (ilium, ischium, and pubis) are easy to differentiate.

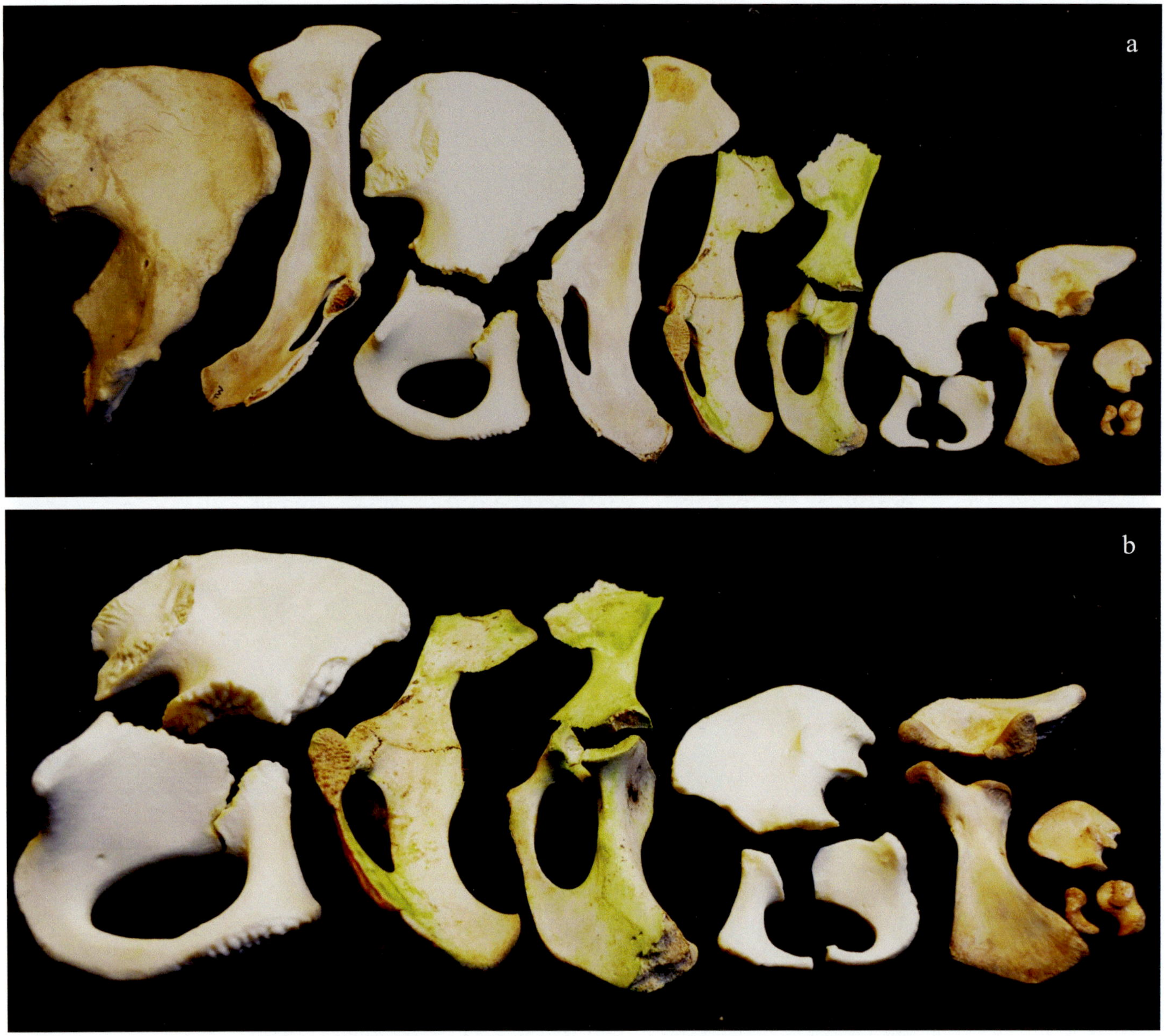

Figure 1.66 Assorted os coxae. (a) From left to right: adult human, deer, 13-year-old human, deer, subadult deer, subadult deer, 5-year-old human, alligator, and infant human. (b) From left to right: 13-year-old human, subadult deer, 5-year-old deer, alligator, and infant human.

Figures 1.67a, b show a deer sacrum on the left and a human sacrum on the right. The first set depicts the anterior view while the second set depicts the posterior views of each sacrum. If found isolated from the rest of the skeleton, it is easy to differentiate a human from a nonhuman sacrum.

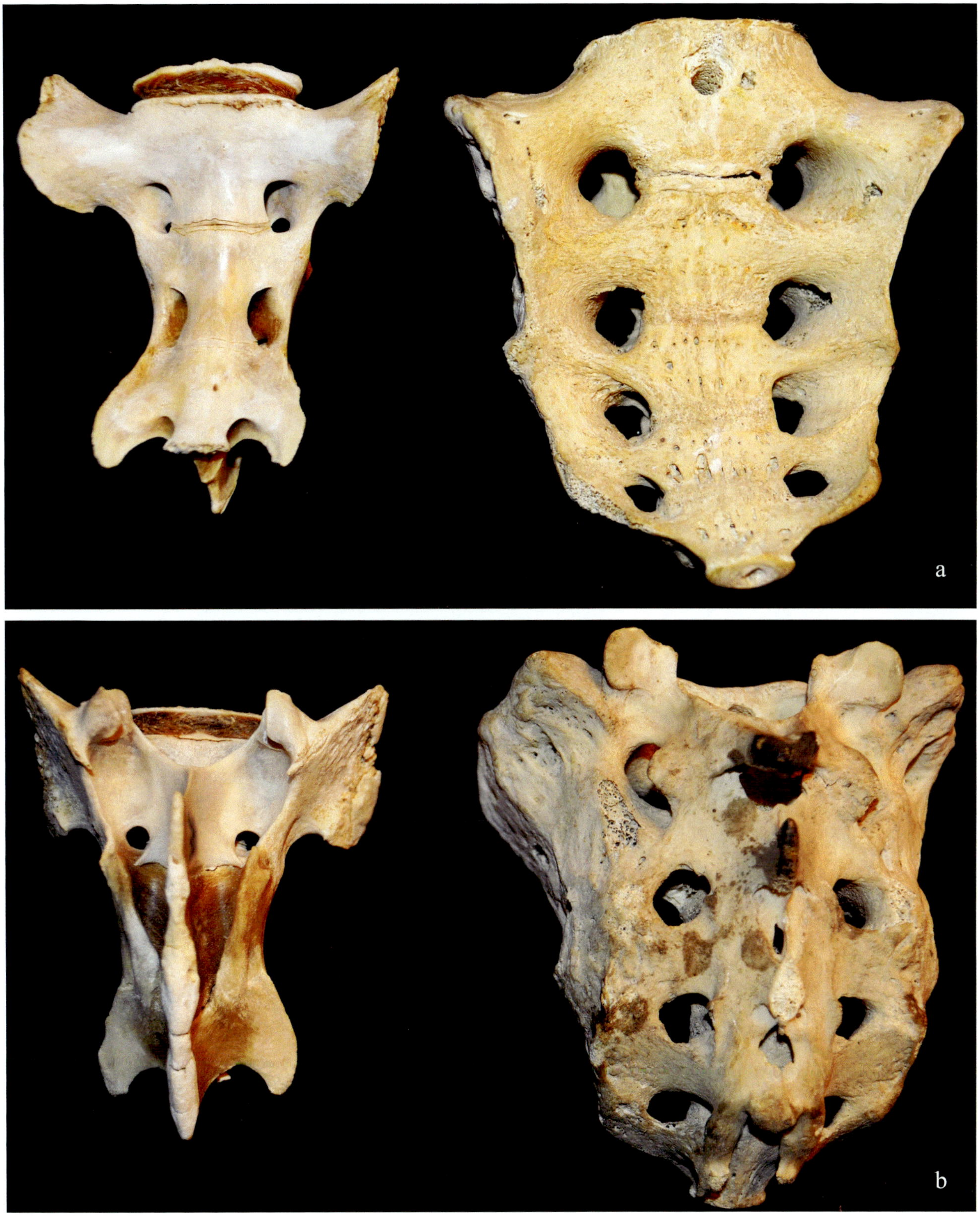

Figure 1.67 Deer sacrum and adult human sacrum. (a) Anterior view of deer (left) and human (right). (b) Posterior view of deer (left) and human (right).

Figures 1.68a, b portray a deer and a human pelvis, which includes both os coxae and a sacrum. They are quite distinct, and therefore not generally mistaken for the other.

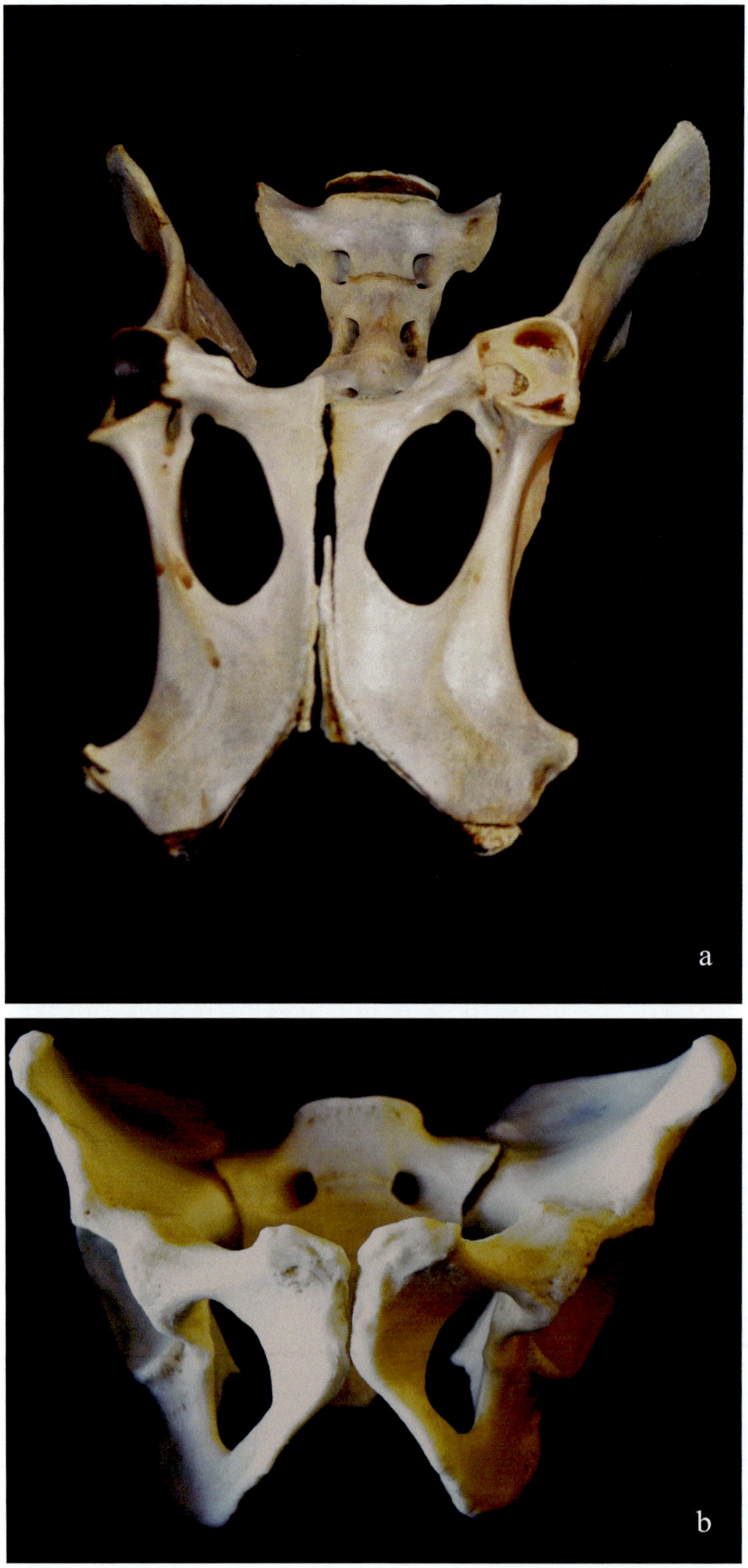

Figure 1.68 Deer and adult human pelvic girdles. (a) Deer (anterior view). (b) Adult human (anterior view).

Figures 1.69a–c show human and nonhuman femora. As explained with the other long bones, the smaller additional bone pictures are epiphyses. Apart from the first bone on the left in Figure 1.69a, which is a horse femur, the rest of the bones have similar shapes on the top (proximal end), middle (shaft or diaphysis), and bottom (distal end). The femur bone can be difficult to differentiate between human and nonhuman. Therefore, anthropologists receive a lot of inquiries about them.

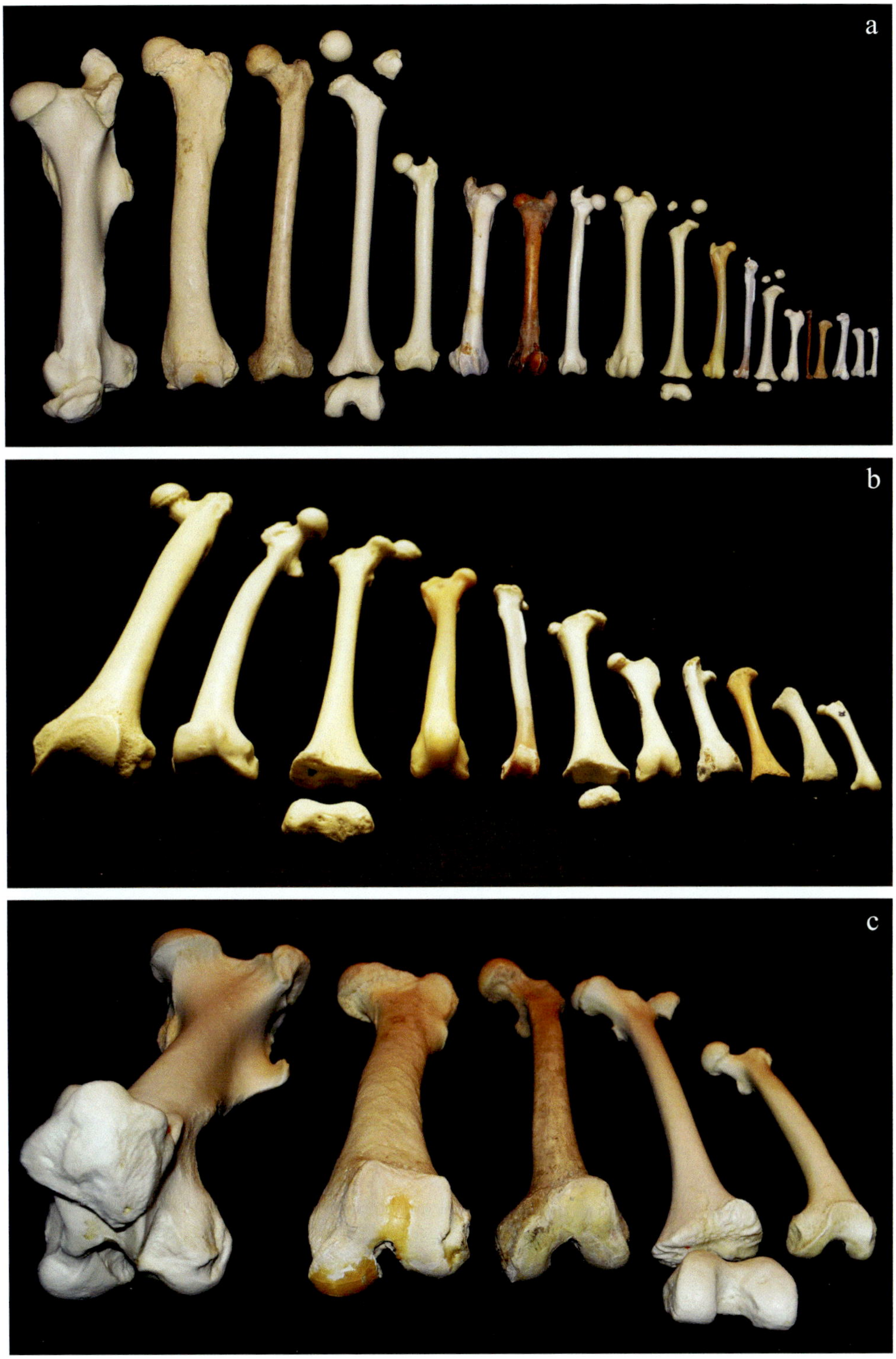

Figure 1.69 Assorted femora. (a) From left to right: horse, bear, adult human, 13-year-old human, bonobo, deer, deer, baboon, dog, 5-year-old human, subadult deer, goose, 14–16-month-old human, raccoon, chicken, newborn human, chicken, chicken, and raven. (b) Various femora. (c) Distal ends of various femora.

Figures 1.70a, b show human and nonhuman tibiae. The small, extra bones, as noted before, are the epiphyses. The tibia like several of the other long bones is difficult to differentiate between human and nonhuman. The tibia is another bone the anthropologist receives from investigators. If the tibia is cut or fragmented, the identification can be even more difficult. If the investigator is unsure, it is always best to send the bone(s) to the anthropologist for analysis.

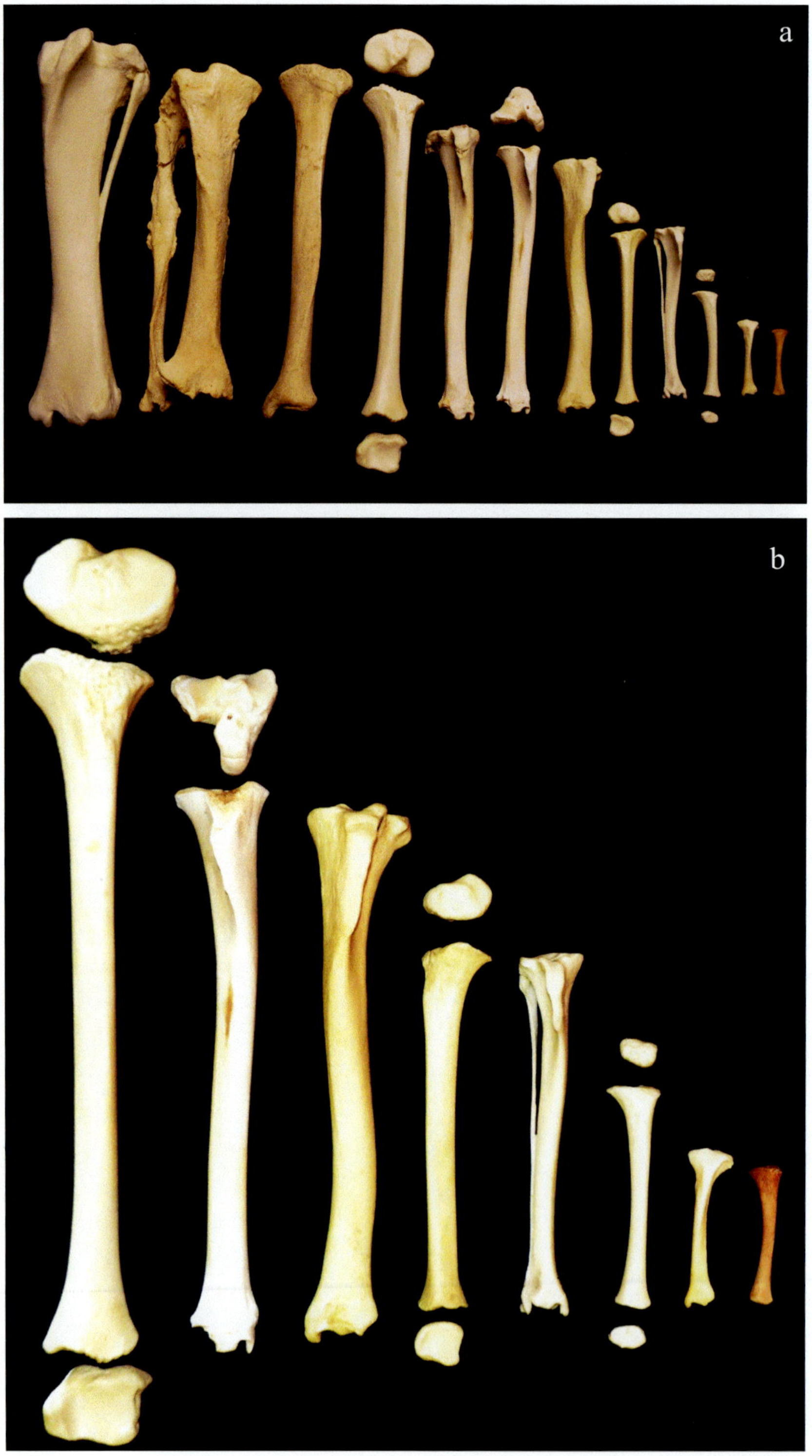

Figure 1.70 Assorted tibiae. (a) From left to right: horse (with fibula), bear (with fibula), adult human, 13-year-old human, adult deer, subadult deer, dog, 5-year-old human, coyote (with fibula), 13–16-month-old human, chicken, and infant human. (b) From left to right: 13-year-old human, subadult deer, dog, 5-year-old, coyote, 13–16-month-old human, raccoon, and infant human.

Figure 1.71 shows a variety of human and nonhuman fibulae. They can be easily confused, so it is best to check with an anthropologist if one is located and isolated from the rest of the skeleton.

Figure 1.71 Assorted fibulae. From left to right: adult human, 13-year-old human, dog, 5-year-old human, 13–16-month-old human, and infant human.

Figure 1.72 shows both human and nonhuman tibiae and fibulae. Some fibulae are fused to the tibia. Human fibulae are not fused to the tibia, giving more range of movement. The fibula bears little weight which is why several animals have reduced or no fibulae.

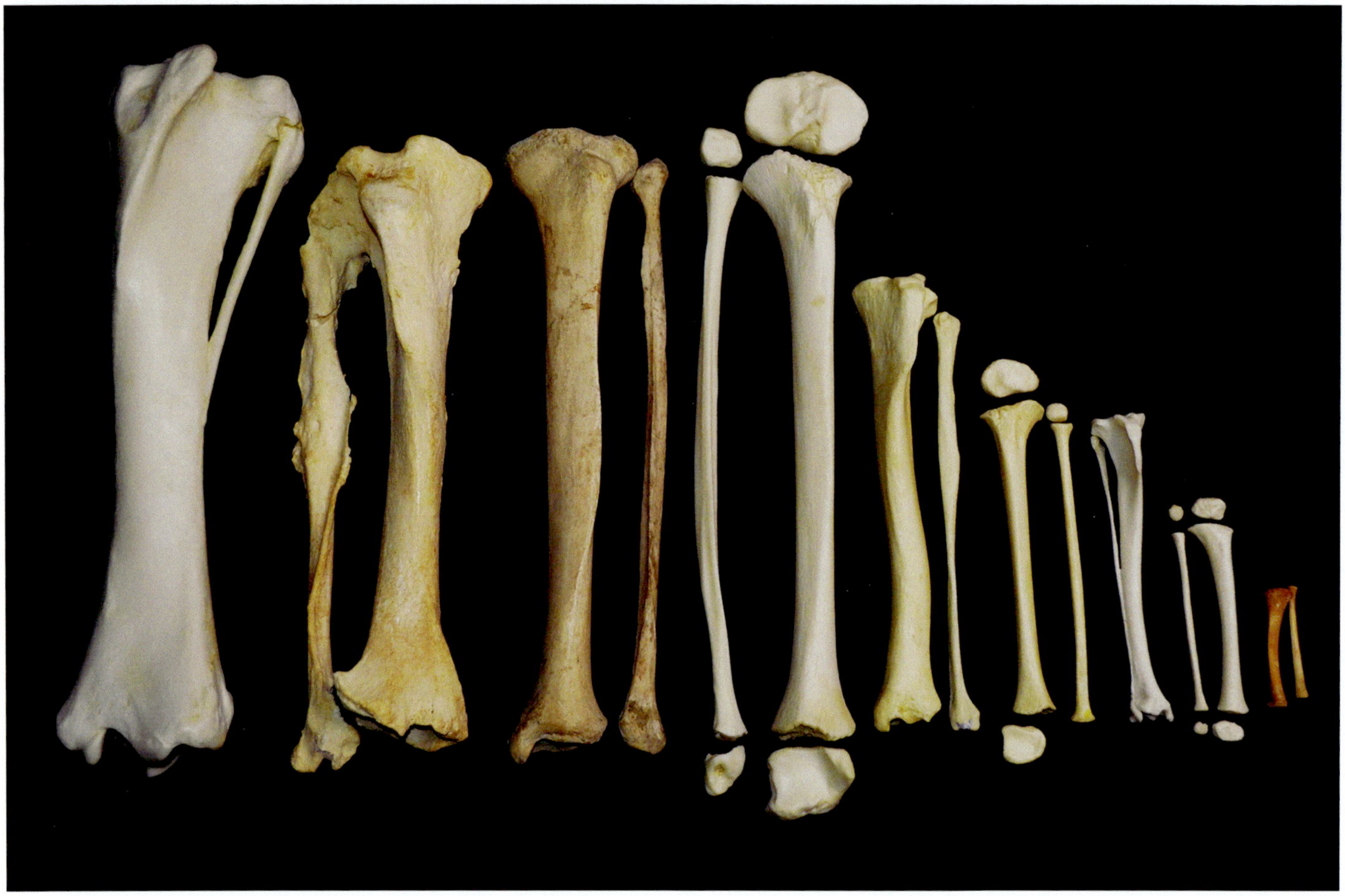

Figure 1.72 Assorted tibiae and fibulae. From left to right: horse, bear, adult human, 13-year-old human, dog, 5-year-old human, coyote, 14–16-month-old human, and infant human.

Figures 1.73a, b show a deer and human calcaneus. If found isolated from the rest of the skeleton, the human calcaneus can be differentiated from a nonhuman calcaneus due to its unique shape. Figures 1.73c, d show two deer astragalus/talus and one human talus, which are bones of the foot. The deer astragalus allows the deer to walk on their "toes."

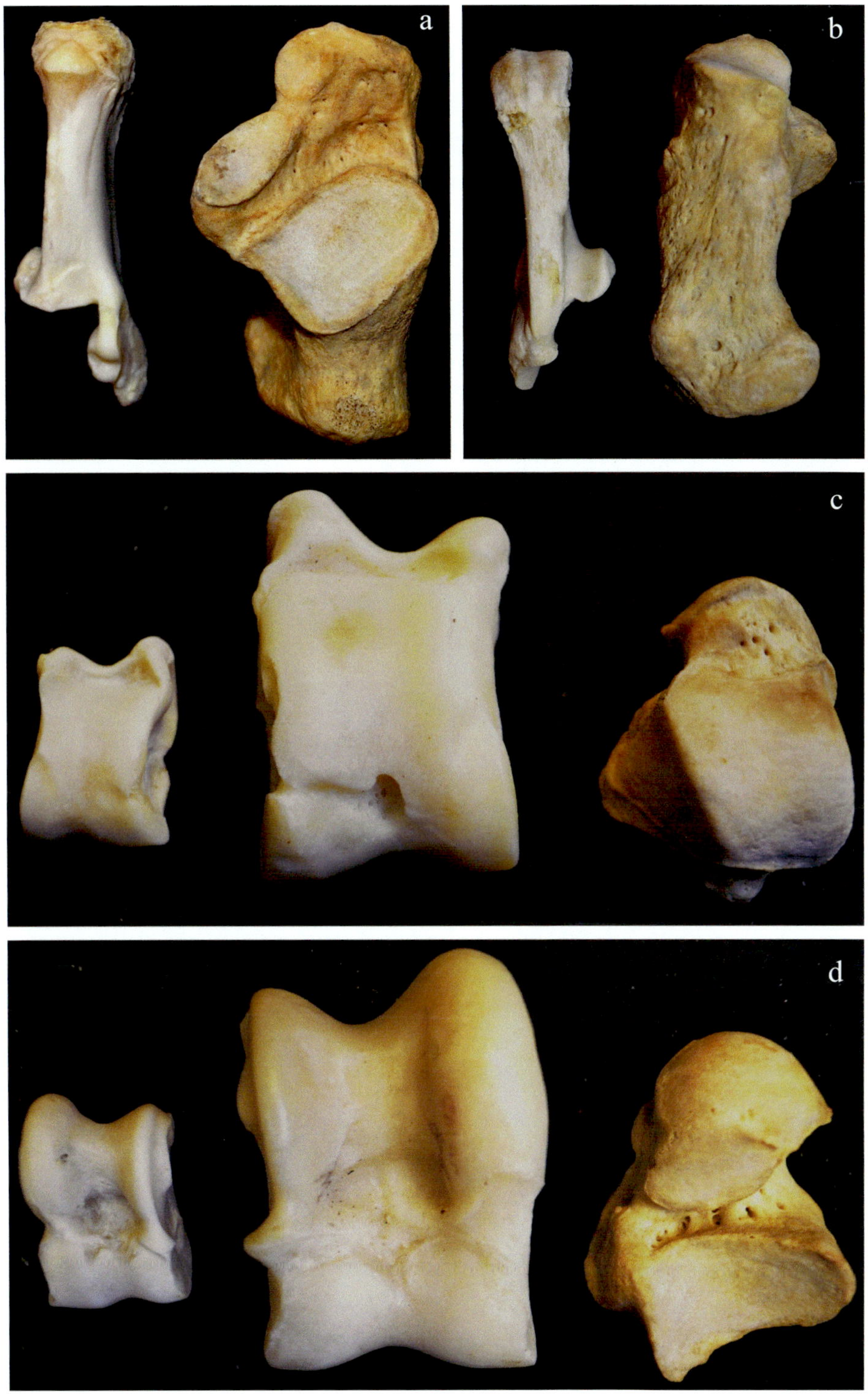

Figure 1.73 Assorted tarsal bones. (a) Superior view of deer (left) and human (right) calcanei. (b) Inferior view of deer (left) and human (right) calcanei. (c) Superior view of subadult deer astragalus (left), adult deer astragalus (center), and adult human talus (right). (d) Inferior view of subadult deer astragalus (left), adult deer astragalus (center), and adult human talus (right).

Bibliography

Dupras TL, Schultz JJ, Wheeler SM, and Williams LJ. 2012. *Forensic Recovery of Human Remains, Archaeological Approaches*. Boca Raton, FL: CRC Press.

France DL. 2008. *Human and Nonhuman Bone Identification: A Color Atlas*. Boca Raton, FL: CRC Press.

France DL. 2011. *Human and Nonhuman Bone Identification: A Concise Field Guide*. Boca Raton, FL: CRC Press.

Scheuer L and Black S. 2000. *Developmental Juvenile Osteology*. London: Academic Press.

White TD, Black MT, and Folkens PA. 2012. *Human Osteology*, 3rd edn. London: Academic Press.

Note

All photographs in this chapter were taken by Teresa A. White.

Recovery

2

HILLARY R. PARSONS AND TERESA A. WHITE

Contents

Scattered human remains

Introduction

The recovery of human skeletal remains from outdoor contexts is one of the most important aspects of a forensic investigation of death. The presence of a qualified forensic anthropologist at a scene is ideal, however, one may not always be available. This section provides simple and effective recovery methods for use by any forensic investigator. Although no scene is the same, basic recovery methods can be adapted to almost any situation.

The recovery of human skeletal remains is a destructive process, and the scene is altered the moment the investigation begins. When recoveries are done properly, the context of evidence and the scientific integrity of the scene can be preserved. Systematic, scientifically defensible, replicable, and easy-to-implement recovery procedures are essential for the investigation of scenes. There are several ways to document a scene including the use of high-technology equipment and advanced imaging; however, this field guide focuses on methods that can be used by any forensic investigator, anywhere, and at any time.

This section details two control-point mapping methods for the recovery of scattered human remains: **baseline mapping** and **rose-azimuth mapping**. These methods are simple, expedient, accurate, and adaptable to any scene. They are also nonintrusive and low technology, allowing any investigator with a simple tool kit to implement quickly.

High-technology mapping tools such as 3D laser scanners, drones, and transit survey systems are available to digitally map scenes. These technologies can be useful; however, not every agency has access to the equipment, funding, or qualified personnel to operate the technology and interpret the results. These technologies can come with challenges such as equipment breakage and failure, drained batteries, compensation and/or calibration issues, or other limiting factors such as thick forest canopies, varying terrain, and other unfavorable environmental conditions. The methods outlined in this field guide give the investigator complete control over the scene without specialized equipment, software, or advanced training.

Steps for a surface recovery

The most important factor in a successful scene recovery is the construction of a solid plan. The following steps describe the key components of an organized recovery adaptable to any scene and to your agency's protocol. Implement the plan prior to recovering skeletal remains or evidence to preserve the integrity of the scene. Ensure all safety and security measures are in place to protect the scene and investigators.

Steps for conducting a surface recovery:

1. Secure the scene.
2. Photograph the general area.
3. Gather the proper equipment, paperwork, and personnel.
4. Conduct a search to delineate the boundaries of the scene.

DOI: 10.4324/9781032623320-3

5. Evaluate the scene for spatial distribution.
6. Identify and record site datum.
7. Identify secondary datum.
8. Use a control-point mapping framework appropriate for the type of scene and the spatial distribution of evidence within the scene.
9. Photograph, sketch, map, and record human remains and other evidence.
10. Carefully remove and package all evidence for transportation and storage.

If the recovery is made without following proper procedures, important evidence and context may be compromised or lost.

Step 1: Secure the scene The area surrounding the site should be secured prior to recovery efforts. Take care to control ingress and egress points and outline the scene with police tape. If the discovery was made in the early evening or at night, secure the scene and wait until daylight to proceed.

Step 2: Photograph the general area Photo documentation of the scene should occur early and often. Initial photos of the scene should include overall photographs from all directions, photos of ingress and egress points, and photographs of areas of interest. Figure 2.1 shows investigators taking midrange and close-up photographs of their scenes.

Figure 2.1 Investigators photograph the scene (a) Midrange photography. (b) Close-up photography.

Step 3: Gather the proper equipment, paperwork, and personnel Prior to recovery, make sure to gather the required equipment, paperwork, and personnel (Figure 2.2). In addition to the paperwork required by your agency (chain of custody forms, photo logs, evidence inventory forms, etc.), recovery forms specific to the type of scene are required to record the location of evidentiary items at the scene. These forms are located in Appendix A, Appendix B, and Appendix C.

Figure 2.2 (a) Formulating a plan for the recovery. (b) The equipment required for baseline recovery. (c) The equipment required for a rose-azimuth recovery. (d) Investigators gathering all equipment in advance of the recovery.

Step 4: Conduct a search to delineate boundaries of the outdoor scene Once the plan is in place, conduct a methodical search of the area where suspected human remains are located. A search should be thorough and conducted without assumptions about the scene or distribution of evidence. Items should be flagged, but not touched or moved. The type of search will depend upon the size of the area and how many searchers are present (Figure 2.3). If several people are present, conduct a pedestrian **line search**.

Pedestrian line searches are organized through the following steps:

a. Provide each person with several pin flags to mark human skeletal remains and other potential evidence, then choose which color flag will mark each type of evidence.
b. Form a straight line at the outer perimeter of the potential scene. Space personnel appropriately to ensure maximum coverage; generally, outstretched arms are touching.
c. Choose a line leader to call out directions and keep the line straight.
d. Following the line leader's vocal commands, advance forward carefully and deliberately until suspected evidentiary items are located. The line leader will stop movement so item(s) can be marked with pin flag(s).
e. Periodically look up, as items can be in trees, on rock ledges, etc.
f. The line leader resumes the forward advancement after suspected evidentiary items are marked. If a forensic anthropologist is present, they can follow the line search to check whether human or nonhuman skeletal remains have been flagged.
g. The line leader will continue the search until the suspected outer boundary of the scene has been determined. Always search further than suspected to ensure all potential evidentiary items are located and flagged.
h. To provide an optimal search of the area, the leader will now move the line to conduct a **grid search**, which is described below.

Grid search instructions:

a. Conduct a pedestrian line search as previously described.
b. Upon reaching the outer boundary of the scene, the leader instructs participants to shift perpendicular to the original line and conduct another pedestrian line search. This grid search provides an additional opportunity to locate and flag evidentiary items. For example, items may be located within long grass, behind trees or other obstructions, or in other areas not visible during the initial pedestrian line search.
c. The leader will move the line forward until the outer boundary of the scene is reached, which will be perpendicular to the previously delineated boundary.

If only one person is available to search, employ a **spiral search**.

Spiral search instructions:

a. When searching the scene alone, begin at the location of suspected human skeletal remains or another evidentiary item.
b. Walk in a circular manner outward from the item, creating a spiral that gradually expands in surface area.
c. A spiral search may be repeated in other areas, if necessary, to ensure the entire scene has been thoroughly searched.

Figure 2.3 Investigators conduct pedestrian line searches to locate and flag items of evidentiary value. (a) Schematic of a one-way pedestrian line search. (b) Demonstration of an on-way pedestrian line search. (c) Schematic of a grid search. (d) Demonstration of a grid search. (e) Schematic of a spiral search. (f) Demonstration of a spiral search.

Flag items of evidentiary value with pin flags of different colors. Flagging items helps to visualize the distribution of evidence at a scene. Potential evidentiary items can be flagged individually or as a group. Flagging items individually may become visually distracting if the scene contains areas of concentrated skeletal elements and evidence. One flag to denote a grouping of items is sufficient, however, use one flag of each color if the grouping contains both skeletal elements and evidence. Ultimately, how items are flagged will depend on time and scene conditions (Figure 2.4).

Flag all skeletal elements even if they may not be human. It is best to identify all bones for the on-scene forensic anthropologist to review. If an anthropologist is not present, document and collect all bones for the anthropologist to analyze at the laboratory.

Figure 2.4 (a) Items of evidentiary value are marked individually with flags. These items can be marked as a group using fewer flags. (b) Investigators on this scene use yellow flags to identify skeletal elements and pink flags to identify nonskeletal evidence.

Step 5: Evaluate the scene for spatial distribution Upon completion of the search, observe the distribution of the flags. The scene may contain a **linear distribution** of evidence where items are spread out in a long and relatively narrow pattern (Figure 2.5). A **control-point mapping** method called baseline mapping will be used for these types of scenes. Alternatively, a **nonlinear distribution** describes evidence widely dispersed without a linear pattern. A control-point mapping method called rose-azimuth mapping will be used for these types of scenes.

Figure 2.5 (a) A scene with a linear distribution pattern of evidence (red dotted line). In this scenario, a baseline mapping method can be used. (b) A scene with a nonlinear distribution pattern of evidence (red dotted line) where the rose-azimuth mapping method can be used.

Mark each flag with a numbered or lettered evidence marker. These markers will be the known **reference points** used to document evidence. These reference points may represent individual or grouped items depending on how the scene was flagged (Figure 2.6).

Figure 2.6 (a–d) Skeletal remains and items of evidentiary value are marked with pin flags and photograph reference markers. Yellow flags mark skeletal remains and pink flags mark nonskeletal evidence.

Take photographs of the scene and document the process. If available, a drone can take photographs of the scene to document the spatial distribution of evidence (Figure 2.7).

Figure 2.7 (a–c) Drones can be used to help visualize the search area and distribution of evidence. Drone operators can be hired if your agency does not have access. Zack Sybert, owner of Flathead Lake Drone LLC (and photographed here), took all of the drone pictures in this section of the field guide.

Step 6: Establish a site datum To establish a **site datum**, locate the nearest fixed or permanent structure near the flagged scene. This structure will become the site datum and used to define the location of the scene. In remote areas, natural landmarks such as large rocks can be used (Figure 2.8). For urban or developed scenes, the corner of a building, bridge, or power pole works well (Figure 2.9). Place a flag at the chosen location and

Figure 2.8 (a) Example of a site datum for remote areas. The rock is likely to remain in place over a long period of time providing a site reference point for future use. (b) Close-up of the specific datum point on the rock denoted by the blue flag. Photograph the site datum with a north arrow and the compass bearing.

Figure 2.9 (a) Midrange photograph of a bridge used as a site datum in a developed area. The red circle highlights the blue flag marking the exact datum. (b) Close-up photo of the exact datum location marked with a blue flag.

take the GPS coordinates of this site datum. Finally, use a compass to find magnetic north (Figures 2.10 and 2.11). The site datum should be permanent, as it might be accessed at a future date. For instance, another investigator may take on the case in the future and need to locate the site datum.

If there is no permanent structure near the scene, hammer a long piece of rebar or a 10-in. carpenters nail into the ground to create a site datum. This rebar (or nail) will be hammered completely into the ground upon departure of the scene so it can be relocated with a metal detector later, as needed. Photograph the datum with a north arrow and/or a compass on the ground.

Figure 2.10 (a) Investigators use a cell phone to record GPS data for the site datum. (b) An example of GPS coordinates on a cell phone.

Figure 2.11 (a) Investigators denote the corner of a building for the site datum with a pink flag. (b) A compass is used at the datum to locate north.

Step 7: Identify secondary datum, tie in secondary datum to site datum, and use control-point mapping with baseline A **secondary datum** is an established point at a recovery scene from which all measurements are taken. This point is established by the scene investigator and marked with a piece of rebar or a 10-in. carpenter's nail driven into the ground. The secondary datum needs to be tied into the site (scene) datum.

When using baseline control-point mapping, the secondary datum is placed at the furthest point on one edge of the scene. Place a flag and a 10-in. carpenter's nail several feet (approximately 3 ft) away from the furthest flagged item, from the edge of the scene, to ensure everything within the scene is mapped/documented. Scene measurements will be recorded from this secondary datum. Record the GPS coordinates of this point on the data sheets.

Steps used to tie in secondary datum to site datum:

a. Stand at the secondary datum. Hold the compass flat and at eye level with the mirror tilted to a 45-degree angle.
b. Look through the compass sight to find the site datum pin flag (Figure 2.12).
c. While looking through the sight, rotate the bezel of the compass until the magnetic needle (i.e., solid, red arrow) is within the orienting arrow/doghouse/"Red in the Shed" (i.e., hollow, red lines).
d. Read the number at the index line on the top of the compass. This number is the front bearing/front azimuth. Record this number.
e. Using a reel measuring tape, walk from the secondary datum to the site datum. Record the distance between the two datums.
f. Finally, record the **back azimuth**. Stand at the site datum and look back through the compass viewfinder to the secondary datum. The white end of the magnetic needle should now be lined up within the orienting arrow/doghouse. This is the back azimuth. There is a 180-degree difference between the front and back azimuths. These degree readings are on the top and bottom index lines of the compass (Figure 2.13).

Figure 2.12 (a) A compass is used to gather the degree bearings from the site datum (power pole) to the secondary datum. Here, the investigator is standing at the pole and looking through the viewfinder to locate the secondary datum. (b) To record the back azimuth, simply repeat the process except stand at the secondary datum and line up the site datum in the viewfinder.

Figure 2.13 (a) A view of the secondary datum (blue flag) through the compass sight. (b) Close-up of the compass face showing the azimuth bearing from the site datum to the secondary datum. The red compass needle is in the red doghouse on the compass face. (c) Close-up of the back-azimuth bearing showing the white compass needle in the red doghouse.

Step 8: Identify the mapping method most appropriate for your scene Step 8 outlines two different control-point mapping methods. The first method is called baseline mapping. The second method is called rose-azimuth mapping. Baseline mapping will be discussed first in this section. As mentioned earlier, control-point mapping using baseline can be used on any scene but works especially well with a linear distribution of evidence, where evidentiary items are spread out in a long, but narrow pattern.

Baseline mapping

When the scene is ready, a baseline mapping framework can begin. Figure 2.14 shows the overview of a baseline scene taken from a drone and a corresponding overview map created of the scene. The horizontal red line shows the **x-axis** of the baseline. It begins on the left side, at the zero end of the reel tape measure, and extends to the right end of the tape which is the other end of the scene. The red arrows, running perpendicular to the x-axis, are measurements for the **y-axis**. Each perpendicular red arrow ends at a flagged reference number.

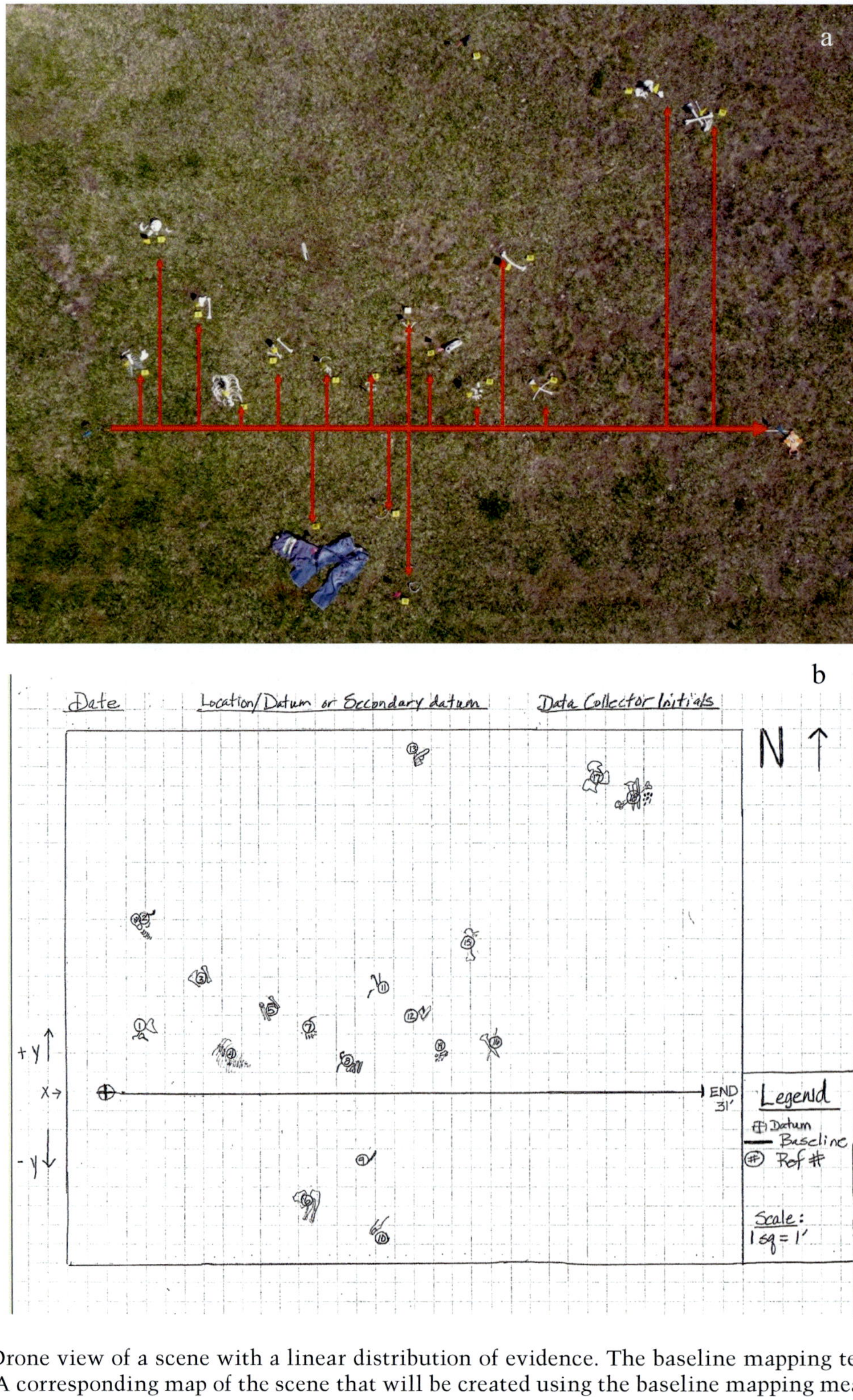

Figure 2.14 (a) Drone view of a scene with a linear distribution of evidence. The baseline mapping technique is used in this example. (b) A corresponding map of the scene that will be created using the baseline mapping measurements.

Figures 2.15 and 2.16 illustrate how to map a scene with the baseline mapping technique from the overhead perspective. Figures 2.17–2.19 show the same process from the ground level.

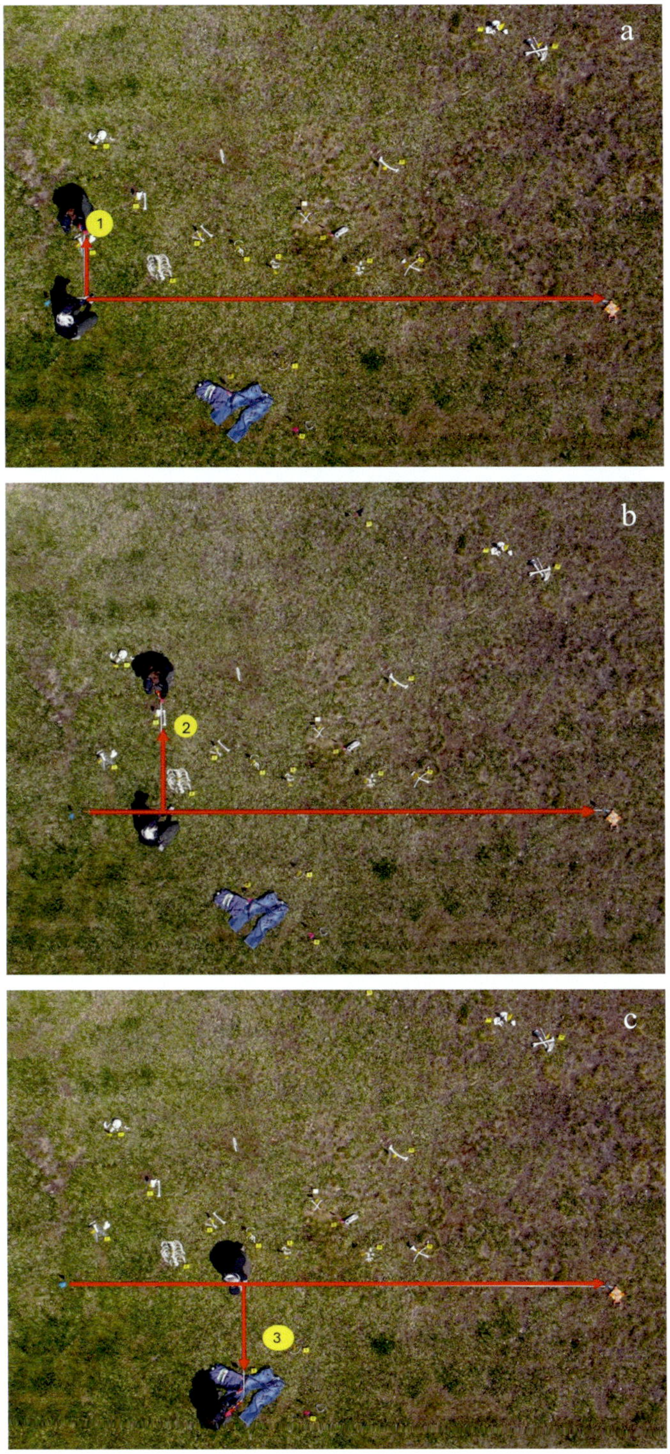

Figure 2.15 Drone photographs showing scene mapping using the baseline method. (a) The evidence (yellow circles) is mapped starting with the first piece. (b) One investigator moves down the baseline (x-axis) to record the measurement. The second investigator travels to each piece of evidence to record the y-axis measurement. (c) Item number three falls below the baseline. The y-axis measurement for this item is recorded as a negative number.

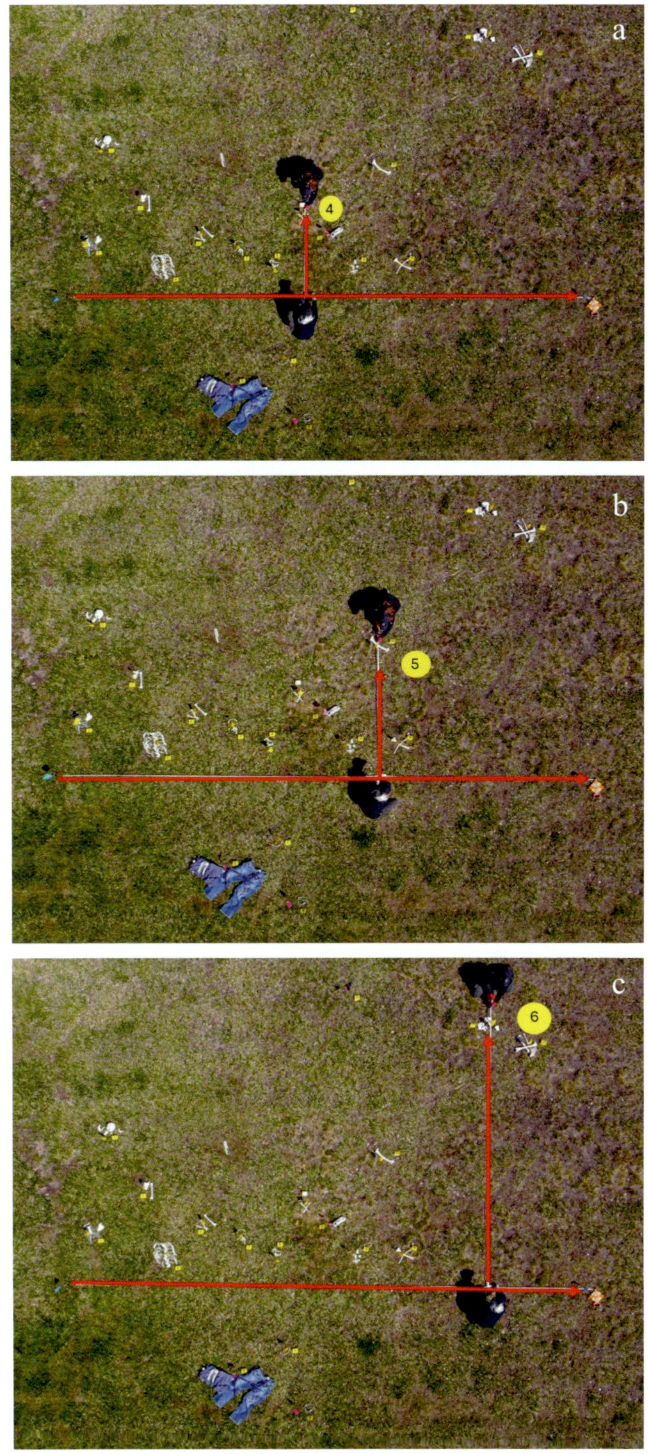

Figure 2.16 (a–c) Drone photographs showing the continuation of mapping items using the baseline mapping method.

Figure 2.17 Ground-level photographs showing the baseline mapping method. (a) Midrange photograph showing the scene. (b) Investigators map the first item (white circle) from the measuring tape baseline (red line). (c) Item number two is measured in the same manner. Notice the measuring tape runs through the scene with the blue flags on each end.

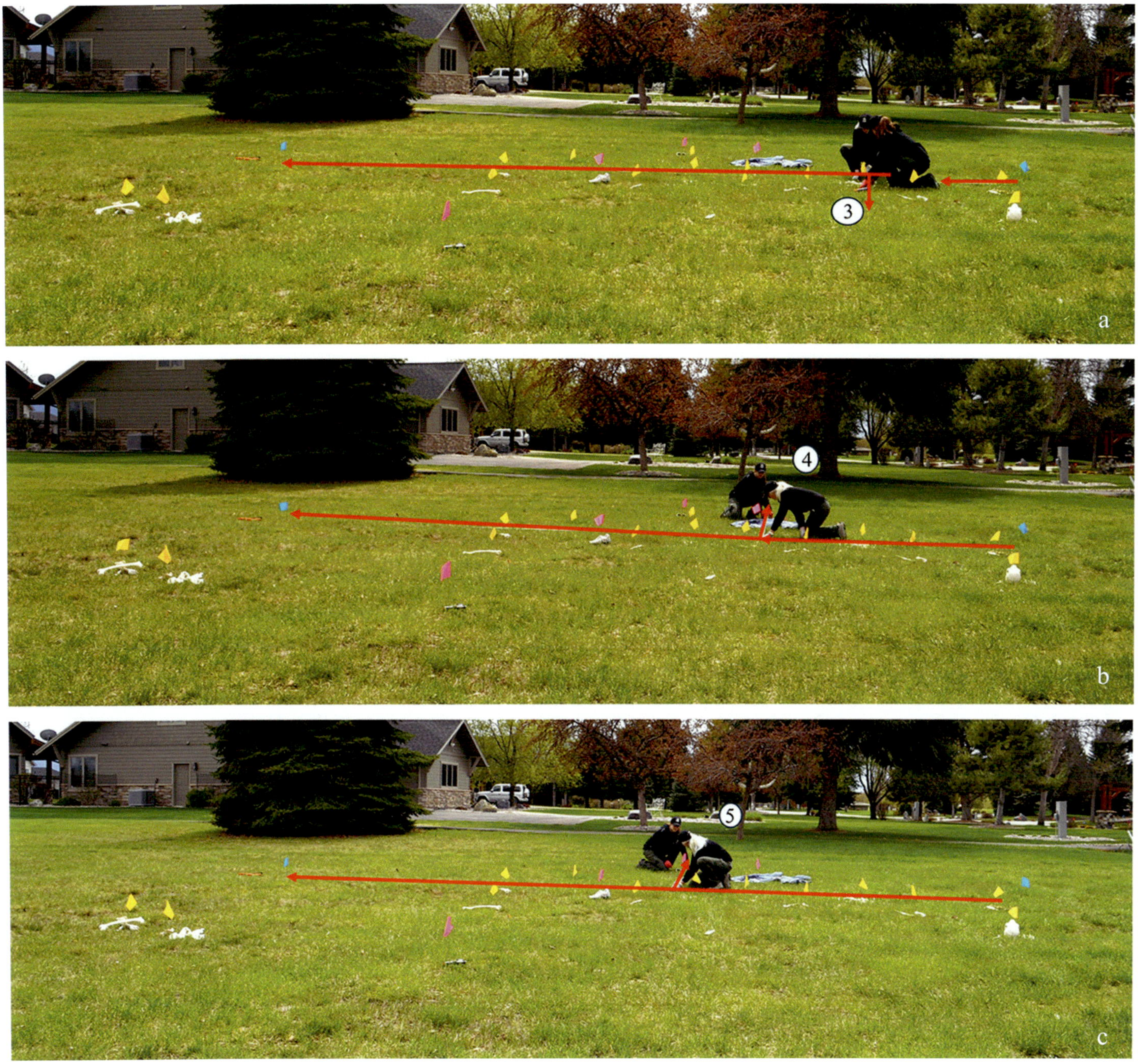

Figure 2.18 (a–c) Ground-level photographs showing the mapping of items 3–5 using the baseline mapping method.

Figure 2.19 (a–c) Ground-level photographs showing the mapping of items 6–8 using the baseline mapping method.

Steps to setting up a baseline:

a. The baseline (x-axis) is created by placing an open reel measuring tape through the middle of the scene. Place the zero end of the measuring tape on the secondary datum carpenter's nail. The tape should be secured in place until all reference point measurements are taken.
b. Take measurements from the secondary datum, beginning at zero, to each reference point on the x-axis. The y-axis runs perpendicular to the x-axis. The y-axis measurements are taken by physically moving along the x-axis with an additional tape measure that runs to each evidentiary item. It is not secured to the ground like the x-axis.
c. X- and y-axis measurements are taken for each reference point. For example, reference point number one is 1 ft, 3 in. along the x-axis and 2 ft 5 in. along the y-axis. Any items located on the opposite side of the x-axis will be given a negative number for the y-axis measurement.
d. Continue to move along the x-axis (baseline) to each reference point until all evidence is mapped.
e. When taking baseline measurements, keep all measuring reels tight so there is no slack which would create incorrect measurements. When possible, use a 90-degree scale to ensure right angles for proper measurements (Figure 2.20).

Figure 2.20 (a–f) A 90-degree angle scale is used to help keep the y-axis measurement line at a 90-degree angle from the x-axis (baseline) to ensure the most accurate measurement.

When evidence is located above or below ground level, it is recorded as the **z-axis** measurement. Figure 2.21 shows investigators obtaining the z-axis measurement. After measuring x and y, the z-axis measurement is taken off the y-axis using a 90-degree angle. Run a tape measure from zero to the piece of evidence. Record x-, y-, and z-axis measurements on the data sheets. Items located above ground level are recorded as positive numbers and items located below ground level are recorded as negative numbers. Note: reference marker #4 is in the tree identifying evidence.

Evidence can be carefully packaged after each reference point has been documented and mapped. Alternatively, all measurements can be taken first, and evidence then carefully packaged for transportation to the proper professionals.

Figure 2.21 (a–c) Investigators working together to map the z-axis measurement of items encountered in trees. Notice how the z-axis measurement is taken 90 degrees vertically from the y-axis. The white arrows in (c) indicate where the x-, y-, and z- measurements are derived.

Rose-azimuth mapping

If pin flags are distributed in a nonlinear pattern, you may use the baseline method. Alternatively, you can use a control-point mapping method called rose-azimuth mapping to map both linear scenes and nonlinear scenes. The rose-azimuth method requires one measuring tape and a **rose-azimuth board** (can be purchased online). The following figures detail how to map a scene using the rose-azimuth method.

A rose-azimuth board is essentially a large compass secured on the ground surface within a scene. For this method, the reference points are measured using distance and degrees (i.e., 0–360) on the board, versus measurements along x- and y-axes, as demonstrated with baseline mapping. An open reel measuring tape is used to measure the distance from the center of the board to each reference point.

Before beginning, establish a secondary datum for your scene. When using the rose-azimuth method, the secondary datum will be the *center* of the rose-azimuth board. There is a hole in the middle of the board for a nail which will be left in the ground for future reference, as needed (Figure 2.22). It is a good idea to place the

Figure 2.22 (a) Using a compass, investigators align the zero-degree hash mark on the rose-azimuth board with north. (b) The center nail serves as the secondary datum for the scene and the point from where all measurements are taken. (c) Once the back-azimuth bearing is obtained, large nails are used to secure the board to the ground at each corner.

rose-azimuth board near the center of your scene. After the secondary datum is identified, use the compass to find magnetic north and line up the zero-degree hash mark on the board with north. Then, secure the board to the ground by hammering carpenter nails into the four corners of the board. Tie in the site datum and record the back azimuth, as described previously in the baseline mapping section (Figure 2.23).

Figure 2.23 (a) The distance measurement between the datum and the secondary datum (center nail of the board) is taken. (b) The view of the back azimuth from the secondary datum.

Figure 2.24 shows an overview of a scene where a rose-azimuth board is used to take measurements for reference points number one through ten and the corresponding overview map created of the scene. Notice the center of the board is where all measurements are taken.

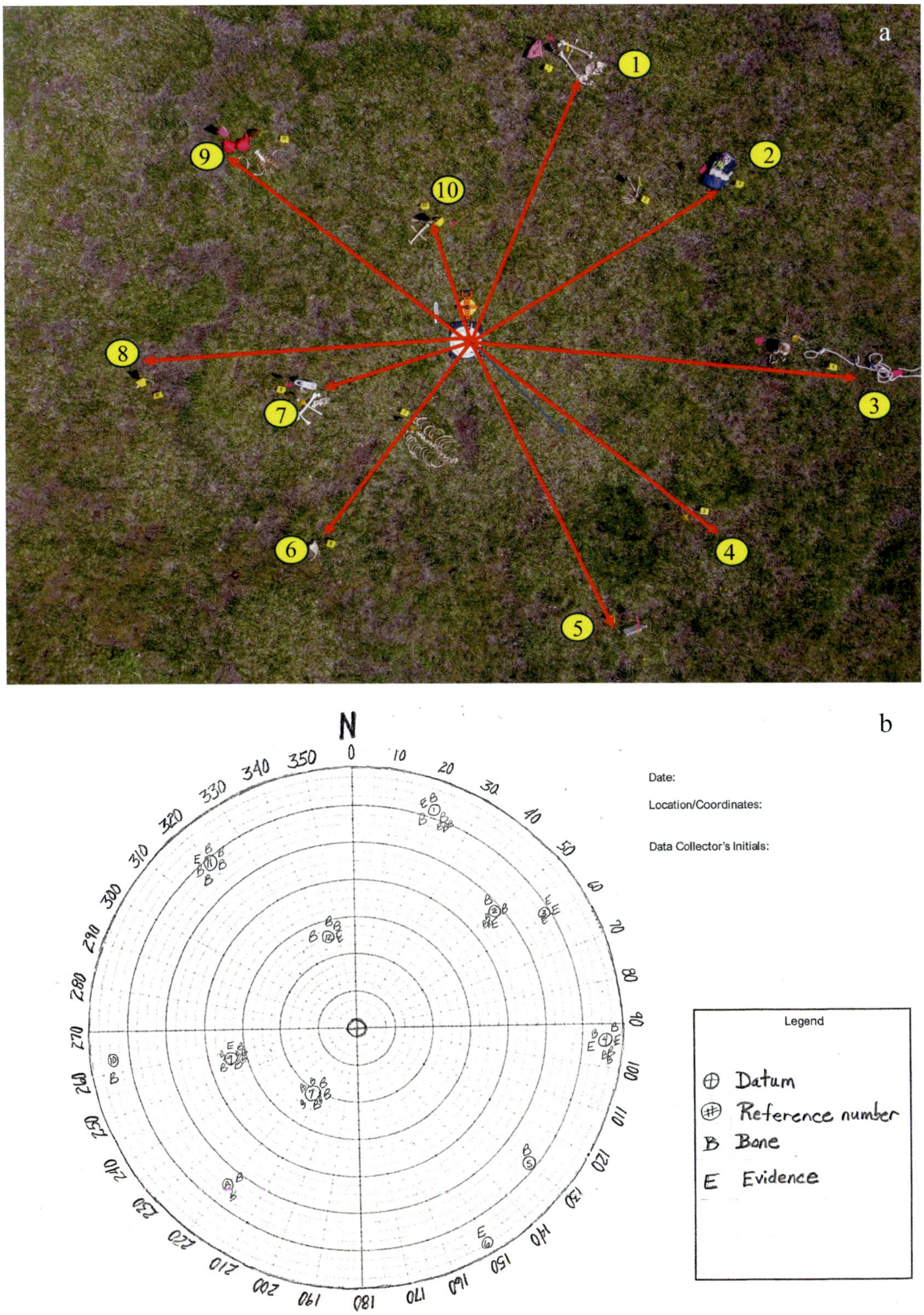

Figure 2.24 (a) Drone photograph of a scene where rose-azimuth mapping is used. The items of evidentiary value are marked with yellow circles and the measurements from the center of the board to the items are marked by red arrows. (b) A corresponding map of the scene that will be created using the rose-azimuth mapping measurements.

Figures 2.25–2.27 show the process of measuring each reference point from the center of the rose-azimuth board from above. Notice the reference points are recorded in a clockwise manner. One person remains stationary at

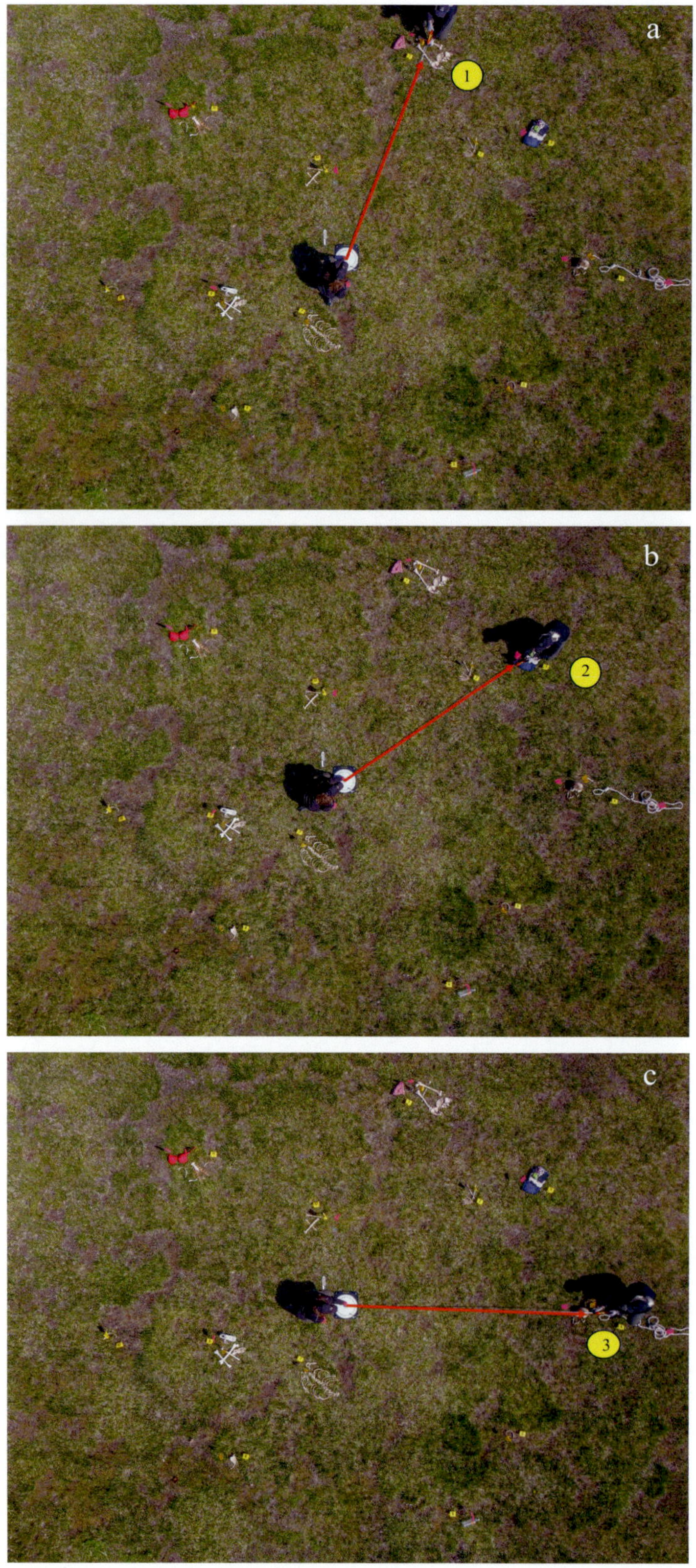

Figure 2.25 (a–c) Overhead photographs of investigators mapping the items of evidentiary value (yellow circles) from the center of the rose-azimuth board (red arrow). Notice how the investigator systematically moves to each item around the compass.

the azimuth board to document the degree angle for each reference point. The other person physically moves to each reference point with the tape measure to record the distance from the center of the board to each reference point.

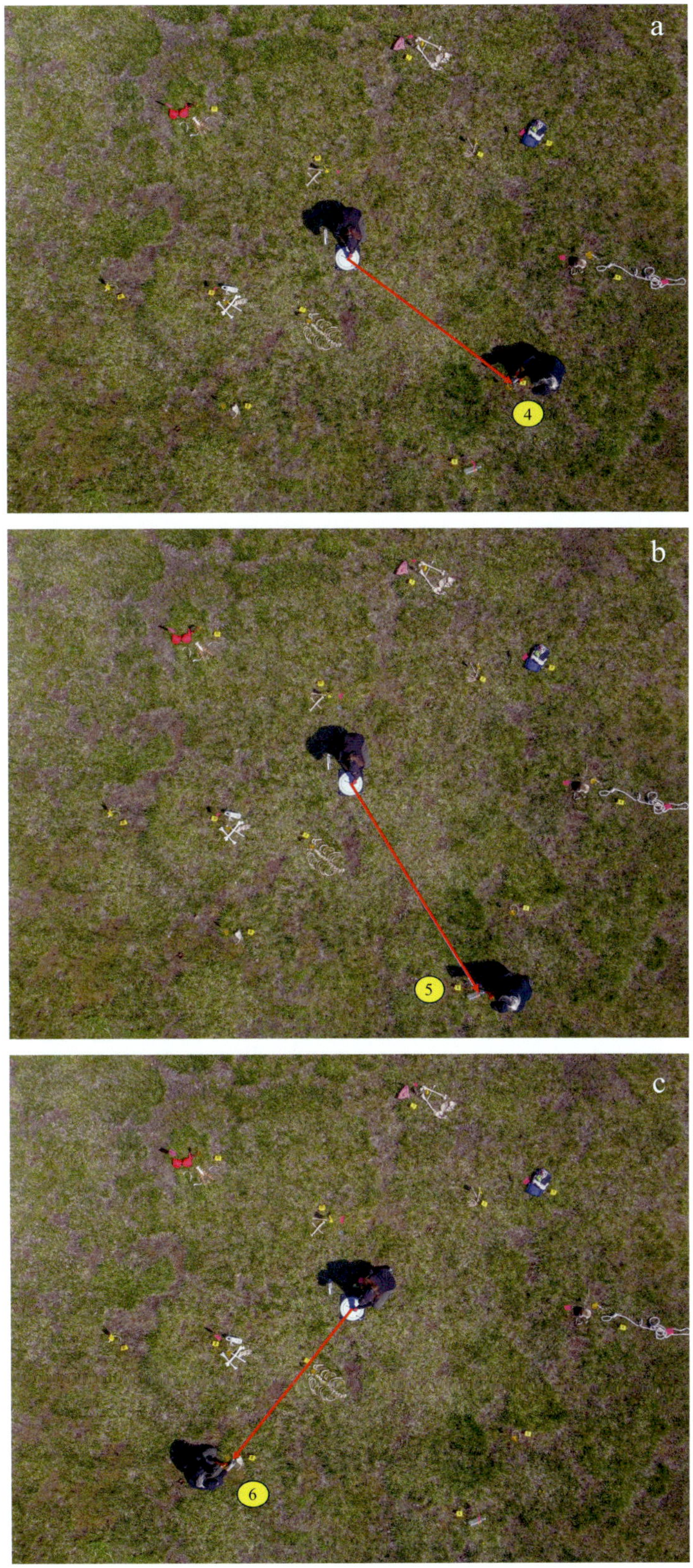

Figure 2.26 (a–c) Overhead photographs showing mapping of items 4–6 using the rose-azimuth mapping method.

The tape should be pulled taut to ensure the most accurate measurement. One measurement is usually sufficient for each reference point; however, multiple measurements can be taken if desired. For example, a large cluster of bones may require more than one measurement to adequately demonstrate the size of the assemblage.

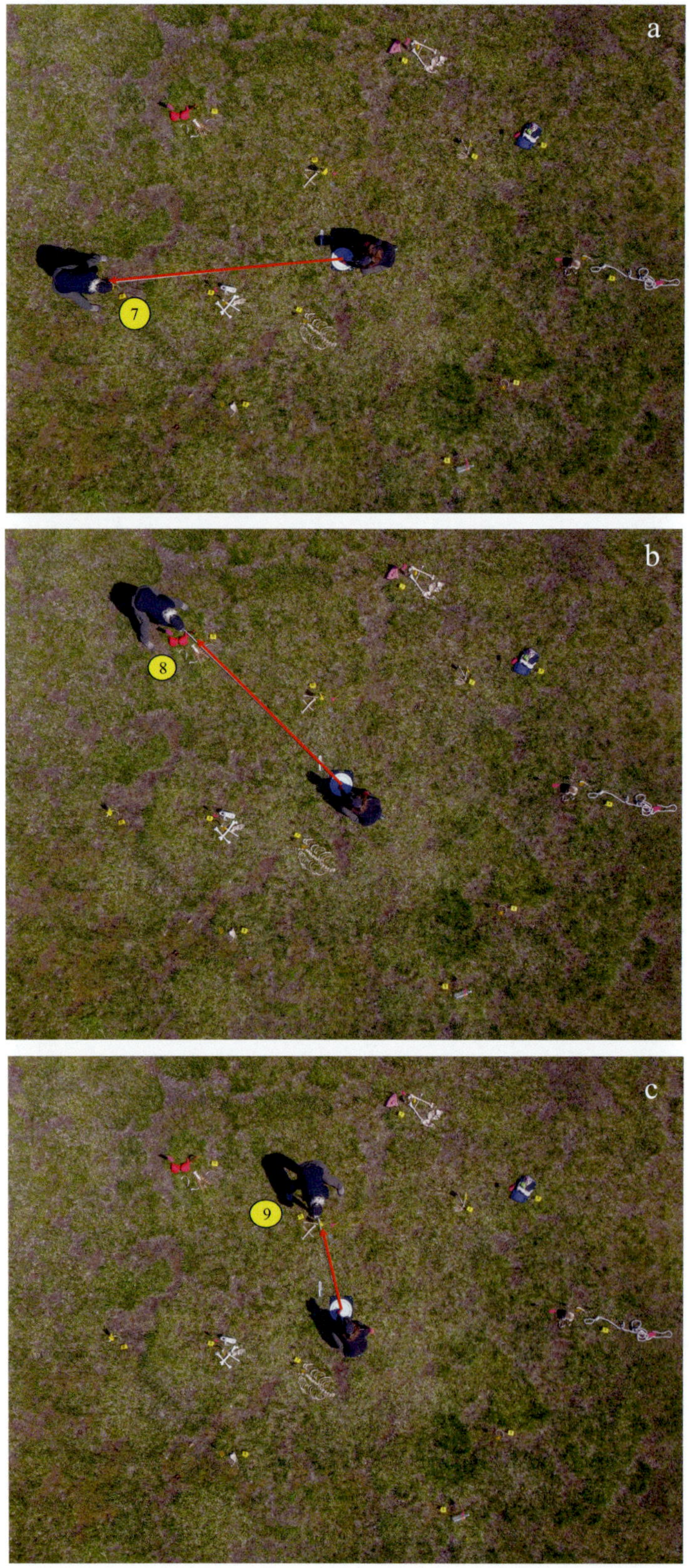

Figure 2.27 (a–c) Overhead photographs showing mapping of items 7–9 using the rose-azimuth mapping method.

Figures 2.28 and 2.29 show the process from the ground level. This method goes quickly with two people but can be performed alone. If performing this method alone, pull the tape measure to the evidentiary item and

Figure 2.28 (a–d) Ground-level view of investigators mapping items 1–4 (white circles) using the rose-azimuth mapping method.

record the distance. Carefully leave the tape measure on the ground and read the degree marking on the board. To prevent the tape measure from moving, you can anchor it with a heavy object, such as a rock.

Figure 2.29 (a–b) Ground-level photographs showing mapping of items 5–6 using the rose-azimuth mapping method. (c) Demonstration of the method with two people. (d) Demonstration of the method with one person. Secure the hook at the end of the measuring tape to the center nail.

Figure 2.30 shows investigators using the rose-azimuth mapping method to document a variety of scenes.

Step 9: Photograph, sketch, map, and record skeletal remains and other evidence Multiple methods of documentation reduce the chance of unintentionally excluding information about the scene. Photographs, sketches, data collection forms, and maps are all important in telling the story of the scene.

- Photograph the scene early and often including overall, midrange, and close-up shots.
- Take additional photos of the scene after all evidence is flagged.
- Take photos of the site datum and the secondary datum(s).
- When the mapping method is established (i.e., baseline or rose-azimuth) take photographs to show the mapping system process.

Figure 2.30 (a–f) Investigators employing various methods of scene documentation while using rose-azimuth mapping. All data points are recorded on paper, and photographs of the evidence and recovery methodology are taken.

- Photographs should include a north arrow or something to indicate north.
- Use the data collection forms provided in Appendices A–C and graph paper to collect all necessary scene information.

Figure 2.31 shows an example of the paperwork used to document the reference points. The tables contain columns to record the measurements taken from the scene. Additionally, there is a column to provide a description of the item(s) within each reference point and a column

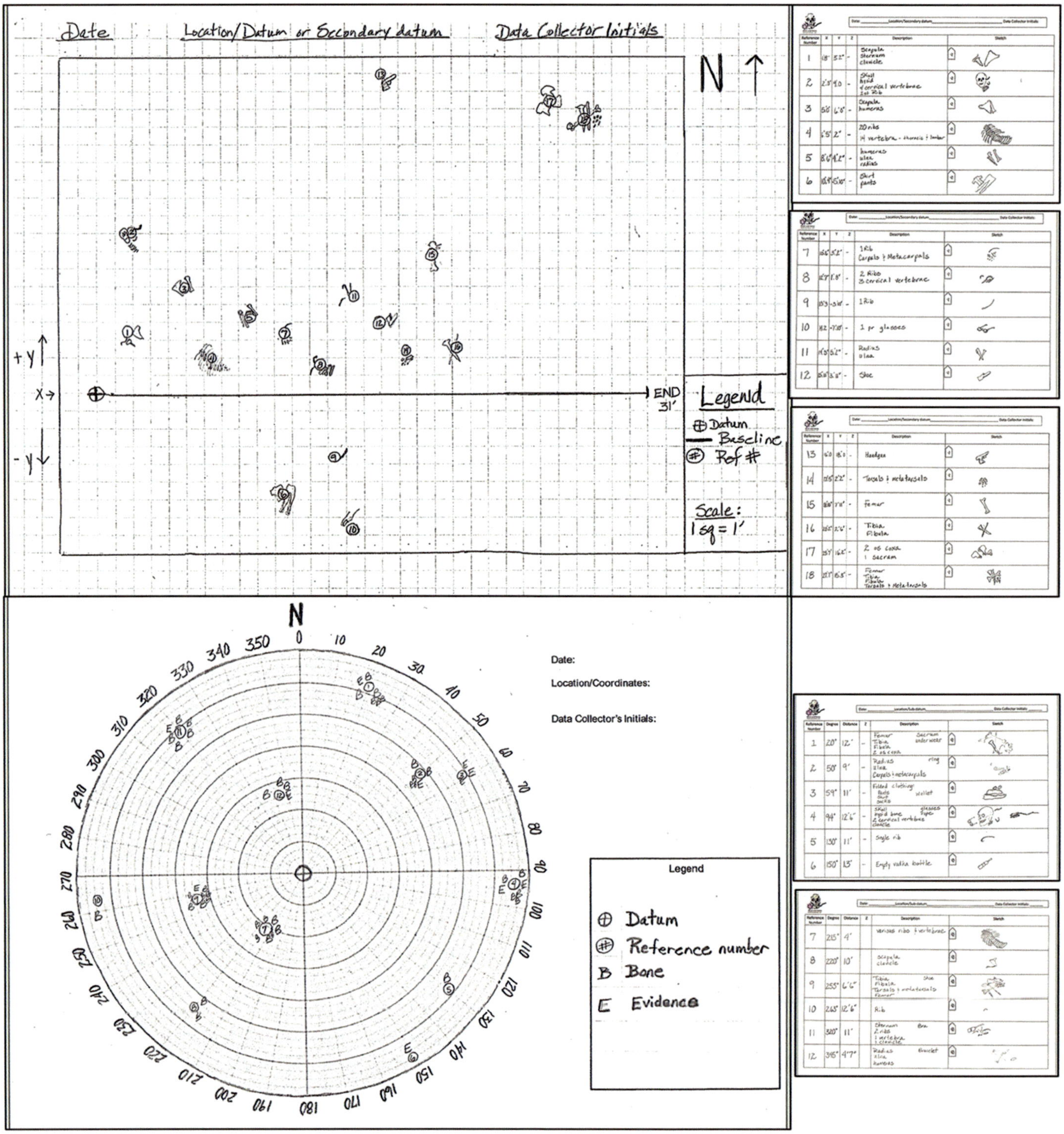

Figure 2.31 Map of the baseline scene with baseline mapping worksheets (top). The worksheets provide space to record x-axis, y-axis, and z-axis data, descriptions of items, and sketches. Map of the rose-azimuth scene with worksheets (bottom). The worksheets provide space to record distance, degree, and z-axis data, descriptions of items, and sketches.

to draw a quick sketch. Do not worry, the descriptions can be as simple as counting the number of bones, and the sketches can be rudimentary.

Baseline maps are created from the x- and y-axis measurements recorded on the data sheets. These scenes can be mapped on traditional graph paper. Similarly, rose-azimuth maps are created from the distance and degree measurements recorded on the data sheets. However, rose-azimuth scenes are mapped on circular graph paper. The center of the azimuth board (the secondary datum) is the point in the middle of the graph paper. When mapping, remember to include a legend and important location data, such as GPS coordinates.

Step 10: Carefully remove and package all evidence for transportation and storage Follow agency protocols for evidence packing and labeling. However, use paper bags for skeletal elements and be sure to record the reference number on the bag. Paper bags and cardboard boxes are recommended because mold can grow in plastic bags which can cause bone damage and hinder DNA analysis (Figure 2.32).

Figure 2.32 (a–f) Packaging remains for transport. All skeletal remains should be carefully placed in labeled paper bags by their reference number. Skeletal remains and other items of evidentiary value should be packaged in separate bags.

Items can be collected when they are measured and photographed or at the end of scene processing. Place the marked paper bags/boxes into the body bag and avoid placing loose bones directly into the body bag. The bags/boxes will provide a reasonable amount of protection for human remains (Figure 2.33). Crania should be packaged with plenty of cushions and loose teeth should be packaged separately. Do not attempt to put loose teeth back into tooth sockets. Mummified, partially mummified, or partially decomposed remains can be placed directly in the body bag and sealed for transport.

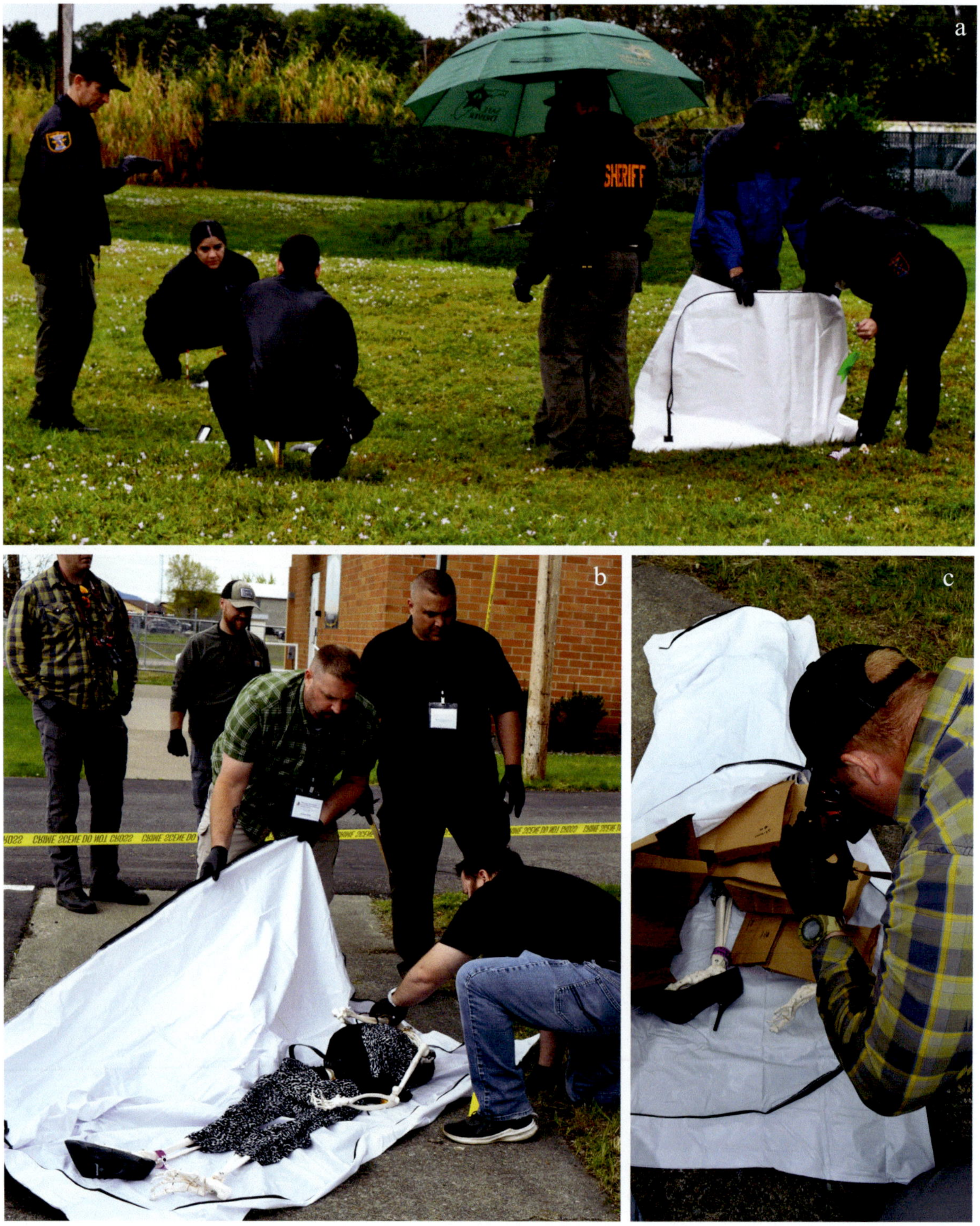

Figure 2.33 (a–b) Dry and/or disarticulated human remains are placed in paper evidence bags inside the body bag. (c) Photograph the packaged remains and the evidence seal.

Buried remains

Introduction

Excavating a **clandestine grave** involves careful planning and attention to detail. In general, burial excavation requires locating the grave, setting up the mapping system, digging, screening soils, photography, documentation, and recovery of skeletal remains and evidence.

There are two types of burial circumstances: **primary burials** and **secondary burials**. A primary burial is the original deposition of a body or bodies within a grave. A secondary burial results from the removal of a body or bodies from the primary burial to another grave. A secondary burial may be completely empty or contain incomplete skeletons, as elements could be left behind.

Like other types of scenes, the moment the burial excavation begins is the moment the context is altered. There is only one chance to get it right, which is why it is essential the investigator thoroughly document all aspects of the burial recovery.

Organization and preparedness are essential for the successful recovery of skeletal remains from a burial. Excavation is a time-consuming process that will vary for each scene and should not be rushed. Consider the environmental conditions such as weather, terrain, and soil type, as well as the time of day, the number of personnel available to help, and the equipment required for the excavation. *Never conduct excavation activities at night, even if scene lighting is available.* The risk of inadvertently destroying context or missing something is far too great. If a grave is discovered late in the day, take the time to plan the excavation, assemble the equipment, secure the scene, post an officer overnight, and begin the excavation the first thing the following morning. Similarly, if excavation is not completed by dark, identify a stopping point and cover the burial overnight by securing plastic tarps over the grave.

In the event of inclement weather, tarps and tents may be used to provide cover for the grave and those conducting excavations. However, if the weather is unfavorable with high winds and/or heavy rain, it is a good choice to delay the excavation until conditions improve. No number of tarps or tents will prevent disruption to the excavation under these circumstances.

This section discusses one method for burial recovery – baseline control-point mapping. This method is preferred by the authors because it is field expedient and accurate. Other mapping methods such as grid mapping require the placement of a grid over the top of the grave. This method works well for singular graves and graves containing more than one individual, but it can be time-consuming.

Steps for a burial recovery

First, follow steps 1–3 of the surface recovery section. Then:

1. Visually identify suspected grave sites.
2. Probe the suspected grave(s) to delineate boundaries.
3. Identify and record the site datum.
4. Construct the burial unit.
5. Create the burial secondary datum.
6. Excavate the grave by following these steps:
    a. Remove vegetation or obstructions from the top of the grave.
    b. Screen all vegetation and topsoil for evidence.
    c. Identify and examine the burial cut.
    d. Excavate across the grave, keeping everything level.
    e. Maintain the walls of the burial.
    f. Screen all soil.
    g. Carefully expose the human remains and other evidence.
    h. Document evidence within the grave (photograph, sketch, map, and record evidence from top down).
    i. Carefully remove skeletal elements. Inventory and package remains for storage/transportation.
    j. Excavate the bottom of the grave.
7. Take final photos.

Finally, maintain a tidy work area by keeping personal items away from the scene (e.g., water bottles, clothing, cigarettes, snacks, etc.) Not only does a messy scene increase the chances of unintentional contamination, but it also makes taking clean photographs of the scene more difficult. Take breaks early and often to avoid fatigue and dehydration.

A variety of small and large hand tools are required for excavation. Figure 2.34 shows the small tools required to conduct a burial recovery. Large tools such as shovels, buckets, screens, and tarps are also required. A complete list of required equipment is listed in Appendix D.

Figure 2.34 (a–b) Small tools required for a burial recovery.

Step 1: Visually identify suspected grave site Identifying a clandestine grave can be difficult, especially if several years have passed since the grave was initially dug. However, there are several physical signs that can indicate a possible burial location.

Common characteristics of burials include signs of recent disturbance such as disturbed ground soil, different color soils, **backfill piles,** a mound of soil, and items placed on top of the grave to conceal it (e.g., leaves, branches, and logs) (Figure 2.35). Signs of older graves include depressed areas of soil, cracks in the soil, and vegetation changes (e.g., new growth, different species of vegetation).

Figure 2.35 Burials can be identified by changes in the ground surface including disturbed soils, depressions, and differences in vegetation. (a) An area where two different colors of soil are present, possibly indicating a burial and a backfill pile. (b) Depressions of the ground surface may be visible. The red line highlights a depression line on the ground. (c) Areas of recent ground disturbance visible in the snow.

Step 2: Probe to search for the grave outline Clandestine graves can be hastily dug and shallow, typically reaching depths of only 12–19 in. in total. When the ground is disturbed or dug into, the soil becomes loosened, broken up, and aerated. These disturbed soils are loose and less dense compared to compacted undisturbed soils surrounding the hole. **Soil probing** is a low-tech and common method for distinguishing disturbed soils from undisturbed soils.

The probe allows the investigator to test the soil density and discover the outline of the grave by poking holes into the ground with the probe (Figure 2.36). Probing is an intrusive search method and should be conducted carefully, so as not to damage anything below the ground surface. Misuse of the probe can result in damage to the skeletal remains, which can hinder anthropological analysis.

When the grave outline is identified, mark it with pin flags to visually delineate the line between undisturbed and disturbed soil (Figure 2.37). Photograph this area for your records.

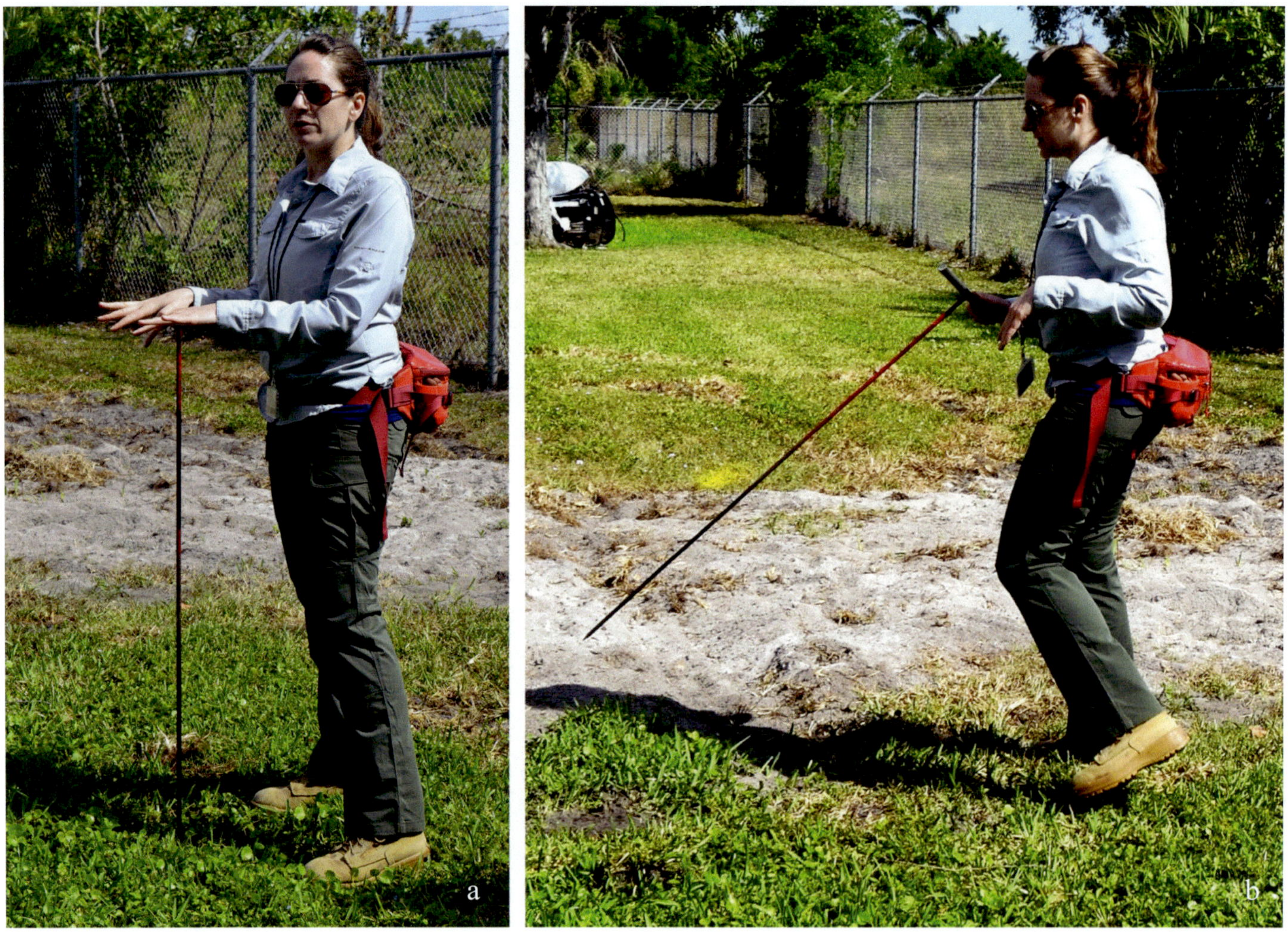

Figure 2.36 (a–b) The soil probe is an effective tool for delineating the boundaries of graves. Simply walk alongside the suspected grave while gently poking the ground surface with the probe to test for soil compactness.

Figure 2.37 (a–b) Working as a team, investigators use the soil probe to delineate the boundaries of the grave, which are marked by flags. (c–d) Flags mark the boundaries of the suspected graves.

Step 3: Identify the site datum Refer to the surface scatter section for instructions to identify a site datum

Step 4: Construct the burial unit After probing and outlining the suspected burial with pin flags, determine the size of the area to be mapped. As a rule, leave at least 12-in. between the flagged area and the undisturbed soil on all sides of the **burial unit**. A burial unit is an area surrounding the burial outline created by using the **Pythagorean theorem** ($a^2 + b^2 = c^2$). It is best to have more room to work with than too little. Furthermore, with extra room on the edges, there is less chance of collapsing the burial walls once excavation commences.

Setting up the burial unit requires two measuring tapes and four 10-in. metal carpenter nails. Figures 2.38 and 2.39 provide visual representations of the process. Follow these steps:

1. Decide how large to make the burial unit (e.g., 4′ × 4′, 4′ × 7′, 5′ × 5′, 6′ × 8′, 8′ × 10′). Figure 2.38 is a chart of unit length measurements with the hypotenuses calculated. Appendix F also shows the side lengths for mapping burial units or grids.
2. Locate magnetic north on a compass and move to the southwesternmost portion of the flagged area. Hammer a 10-in. carpenter's nail halfway into the ground.

3. Run a tape measure north, approximately 12 in. outside the flagged area. This line will be the west side of a four-sided box or rectangle. Hammer a 10-in. carpenter nail halfway into the ground at this northwest corner.
4. From the northwest corner nail, run a tape measure to the northeast corner of the burial unit. Before placing the next nail, run an additional tape measure diagonally from the southwest corner pin across the burial unit to the northeast corner. This measurement should fit the calculation from the baseline hypotenuse chart. The location of this northeast corner pin is where the two tape measures meet. Hammer a 10-in. carpenter nail halfway into the ground.
5. Run a tape measure from the northeast corner nail to the south. This will become the east side of the four-sided box or rectangle. Before placing the next nail, run an additional tape measure diagonally from the northwest corner pin across

Side lengths for mapping burial units or grids

Side Length	1	2	3	4	5	6	7	8	9	10
1	1.41	2.24	3.16	4.12	5.10	6.08	7.07	8.06	9.06	10.05
2		2.83	3.61	4.47	5.39	6.32	7.28	8.25	9.22	10.20
3			4.24	5.00	5.83	6.71	7.62	8.54	9.49	10.44
4				5.66	6.40	7.21	8.06	8.94	9.85	10.77
5					7.07	7.81	8.60	9.43	10.30	11.18
6						8.49	9.22	10.00	10.82	11.66
7							9.90	10.63	11.40	12.21
8								11.31	12.04	12.81
9									12.73	13.45
10										14.14

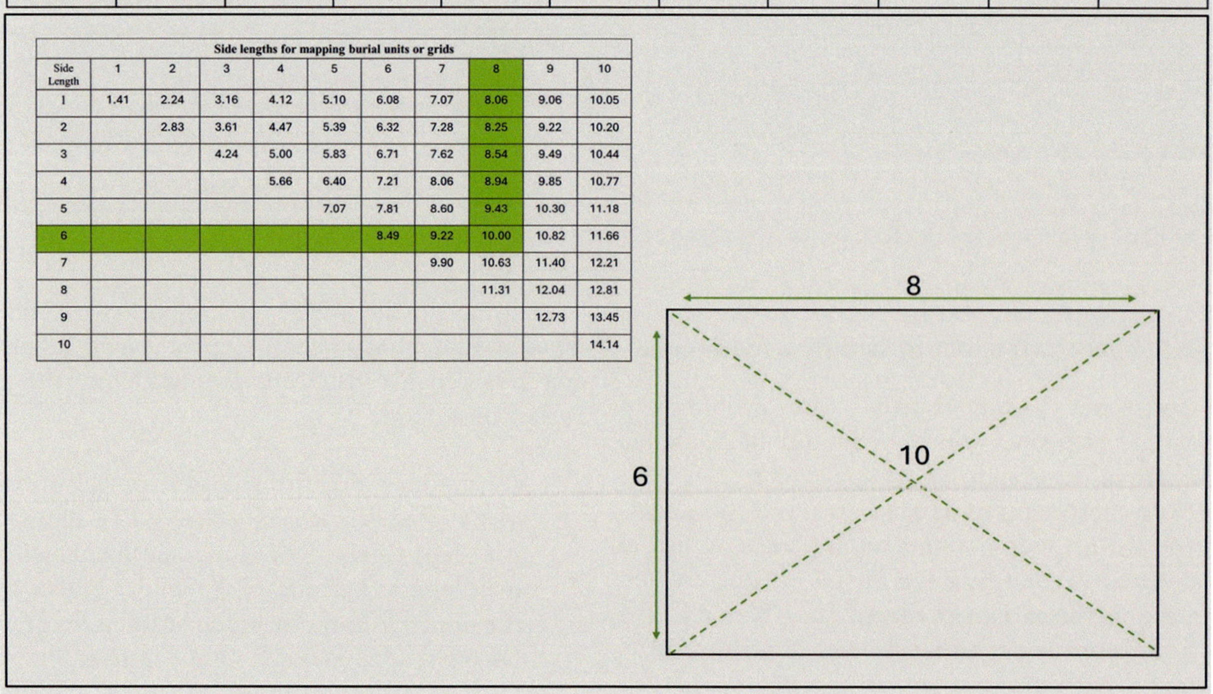

Figure 2.38 Side lengths for mapping burial units or grids. For example: a six by eight (6 × 8) burial unit has a hypotenuse of 10. This chart can be used for measurements in feet or meters.

the burial unit to the southeast corner. The location of this southeast corner nail is where the two tape measures meet. Hammer a 10-in. carpenter nail halfway into the ground.

6. Run a tape measure from the southeast corner nail to the southwest corner nail. This length should be the same as the length from the northwest corner nail to the northeast corner nail. Double-check to ensure all measurements are accurate. If these measurements are accurate, the square or rectangle will have four 90-degree angles.

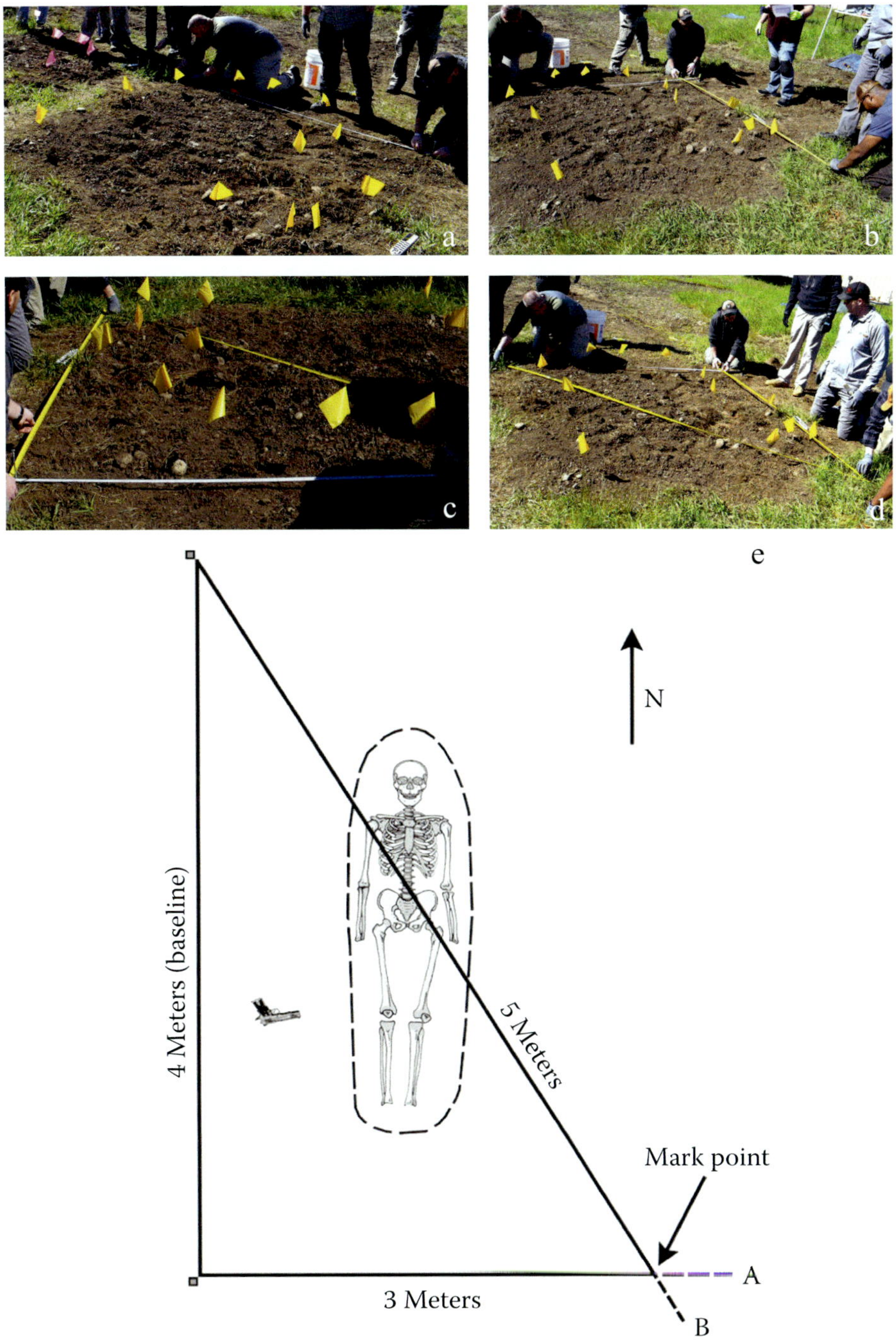

Figure 2.39 Create a burial unit using the Pythagorean theorem. (a) Investigators set the first corner of the burial unit by hammering a large nail halfway in the ground outside the boundaries of the burial. From the nail, measure out the first edge of the unit (a^2) and then place a second corner by hammering another nail halfway into the ground. (b–c) The second edge (b^2) is set from the second nail. Another measuring tape is used to measure the hypotenuse (c^2). (d) Investigators repeat the process for the remaining edges of the unit and completely hammer all the nails into the ground. (e) A schematic illustration of the Pythagorean theorem (taken from Dupras et al. 2012).

All measurements will be taken off one side of the burial unit using a similar method as explained earlier in baseline mapping (i.e., from the x-axis use a measuring tape to record the y-measurement and then find the z-measurement for elements found lower in the unit). Every reference point should be photographed and documented.

String up the burial unit once all sides of the unit are set. Hammer all four carpenter nails into the ground. Wrap fluorescent nylon mason string tightly around the nails of the burial unit. Ensure the string is flush with the ground to prevent tripping (Figure 2.40).

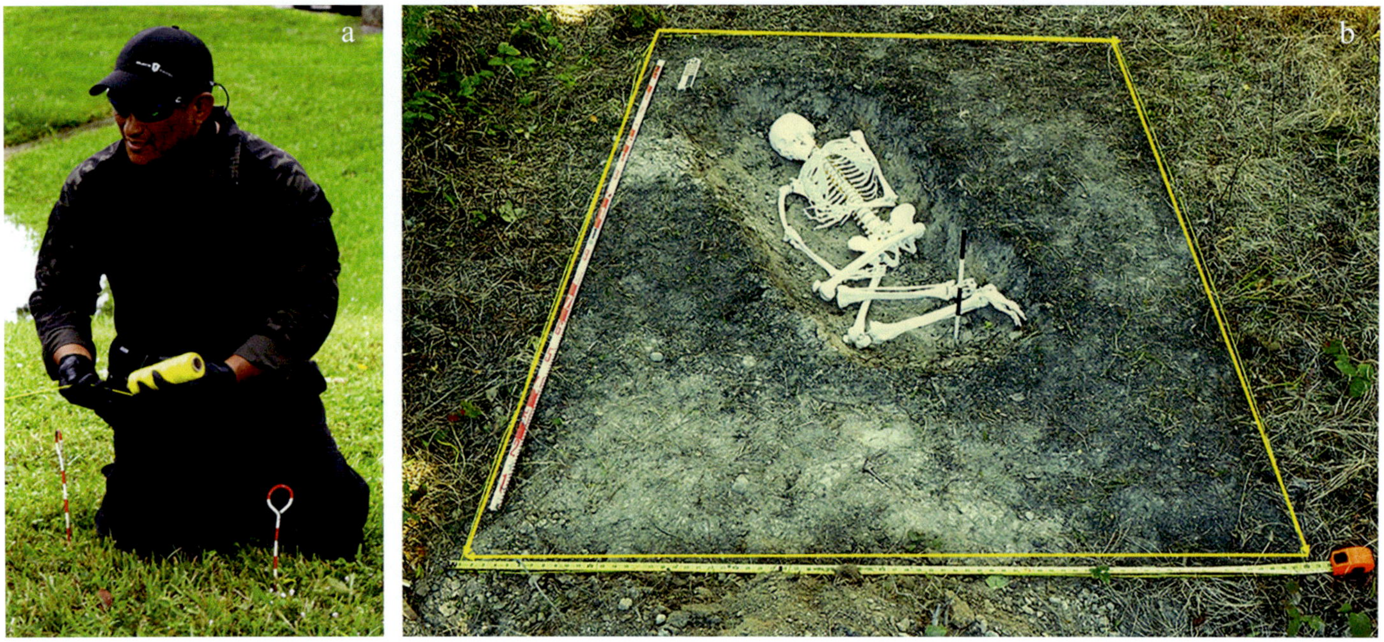

Figure 2.40 (a) A spool of nylon mason line is used to outline the burial unit. Tie the string taut around each corner nail keeping the string flush with the ground to prevent a tripping hazard. (b) The burial unit surrounding the grave after stringing. A tape measure is used along one edge of the grave and is the baseline from which all measurements are taken.

Step 5: Create the burial secondary datum The burial secondary datum is typically offset from the southwest corner nail of the burial unit. However, if the burial unit is on a slope, the secondary datum should be set from the corner with the highest elevation. Figures 2.41 and 2.42 show the process of setting the secondary datum.

Figure 2.41 Setting the secondary datum stake. (a) The stake is placed 10 cm (or 4 in.) diagonal from the burial unit's southwest corner. (b) The stake is hammered in the ground to the demarcated measurement line. (c) Mason string long enough to reach all edges of the burial is tied around the stake and a line level is attached. The line attached to the stake is used for all depth measurements within the grave.

From the southwest corner nail of the burial unit, measure 4 in. (10 cm) diagonally to the southwest. Hammer in a wooden datum stake so the black measurement mark is flush with the ground.

Tie a string around the datum stake 4 in. (10 cm) above the black measurement mark on the ground. The string should be long enough to reach all edges of the burial as it will be used to record the depth measurements (i.e., z-axis) for evidentiary items. Attach a line level to the string and record the GPS coordinates of the stake. Tie in the site datum (refer to the site datum description in the scattered remains section for details). See Appendix E for instructions on how to make the datum stake.

Figure 2.42 (a) The secondary datum stake is set in the southwest corner of the burial unit. (b) GPS coordinates of the secondary stake are taken and recorded on paperwork.

Step 6: Excavate the grave

a. Remove vegetation or obstructions from the top of the grave.

 Photograph and document the burial unit. Remove all vegetation and debris from the top of the suspected grave, including the sod layer (Figure 2.43). Clip vegetation including roots with clippers instead of pulling them out of the ground. Pulling a root at any point in the excavation can disturb evidence and destroy context (Figure 2.44).

Figure 2.43 Excavations begin with the removal of topsoil within the burial unit. (a–b) Investigators use flat-edge shovels to remove the sod layer from the suspected grave.

Figure 2.44 (a–b) Clippers are used to cut vegetation and roots to avoid unintentionally pulling on roots and accidentally destroying the context of evidence.

Flat shovels can also be used to carefully remove topsoil. A technique called **shovel skimming** is the preferred method (Figure 2.45). Notice how the shovel is skimming the surface instead of digging down into the burial unit. Proceed with caution and do not dig deep into the grave. The purpose of removing the vegetation and the sod layer is to help show the burial outline.

Figure 2.45 (a–d) Demonstration of the shovel skimming technique. Notice how the flat-edge shovel remains flat to carefully skim soil from the ground surface. This technique allows for soil removal to expose the edges of the grave shaft without digging directly into the ground and destroying context or damaging evidence.

b. Screen all vegetation and topsoil for evidence.

The sod layer and surface soils should be transferred into buckets for screening (Figure 2.46). Wear gloves when screening and look for anything of evidentiary value (e.g., skeletal remains, cigarette butts, projectiles, etc.).

Figure 2.46 Topsoil including the sod layer is placed into buckets and transported to the screen for inspection.

c. Identify and examine the burial cut (disturbed vs undisturbed soils).

Once surface vegetation has been removed and screened, identify the **burial cut**. The burial cut is where the grave was dug by using tools (e.g., shovels and entrenching tools, skid steers, backhoes). The cut is identified by observing the disturbed and undisturbed soils on the ground surface. Because it is difficult to see in photographs, it is outlined in red in Figure 2.47.

Figure 2.47 (a) A burial unit showing the outline of the grave shaft following removal of the topsoil. (b) The same burial unit showing the excavation of the soils within the grave. Notice how the edges of the grave shaft are maintained during excavations (red outline for emphasis).

d. Excavate across the burial, keeping everything level.

When the burial cut is identified, excavation can begin. Burial excavation should be conducted carefully, and shovels should be abandoned. Small hand tools such as mason trowels, various-sized brushes, and dustpans should be used to gently remove soil from the grave. To preserve context, excavate across the grave in even levels, referred to by archaeologists as **excavating in spits**. If excavating with team members, take a moment to look around at their progress to ensure everyone is excavating at a consistent depth (Figure 2.48).

Figure 2.48 Commencement of excavations using small hand tools to carefully remove soils. (a) Investigators observe each other's work to ensure the grave excavations occur evenly and at the same pace (excavating in spits). (b) An evenly excavated grave.

In archaeology, the **law of superposition** is a theory describing the position of contents in the ground. It states that objects lower in the ground are older than objects located closer to the ground surface. For clandestine graves, the law of superposition clarifies the sequence of events. If items are located at the bottom of the grave and under the body, they were likely deposited in the grave before the body. If items are located above the body, they were likely deposited after the body was positioned in the grave. It is possible to encounter evidence before reaching the level of the skeletal remains so caution should be taken throughout the entire excavation (Figure 2.49).

Figure 2.49 Encountering evidence within the grave. (a) An investigator photographs a piece of evidence with a scale. Notice the team used a spade trowel with the point facing north as a stand-in for a north arrow when one was not available. A north arrow is preferred. (b) The team uncovers skeletal remains and other evidence evenly across the burial to show the spatial distribution including the depth.

If an item of evidentiary value is encountered prior to reaching skeletal remains:

1. Stop all excavation.
2. Assign a reference number to the item.
3. Photograph the item with a north arrow and scale.
4. Measure the item using x, y, and z and document the location information on the data sheets.
5. Sketch the item on the map and associated forms.
6. Collect and place the item into an evidence bag with the reference number written on the bag.

e. Maintain the walls of burial.

Maintain the walls of the burial during excavation. The **burial walls** are the edges of the grave from the top of the grave to the bottom of the grave. The walls of the grave can be identified by the soil composition. Burial walls consist of compact undisturbed soils at the border of the grave. There are two main reasons to maintain these walls:

1. It may be possible to identify marks from the tool that created the burial cut (e.g., shovel marks and backhoe bucket marks).
2. To ensure the entire grave is excavated and all items are found. Conversely, do not dig into the hard undisturbed soils beyond the grave cut.

Figure 2.50 demonstrates how to maintain the walls of the burial. Because the soil inside of the grave is typically loose compared to the undisturbed ground outside the grave, the soil should fall away from the edge of the grave without having to aggressively scrape the side of the grave. Notice how the investigators use the trowel to gently pull loose soil away from the burial edge toward the center of the grave. As excavation continues, do not push soil up against the already excavated wall from other portions of the grave (Figure 2.50).

Figure 2.50 Maintain the burial walls from the top of the grave to the bottom. (a) The investigator uses a rectangular mason trowel to carefully remove soil from the edge of the grave. (b) Even walls are maintained throughout the duration of the excavation. (c) Loose soil should be pulled away from the compact burial walls. Do not push or pile soil from the middle of the grave against the walls.

f. Screen all soil.

All grave contents must be screened for evidence (Figure 2.51). Small evidentiary items and skeletal remains are easy to miss due to size and color and/or because they are clumped within soils. If an item is found in the screen, immediately inform the excavators to verify the approximate location and depth from within the grave where the bucket containing the item came from. Consider using two different color buckets to denote different ends or sides of the burial to help identify where the item came from. Assign the item a reference number, photograph it, and package it in a bag noting it was found in the screen with the location information (e.g., north end of burial, approximately 7–9 in. in depth).

Figure 2.51 (a) Screeners work as a team over a large homemade screen. (b) Excavators use two different color buckets to keep soil from different areas of the grave separate. For example: blue buckets are used on the east end of the grave and orange buckets are used for the west end of the grave. (c) The investigator is taking their time while screening. It can be a slow process especially if the soil is compact, rocky, or wet. Often digging and screening occur at different paces. (d) A bucket of soil is dumped in a stand-up rocker screen for inspection.

g. Carefully expose the human skeletal remains and other evidence.

When working around skeletal remains, replace the trowel with clay modeling tools, wooden picks, brushes, and plastic dust pans (Figure 2.52). Metal tools can easily damage skeletal remains.

Figure 2.52 (a–b) Soft-bristled brushes are used to remove soils from the skeletal remains.

Excavate carefully without bumping or moving items around in the grave. Moving items destroys its original position and relationship to all others (i.e., its context). If an item is accidentally moved within the grave, simply remove the item, bag it, and record its approximate location and depth noting that it was inadvertently moved during excavation. Notice how the investigators maintain a consistent depth across the grave (i.e., excavating in spits) even when skeletal remains are encountered (Figure 2.53).

Figure 2.53 (a) Excavation with brushes continues to expose skeletal remains evenly across the burial to preserve context and allow investigators to document the position of the body in the grave. (b) The investigator uses a very small dustpan to sweep soil for removal in small and cramped spaces.

h. Document evidence within the grave (photograph, sketch, map, and record evidence from top down).

Document evidence within the grave with baseline control-point mapping (Figures 2.54 and 2.55). With burials, the depth measurement (z-axis) is taken for all reference points. Obtain the x-axis and y-axis measurements first, and then use the datum string with line level to record the z-axis measurement (Figure 2.56).

Figure 2.54 (a–b) Basepoint mapping is used to obtain x-axis and y-axis measurements within the grave.

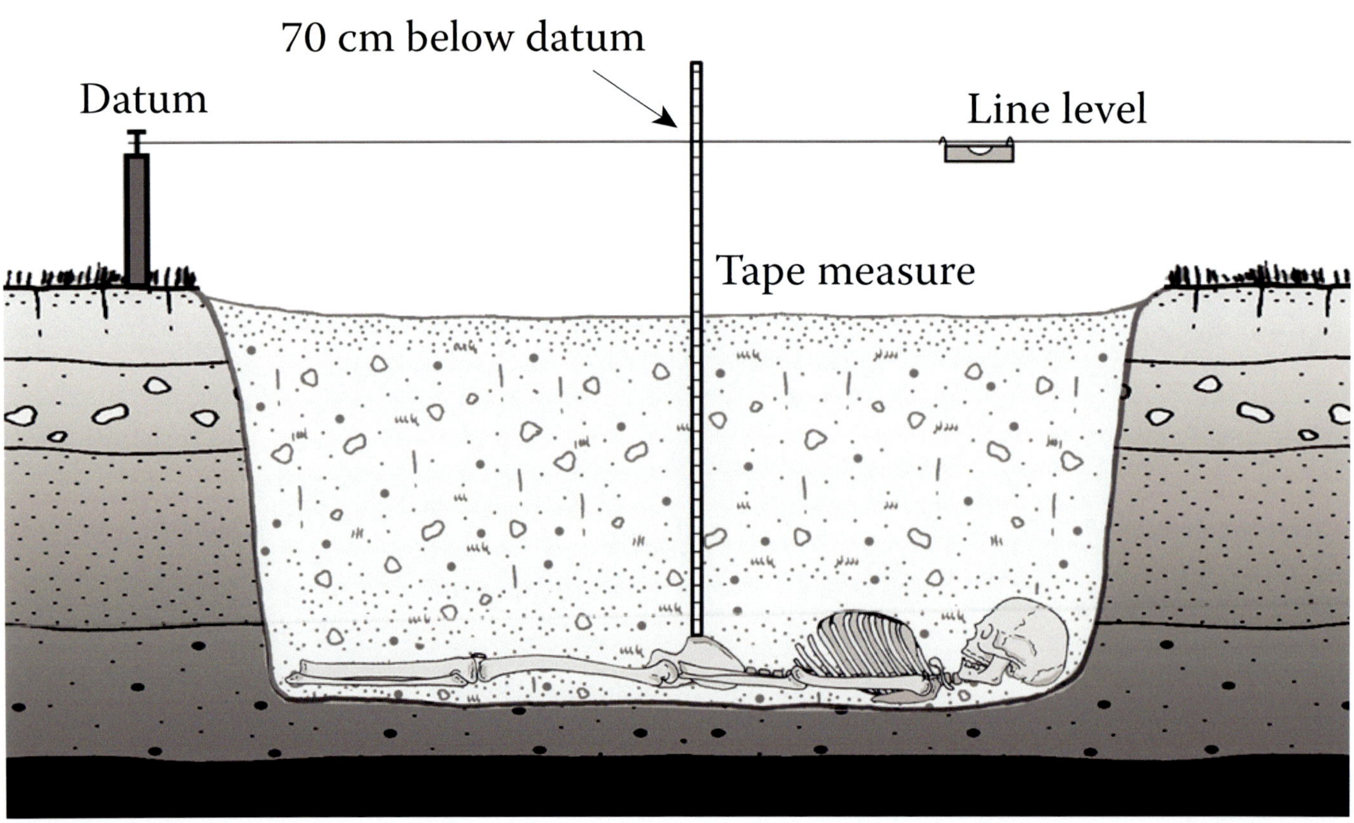

Figure 2.55 Schematic representation for taking depth measurements of evidence within the grave (taken from Dupras et al. 2012).

Refer back to the baseline mapping section, for the technique.

The number of measurements taken within the grave will depend on the complexity of the grave, its contents, and time constraints. Regardless, stay consistent from start to finish. For example, if at the beginning of the excavation, the decision is made to measure multiple points on each bone, ensure all bones are documented in this way to the end. Do not switch to recording one measurement per bone as the day progresses just because it takes too long to record multiple measurements. Remember: measurements are the information used to create the map of the grave. Start with a plan to map the grave and stick to it.

Figure 2.56 Obtaining the z-axis (depth) measurement. (a–b) The mason string from the datum stake is pulled across the grave to the item for measurement. (c–d) The investigators obtain the depth measurement by using a metallic measuring tape to record the distance from the item to the mason string. The line level is used to level the string ensuring a correct depth measurement.

Expose as much of the body as possible for the purpose of documenting the **body position** (Figure 2.57). The body position may offer information about how the person ended up there. For example, the person could be placed **prone** (face down), **supine** (on their back), **flexed** (curled in a fetal position), **semi-flexed** (slightly or partially bent) or **extended** (laid out flat). Document additional information such as the size of the hole and whether it seems planned. For example, the hole may be too small for the person to fit properly, and they seem wedged in. These details can help to determine if the burial was carefully or hastily planned.

If the remains are clothed, it is recommended to keep skeletal items inside the clothing, as best as possible. For example: foot bones can remain inside socks and/or shoes and leg/pelvis can remain within pants. Removing skeletal remains from the clothing risks loss of context and losing small bones or evidence.

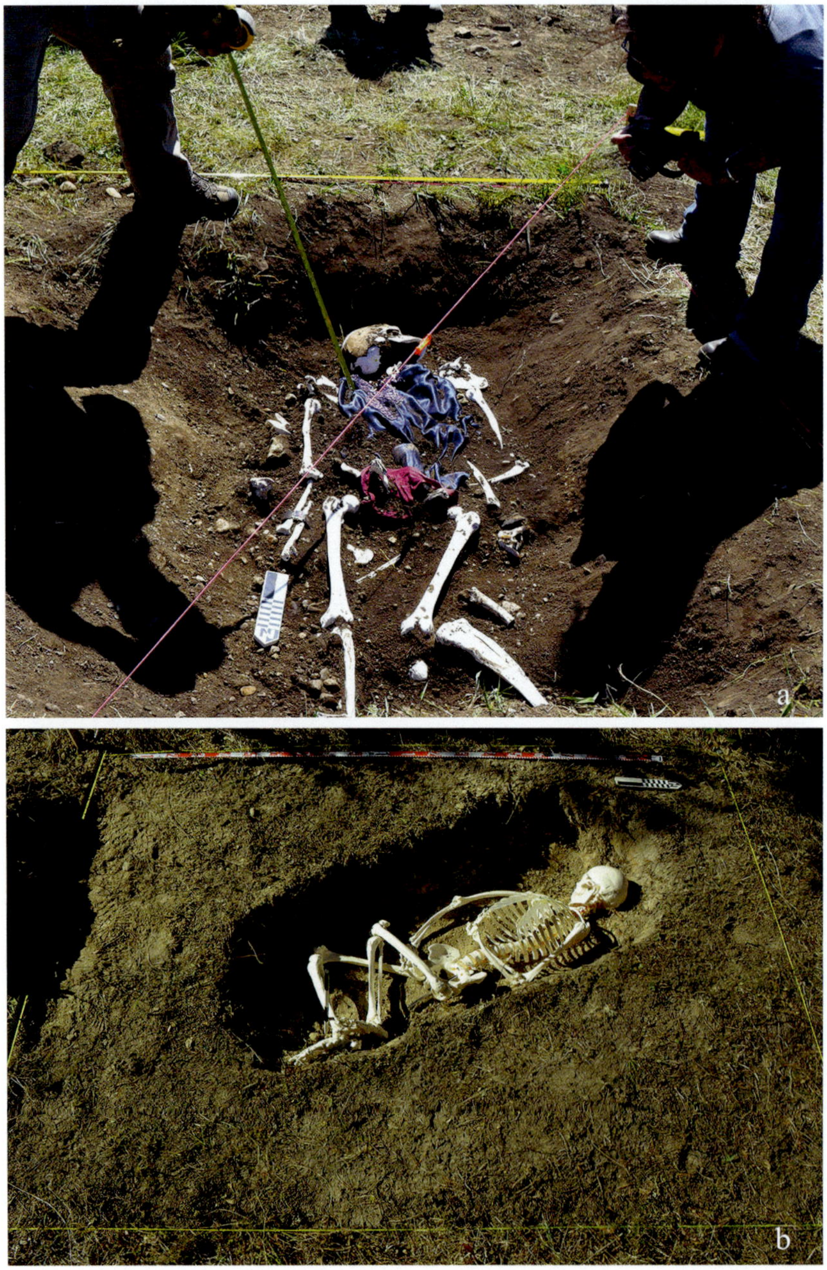

Figure 2.57 Document the body position within the grave including midrange, and close-up photos. (a) The investigator photographs the remains with depth measurements. (b) Final photo of the skeletal remains in situ with a scale and a north arrow.

As mentioned, it is critical to thoroughly document the entire excavation process. This includes photographing, sketching, and mapping each step and evidence in situ and once it has been removed (Figure 2.58). Each type of documentation should back up the other. Work carefully and methodically. Once a piece of evidence is moved, it cannot be placed back in its original location.

Figure 2.58 (a) Photograph any items of evidence in situ prior to removal or further inspection. (b) In this situation, an ID card is encountered within the photographed article of clothing. Document all evidence in situ first and again once it is removed.

Use the baseline mapping recording form in Appendix A and graph paper to record the information about the burial. The measurements will be used to create a map on traditional graph paper (Figure 2.59).

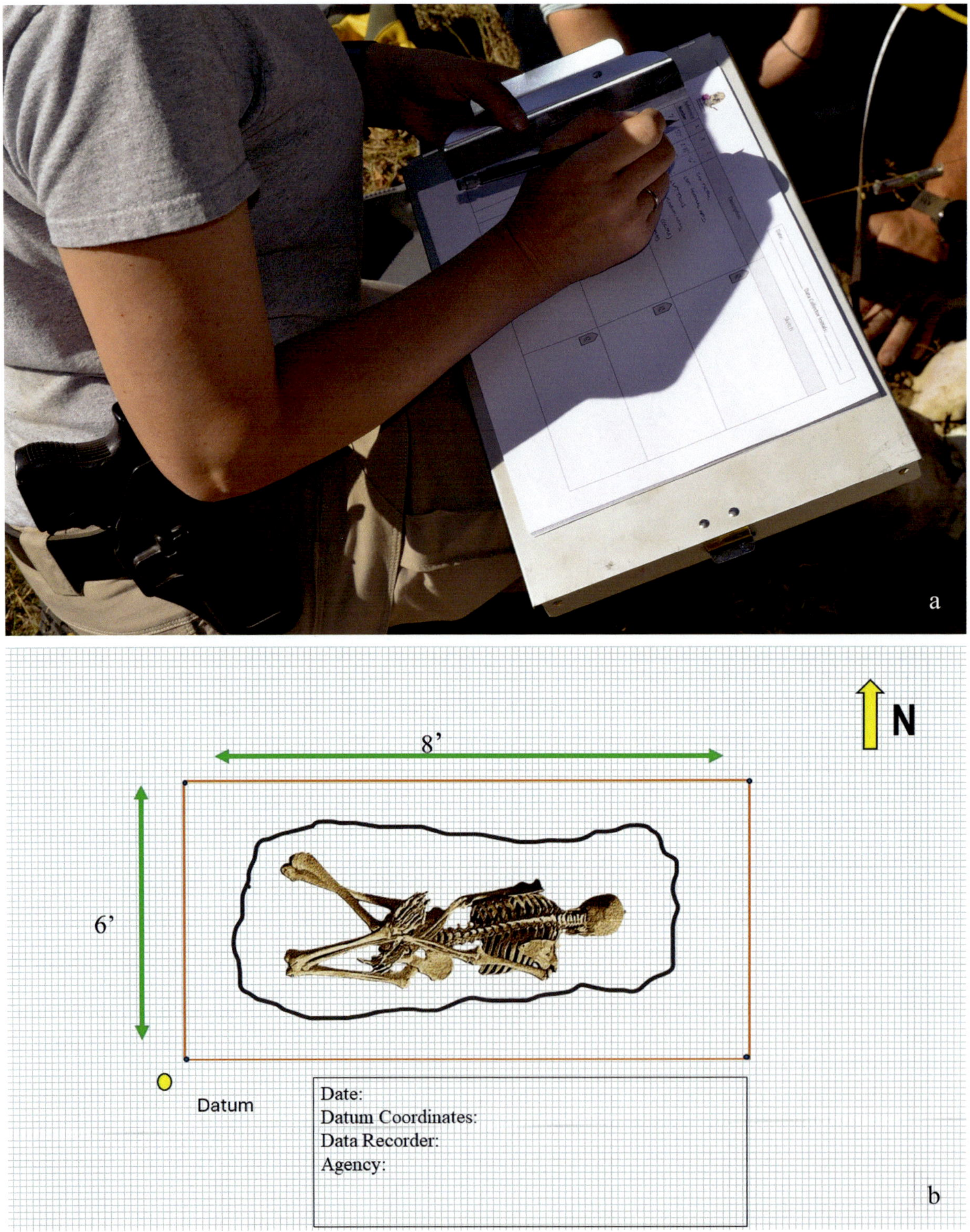

Figure 2.59 (a) All items of evidentiary value are recorded on the data sheets to include descriptions, field sketches, and the x-, y-, and z-axis measurements. (b) The finished map of the burial in digital format although the final map can be hand drawn. Do not worry if your map is not perfect. Everyone's artistic ability varies, and the purpose of the map is to show the spatial relationship of items within the grave.

i. Carefully remove skeletal elements. Inventory and package remains for storage/transportation.

   Package skeletal elements separately into paper bags and/or boxes and then place bags into a body bag with a security seal, per agency protocol. Photograph and document the process. Follow the proper chain of custody.

j. Excavate the bottom of the grave.

   Excavate all loose soil at the bottom of the burial unit to ensure **sterile** and undisturbed soils are reached. There will be a difference in feel, appearance, and consistency in the sterile soil. Use a metal detector to locate any metallic items (e.g., bullets, jewelry) that may have settled into the compact soil beneath the grave. Document, map, and bag any items encountered and indicate their location at the bottom of the grave (Figure 2.60).

Figure 2.60 (a) Use a metal detector to locate projectiles or other metallic evidence that may be within or below the grave. (b) The red circle shows a shell casing found using the metal detector. (c) Always use the metal detector on the sterile soil at the bottom of a finished grave.

Step 7: Take final photos Take final photos of the exhumed grave with a scale to show the dimensions including depth and to show all evidence has been removed (Figure 2.61). Record the final depth of the grave.

Notice how the graves depicted in the figures look different. Every burial is unique, as many factors influence the scene including soil type, terrain, the equipment used to dig the initial grave, and primary versus secondary burial. There is no such thing as over-documenting these types of scenes. Photographs, notes, maps, and sketches are designed to tell the story of the scene. They also allow the investigator to thoroughly understand the circumstances surrounding the burial event.

Remove everything from the scene except for the secondary datum, which should be hammered into the ground. Determine if backfilling the hole with removed soils is necessary before departing the scene.

Figure 2.61 Take final photos of the empty grave. (a) Measuring tapes and a north arrow are used to show the size and orientation of the grave. (b) Take a photo showing the final depth of the grave. This investigator is using a photography rod, but a metallic measuring tape works too.

Bibliography

Dupras TL, Schultz JJ, Wheeler SM, and Williams LJ. 2012. *Forensic Recovery of Human Remains, Archaeological Approaches*. Boca Raton, FL: CRC Press.

Note

All photographs in this chapter were taken by Teresa A. White and Hillary R. Parsons, with the exception of the aerial drone photographs. They were taken by Zack Sybert, owner of Flathead Lake Drone LLC.

Preservation

3

SAMUEL S. WHITE

Contents

Introduction

The goal of this section is to provide information on the preservation of human skeletal remains. If the remains are improperly handled, the efforts to identify the decedent may be difficult if not impossible. This section will also cover the pertinence of legal and ethical issues concerning the treatment of human remains to instill and preserve public confidence in law enforcement and the medicolegal death investigation system. In addition to the importance of the legal aspect of proper preservation procedures, law enforcement and other medicolegal and/or forensic investigators should strive to recognize and understand the need to preserve human dignity. This is not only out of consideration for the deceased individual but also to show deference for their surviving loved ones.

Packaging human skeletal remains

The first consideration discussed here is the preservation of the actual remains themselves. It is important to follow proper protocol and best practices when collecting, packaging, and transporting human skeletal remains to ensure optimal preservation.

Extreme care should be exercised when handling suspected human skeletal remains. Do not place fingers in the eye sockets as it can damage the delicate bones of the face. Wear gloves for protection and to prevent DNA contamination.

When packaging skeletal remains for transportation to a medical examiner or forensic anthropologist for analysis, place elements in breathable paper bags or boxes. Do not place skeletal elements in plastic evidence bags, as bones can retain moisture and develop mold which may hinder DNA analysis.

Clearly label evidence bags and/or boxes on the outside and seal with tamper-proof evidence tape. A second label, with all relevant information, may be placed inside the bag/box. This additional step could be implemented if there is a possibility the label may become illegible (i.e., smeared, faded) due to inclement weather or other unintended circumstances.

When bones are small or conditionally compromised, they can be carefully placed in acid-free paper and then tin foil, which will help stabilize them for transportation. Place the tin foil package into a paper bag or evidence

DOI: 10.4324/9781032623320-4

box, then label and seal it according to the instructions above.

Finally, transfer the human remains to either a medical examiner or a forensic anthropologist following agency protocols. As mentioned earlier in this field guide, only specialists trained in forensic anthropology or osteology should attempt to analyze the remains.

Legal considerations concerning human skeletal remains

The second consideration discussed here pertains to the laws governing the treatment and preservation of human remains and the **chain of custody** of those remains; that is, the documentation of the chronological movement, location, and custodial status of physical evidence from the time it is collected through the final disposition.

Federal, state, and Tribal laws provide a legal framework regarding the proper handling of human skeletal remains. Law enforcement officers and death investigators might encounter human skeletal remains in the course of their work. Knowledge of the laws and regulations pertaining to those remains is essential to their treatment and investigation. In addition to these laws, investigators should follow the **standard operating procedure (SOP)** mandated by their agency.

Although the following laws pertain to human remains and antiquities discovered on federal property, they also provide a basis by which all human remains should be treated. The laws emphasize respect for the remains themselves and empathetic conduct toward surviving family members and loved ones. Integrating a **culturally sensitive awareness**, that is, an informed understanding pertaining to the distinct values, beliefs, and ways of living for a culture, will help effectuate a favorable outcome for all involved in terms of human interactions.

Most laws pertaining to the treatment and preservation of human remains were written to protect those discovered on federal or Tribal lands. Often, encounters with human remains are "associated with historic properties eligible for or listed in the National Register of Historic Places" (ACHP, Policy statement on burial sites, human remains, and funerary objects, 2023). Many of the remains are historic or prehistoric and are not of **medicolegal significance,** meaning they are not "relevant to the medicolegal death investigation system; anthropologically, this term typically refers to human skeletal material of recent origin" (ASB, 2021). Nevertheless, nonrecent human remains may still be consequential in other legal contexts, for example, when human remains are sold in **jurisdictions** where it is prohibited. This will be discussed later in the section dealing with skeletal remains located in homes or other private settings.

In the following section, several federal laws will be discussed concerning human remains. This is by no means an exhaustive list as laws can differ from jurisdiction to jurisdiction.

Federal laws pertaining to the preservation of human remains

Several laws dictate the actions of all members of society in and of the lands upon which they reside. Before the **colonization** of what is now known as the United States and US Territories, these same lands were inhabited by certain groups of people, "including by not limited to Indian Tribes, Native Hawaiians, and other Indigenous Peoples" (ACHP, Policy statement on burial sites, human remains, and funerary objects, 2023).

Through the centuries of colonial occupation, there were few laws governing the proper treatment and removal of human remains or items of **cultural patrimony** from public lands. The need for laws specific to proper handling of skeletal remains and associated burial goods, along with the removal of other antiquities from public lands, became abundantly clear. Government control was required to limit the destruction of culturally important locations for the benefit of generations to come, as well as out of respect for the descendants of the previous inhabitants of these now-public lands.

The Antiquities Act of 1906

The first law enacted to protect culturally sensitive sites, objects, and human remains found on public lands was the Antiquities Act of 1906 (Antiquities Act of 1906 n.d.), which was signed into law by President Theodore Roosevelt. This Act was the first US law to provide general legal protection for cultural and natural resources of historic or scientific interest on federal lands.

In addition, the Act provided punishment for persons caught looting human remains or damaging property while also defining who could legally excavate and conduct research on federally owned property through a permitting process. Overall, the Antiquities Act of 1906 was designed to respond to a federally recognized need to protect culturally sensitive landmarks, historic and prehistoric structures, and other objects of historic and scientific interest located on federal lands.

In the years following the inception of the Antiquities Act of 1906, other laws were introduced that resulted in public policy decisions, yielding tangible public benefits and reflecting the balance between preservation and development of public lands.

The National Historic Preservation Act (NHPA) of 1966 and the Advisory Council on Historic Preservation (ACHP)

The NHPA of 1966 was enacted for the purpose of preserving and maintaining cultural resources in the face of federal undertakings. The NHPA applies Section 106 and Section 110 to determine how to be better stewards over the lands including how to determine the way in which the actions of a government agency will affect historic properties and then take those effects into account when planning an undertaking (Federal Historic Preservation Laws 2018; King 2008).

Additionally, the ACHP administers the requirements of NHPA. On March 1, 2023, the ACHP voted to adopt an updated policy statement on burial sites, human remains, and funerary objects:

> The new policy was adopted in response to unfortunate and traumatic incidents of disturbances of these sites, remains, and objects.... The policy formally recognizes that the places and people most often disturbed are those associated with racial and ethnic minorities, Indian Tribes, Native Hawaiians, Indigenous People, and low-income communities. (ACHP, n.d.)

The Archaeological and Historic Preservation Act (AHPA) of 1974, The Archaeological Resources Protection Act (ARPA) of 1979

After the 1966 NHPA was enacted, there was a need for new laws providing more specific and effective processes for the preservation and treatment of cultural resources. These later laws included the AHPA of 1974, the ARPA of 1979, and the Native American Graves Protection and Repatriation Act (NAGPRA) of 1990, which will be discussed below. These laws apply to federal lands, Native American lands, and in the instances where undertakings involve federal funds and permits. The AHPA authorizes government agencies to fund archaeological research and attempt mitigation at sites affected during an undertaking. In addition to the AHPA, the ARPA was enacted to address the permitting process and impose heavy sanctions and violations on illegal artifact-collecting activities on federal and Indian lands.

The NAGPRA of 1990

Prior to 1990 laws were established primarily for the purpose of preserving the cultural heritage of the United States, while not specifically addressing human remains. In 1990, congress enacted the NAGPRA (Pub. L. 101–601, 25 U.S.C. 3001 et seq., 104 Stat. 3048), which provided for the protection and return of Native American human remains, funerary objects, sacred objects, and objects of cultural patrimony:

> By enacting NAGPRA, Congress recognized that human remains of any ancestry "must at all times be treated with dignity and respect." Congress also acknowledged that human remains and other cultural items removed from Federal or Tribal lands belong, in the first instance, to lineal descendants, Indian Tribes, and Native Hawaiian organizations. (Inouye, 1990)

A January 12, 2024, revision of NAGPRA includes provisions for a more concise process regarding the protection and repatriation of human remains and or cultural items held by museums or federal agencies. As part of the revision, stringent timelines that include sizable penalties for failure to comply with the law were added. The revision also specifically requires deference to the Native American traditional knowledge of lineal descendants, Indian Tribes, and Native Hawaiian organizations (NAGPRA Regulations, 2023, United States of America, 1990).

The African American Burial Grounds Preservation Act

"The legacies of colonization, including **cultural assimilation**, forced relocation, and slavery, have led to an uneven awareness of where and why practitioners are likely to encounter burial sites, human remains, and funerary objects across the United States and its territories" (ACHP, Policy statement on burial sites, human remains, and funerary objects, 2023).

In response to these issues and others, on December 12, 2022, The African American Burial Grounds Preservation Act was enacted into law. "This Act now authorizes the National Park Service to coordinate initiatives designed to identify, interpret, research, preserve, and record African American burial grounds that have been left unmarked, previously abandoned, or underserved" (ASLA, 2024).

While the African American Burial Grounds Preservation Act primarily deals with the preservation and restoration of African American burial grounds, the inherent importance of respectful handling of human remains is apparent throughout the content of the law. Notably, this Act does not pertain to private property.

Other laws pertaining to human skeletal remains

As mentioned earlier, there are several laws pertaining to human skeletal remains, but they differ from state to state and jurisdiction to jurisdiction. For example, the laws with respect to owning or possessing human skeletal remains differ.

In nearly every state in the United States, apart from Louisiana, human skeletal remains are legal to possess if they are legally acquired. In Tennessee and Georgia, individuals can possess human remains, but those remains may not be bought, sold, traded, imported, or exported. This is important because law enforcement and other medicolegal investigators often encounter skeletal remains in homes, garages, storage units, and other places. These remains include 'trophy skulls,' or those used for ritual purposes.

Without professional osteological training, it is difficult for investigators to know how old skeletal remains are, where they came from, and most importantly, to whom they belong. Unfortunately, in the United States, many legislators erroneously assume death investigators have mandated specialized training in human skeletal remains which many do not. Therefore, when in doubt, skeletal remains should be carefully packaged and transported to a medical examiner or forensic anthropologist to determine their medicolegal significance.

Some medical examiner's offices employ full-time forensic anthropologists, which limits the transportation of human remains and prevents excessive handling. In addition, with forensic anthropologists on staff, human remains are not as likely to end up sitting on morgue shelves because the analysis can often begin as soon as the remains are received. This not only helps with the medical examiner's caseload, but it also helps identify the decedent and provide answers to surviving family members or loved ones.

Preservation of human dignity

The final consideration discussed in this section is the preservation of human dignity. Every law enforcement officer, coroner or medical examiner, medicolegal investigator, crime scene investigator, forensic anthropologist, or other specialist working with human skeletal remains should recognize their moral and ethical duty to treat all people with dignity, both in life and in death. The skeletal remains were once a living, breathing person. Therefore, determining who they belong to can be the most important undertaking.

According to the **NamUs** website, an estimated 4,400 dead bodies are located each year. Approximately 25% of those bodies remain unidentified after 1 year. As of 2018, medical examiner and coroner offices alone reported 11,380 unidentified remains (Brooks 2021). There are a number of reasons people remain unidentified including, but not limited to, a lack of **interjurisdictional** communications, errors in scientific identification, transcription errors, depleted human and financial resources, no surviving family members, and other factors. Furthermore, limited access to computerized databases can make identifications unlikely.

Unfortunately, according to Brooks, fewer than half (40%) of coroner offices and about half (54%) of city, county, district, or regional medical examiner offices have a computerized information management system. In contrast, the majority (91%) of state medical examiner offices have a computerized information management system. Offices serving larger populations are more likely to have access to these systems than smaller offices. Without these management systems, it is reasonable to assume that unidentified individuals will continue to go unnamed.

The lack of communication among families is yet another reason people remain unidentified. For example, if families are not in contact or are estranged, they may not know to file a missing persons report or be aware that their family member has died. Furthermore, marginalized individuals can go unidentified due to the lack of social connectedness or visibility. Unfortunately, in these cases, law enforcement personnel would not know that they need to file a report. "To date, there is no federal law requiring a law enforcement report be filed for anyone 21 years or older who goes missing, nor is there a mandate to enter the case into NamUs" (Spamer et al. 2019).

The NamUs program facilitates communication and data sharing among allied forensic professionals while providing an effective tool allowing for the searching and crossmatching of missing persons cases with unidentified human remains records. Additionally, NamUs is the only federal database providing limited access to the public, empowering the families of the missing to assist in search and recovery efforts (NamUs, nd).

As mentioned earlier in this field guide, without the proper identification, recovery, and preservation of human remains, it is difficult, if not impossible, to bring these individuals back home for their **final disposition**. That is why the work is so important. Remember these are not just bones, they are people.

Suggested readings and additional resources

See Appendix G for a complete list of suggested readings and additional resources.

Bibliography

Academy Standards Board. 2021. *Standard for Determination of Medicolegal Significance from Skeletal Remains in Forensic Anthropology.* Colorado Springs, CO. https://www.aafs.org/asb-standard/standard-determination-medicolegal-significance-skeletal-remains-forensic-anthropology

American Council of Historic Preservation. nd. *Burial Sites, Human Remains, and Funerary Objects.* Washington, DC. https://www.achp.gov/treatment-burial-sites.

American Council of Historic Preservation. 2023. *Policy Statement on Burial Sites, Human Remains, and Funerary Objects.* Washington, DC. https://www.achp.gov/treatment-burial-sites.

Ballou S, Kline M, Stolorow M, Taylor M, Williams S, Bamberger P, Yvette B, Brown L, Jones C, Keaton R, Kiley W, Thiessen K, LaPorte G, Latta J, Ledray L, Nagy R, Schwind L, Stoiloff S, and Ostrom B. 2013. *The Biological Evidence Preservation Handbook: Best Practices for Evidence Handlers.* Gaithersburg, MD: NIST Interagency/Internal Report (NISTIR).

Bass WM. 1995. *Human Osteology: A Laboratory and Field Manual*, 4th edn. Columbia: Missouri Archaeological Society.

Brooks C. 2021. *Medical Examiner and Coroner Offices: 2018.* Bureau of Justice Statistics. https://bjs.ojp.gov/library/publications/medical-examiner-and-coroner-offices-2018.

Carter M, Newman J, Seidemann R, and Reedy E. 2022. Review of United States laws pertaining to the recovery and analysis of human skeletal remains. *Journal of Forensic Sciences.* 67(5), 1876–1889.

NamUs. nd. *"What is NamUs?" NamUs National Missing and Unidentified Persons System.* https://namus.nij.ojp.gov/what-namus.

Spamer BJ, Weiss D, and Heurich C. 2019. *Solving the Missing Indigenous Person Data Crisis: NamUs 2.0.*" nij.ojp.gov. https://nij.ojp.gov/topics/articles/solving-missing-indigenous-person-data-crisis-namus-20.

The American Society of Landscape Architects. 2024. *Advocacy Issue Brief: African-American Burial Grounds Preservation Act.* Washington, DC. https://www.asla.org/IssueBrief/BurialGrounds.aspx.

U.S. Department of the Interior Bureau of Indian Affairs 2024. *Native American Graves Protection and Repatriation Act.* https://www.bia.gov/service/nagpra.

Appendix A: Baseline data sheet

Date: ____________ Location/Secondary datum ________________________________ Data Collector Initials: __________

Reference Number	X	Y	Z	Description	Sketch

Appendix B: Azimuth data sheet

Date: ____________ Location/Sub-datum:____ Data Collector Initials: ______

Reference Number	Degree	Distance	Z	Description	Sketch
					N
					N
					N
					N
					N
					N

Appendix C: Azimuth mapping

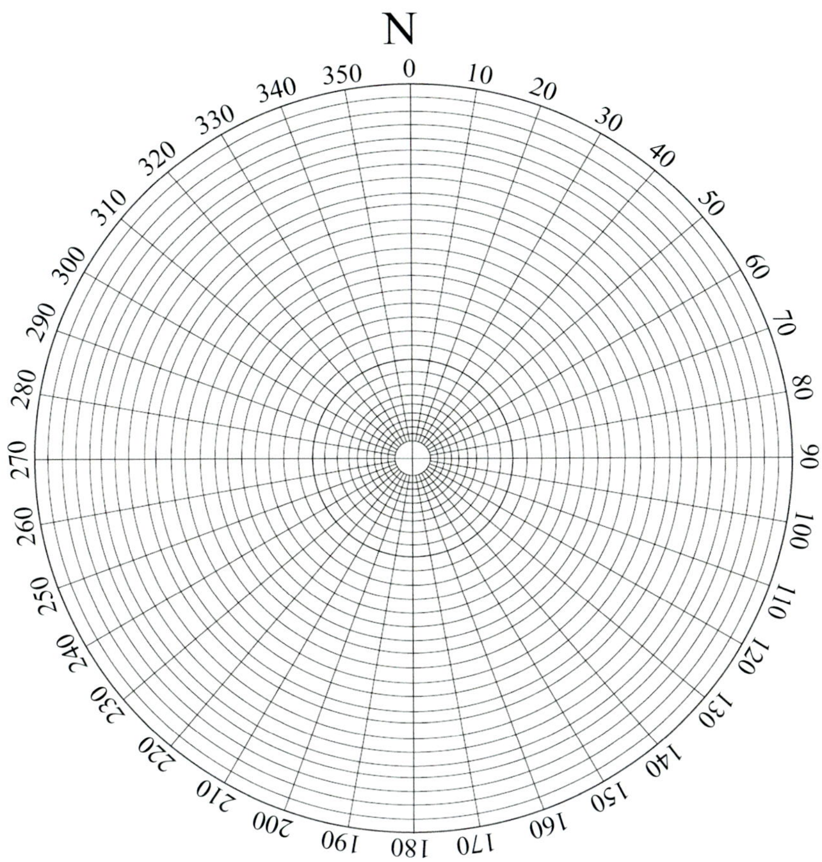

Date:

Location/Coordinates:

Data Collector's Initials:

LEGEND

Appendix D: Equipment list

General equipment list

The following items are the foundation of your scene response kit and should always be on hand. Consumable items such as gloves and paperwork should be replaced after each recovery to ensure the kit is stocked for the next scene.

Pop-up tent(s)
Folding table(s)
Large tarp(s)
North arrow
Different colored pin flags
Compass
Handheld GPS unit
10-inch metal carpenter's nails
Rebar
Hammer or mallet
Metal clipboard(s)
Work gloves
Protective coveralls
Camera
Photographic scales
Evidence markers
Pencils and paperwork for scene documentation
Paper evidence bags and tamper-proof tape
Body bag(s) and evidence seal(s)

Baseline-specific surface recovery equipment list

In addition to the general equipment, the following are used for baseline recovery scenes:

Two 200-feet reel measuring tapes
Metal measuring tape
90-degree right angle ruler (forensic ABFO photo scales work well)

Rose-azimuth-specific recovery equipment list

In addition to the general equipment, the following are used for rose-azimuth recovery scenes:

Rose-azimuth board
200-foot reel measuring tape
Metal measuring tape

Burial recovery equipment list

In addition to the general equipment, the following are used for burial scenes:

Sifting screen(s)
Several five-gallon buckets (at least two different colors)
Flat-edge shovel(s)
Mason trowels (spade and rectangular)
Soil probe
A minimum of two metal measuring tapes or two 200-foot reel measuring tapes
Wooden datum stake(s) with line levels attached (see book figure for example)
Various-sized paintbrushes
Wooden picks and/or wooden clay modeling tools
Small brush and dustpan sets
Plumb bob(s)
Roll(s) of fluorescent mason string

Appendix E: Construct datum stake

How to make a datum stake:

Cut a notch into both sides of a wooden stake.

These notches will keep the line-level and string from sliding up or down the stake.

Place a black mark on the stake 4 inches (10cm) down from the notches.

The datum stake will be hammered into the ground up to this line. All measurements will be taken from 4 inches above this line (ground), using a string with a line level attached.

Appendix F: Burial unit dimensions

Side lengths for mapping burial units or grids										
Side Length	1	2	3	4	5	6	7	8	9	10
1	1.41	2.24	3.16	4.12	5.10	6.08	7.07	8.06	9.06	10.05
2		2.83	3.61	4.47	5.39	6.32	7.28	8.25	9.22	10.20
3			4.24	5.00	5.83	6.71	7.62	8.54	9.49	10.44
4				5.66	6.40	7.21	8.06	8.94	9.85	10.77
5					7.07	7.81	8.60	9.43	10.30	11.18
6						8.49	9.22	10.00	10.82	11.66
7							9.90	10.63	11.40	12.21
8								11.31	12.04	12.81
9									12.73	13.45
10										14.14

Suggested readings and additional resources

Suggested readings

Adams B and Crabtree P. 2012. *Comparative Osteology: A Laboratory and Field Guide of Common North American Animals*. Waltham, MA: Elsevier Academic Press.

Dupras TL, Schultz JJ, Wheeler SM, and Williams LJ. 2012. *Forensic Recovery of Human Remains, Archaeological Approaches*. Boca Raton, FL: CRC Press.

France DL. 2008. *Human and Nonhuman Bone Identification: A Color Atlas*. Boca Raton, FL: CRC Press.

France DL. 2010. *Human and Nonhuman Bone Identification: A Concise Field Guide*. Boca Raton, FL: CRC Press.

Mann RW. 2017. *The Bone Book: A Photographic Lab Manual for Identifying and Siding Human Bones*. Springfield, IL: Charles C Thomas.

Parsons HR. 2009. The postmortem interval: A systematic study of pig decomposition in west central Montana. MA Thesis. The University of Montana, Missoula, MT.

Parsons HR. 2017. The accuracy of the biological profile in casework: An analysis of forensic anthropology reports in three medical examiners' offices. PhD Dissertation. The University of Tennessee, Knoxville, TN.

Parsons HR. 2021. Ancestry estimation in practice: An evaluation of forensic anthropology reports in the United States. Forensic Anthropology. 4(4), 330–340.

Plotkin S and Ogle R. 2026. *Crime Scene Investigation and Reconstruction*, 5th edn. [Manuscript submitted for publication.] Solana Beach, CA: Cognella, Inc.

Scheuer L and Black S. 2000. *Developmental Juvenile Osteology*. London: Academic Press.

White TD, Black MT, and Folkens PA. 2012. *Human Osteology*, 3rd edn. London: Academic Press.

White TD and Folkens PA. 2005. *The Human Bone Manual*. London: Elsevier Academic Press.

White SS. 2015. The Anzick site: Cultural balance and the treatment of ancient human remains (toward a collaborative standard). Masters Thesis. The University of Montana, Missoula, MT.

White SS. 2019. The Anzick artifacts: a high-technology forager tool assemblage. PhD Dissertation. The University of Montana, Missoula, MT.

White TA. 2013. Avian scavenging, mummification, and variable micro-environments as factors affecting the decomposition process in western Montana. Masters Thesis. The University of Montana, Missoula, MT.

White TA. 2019. Constructing distance, responsibility, and memory management theories: An anthropological approach to death notification interactions. PhD Dissertation. The University of Montana, Missoula MT.

Additional resources

AAFS American Academy of Forensic Sciences | American Academy of Forensic Sciences (aafs.org).

ASB American Standards Board Academy Standards Board | American Academy of Forensic Sciences (aafs.org).

ASPR NDMS DMORT Teams NDMS | Disaster Mortuary Operational Response Teams (hhs.gov).

Black and Missing Foundation (Bamfi) (https://blackandmissinginc.com).

Body to Burial Podcast 11: The Forensic Anthropologis – Body To Burial – Apple Podcasts (https://podcasts.apple.com/us/podcast/11-the-forensic-anthropologist/id1612758349?i=1000577761622).

Bone & Stone Anthrosciences, LLC Home | Anthropological Services/Bone & Stone Anthrosciences, LLC (boneandstoneanthrosciences.com).

Critical Incident Stress Management CISM International – Critical Incident Stress Management – What Is CISM? (https://www.criticalincidentstress.com/what_is_cism_).

DNA Doe Project (https://dnadoeproject.org/).

Forensics Found Ep. 23 Unseen Impact: Understanding Death Notifications with Dr. Teresa 'Lilly' White — Forensics Found and, Last Responder Peer Support (https://www.forensicsfound.com/podcast/ep23).

International Association of Coroners & Medical Examiners International Association of Coroners & Medical Examiners (theiacme.com).

International Association of Identification Home – International Association for Identification (theiai.org).

Investigation with Dr. T: NSU's School of Criminal Justice NSU SharkFINS Crime Scene Investigation and Forensic Anthropology – YouTube (https://www.youtube.com/watch?v=6IfYy1ef1lE).

NamUs What Is NamUs? | NamUs (ojp.gov).

National Center for Missing & Exploited Children National Center for Missing & Exploited Children (missingkids.org).

National Inquiry into Missing and Murdered Indigenous Women and Girls Home Page – Final Report | MMIWG (mmiwg-ffada.ca).

National Institute of Standards and Technology National Institute of Standards and Technology (nist.gov).

Odyssey Anthropology, LLC Dr. Hillary Parsons: Expert Forensic Anthropologist | Odyssey Anthropology.

The Voice After Life About | Voice After Life (theval.net).

This Anthro Life Death Work: The Life and Culture of Forensics with Lilly White (thisanthrolife.org).

Trans Doe Task Force LAMMP – LGBT Accountability for Missing and Murdered Persons (transdoetaskforce.org).

Tri-tech Forensics Training Human Osteology, Taphonomy, and Forensic Recovery of Human Remains – TRITECH FORENSICS TRAINING (tritechtraining.com).

Glossary

Acetabulum: A cup-shaped socket in the hip bone.

Anatomical position: The orientation of the body when it is upright, facing forward, with palms forward. Note: with the palms forward, the radius and ulna do not cross over one another.

Anterior: The position of a bone or portion of the bone oriented toward the front of the body when in anatomical position.

Archaeologist: A person who studies human history and prehistory through the excavation and analysis of archaeological sites containing artifacts and human remains.

Articulated: A term used to describe bones that are connected to one another at a joint surface.

Azimuth: The angle or direction of a compass bearing.

Back azimuth: A recorded measurement that is 180 degrees from the recorded azimuth.

Backfill piles: Displaced soils removed from the grave during the burial of an individual. This soil is placed back in the grave once the body is deposited, usually leaving some behind on the ground surface next to the grave.

Baseline mapping: A control-point mapping technique where evidentiary items are measured along a baseline (x-axis) and from the baseline to the item (y-axis). This method requires two measuring reels.

Biological profile: The estimated age, sex, ancestry, and stature of an unknown individual as compiled by a forensic anthropologist.

Bipedal (orthograde): The type of terrestrial locomotion where an animal walks upright on two legs.

Body: The bulky portion of the vertebra consisting mostly of trabecular bone.

Body position: The physical layout of an individual in a grave (e.g., supine, prone, flexed, semiflexed).

Bone fusion: The process by which ossified portions of bones join together to form singular bones during growth and development.

Burial cut: The physical edge of the grave created by the tool used to dig the original grave.

Burial unit: The measured area surrounding a grave. The burial unit is established by triangulation using the Pythagorean Theorem.

Burial walls: The physical edges of the grave from the ground surface to the termination of the grave at its bottom.

Chain of custody: Documentation of the chronological movement, location, and custodial status of physical evidence from the time it is collected through the final disposition.

Clandestine grave: A burial for the concealment of human remains without regard for cultural tradition.

Colonization: The intentional action of settling and exacting control over Indigenous inhabitants of an area.

Context: The relationship between all data points at a scene relative to time and space.

Control-point mapping: A mapping technique utilizing controlled and fixed points to map the position of items or landmarks in relation to a known reference point.

Cortical (compact) bone: The dense outer layer of bone.

Cranial bones: Bones of the head and face.

Cranium: The term used for the bones of the head when the mandible is absent.

Cultural assimilation: The voluntary adoption or forcibly mandated acceptance and practice of customs and traditions of the predominant (majority) culture.

Cultural patrimony: The physical items of a cultural heritage of a group or society.

Culturally sensitive awareness: Tangible and intangible property and knowledge that pertain to the distinct values, beliefs, and ways of living of a culture. It often includes property and knowledge that are not intended to be shared outside the community of origin or outside of specific groups within a community.

Diaphysis: The shaft (long portion) of a long bone.

Disarticulated: A term used to describe bones that are separated and not connected at a joint surface.

Distal: The position of a bone or portion of the bone furthest from the trunk (midline) when in anatomical position.

Dorsal: The position of a bone or portion of the bone toward the back of the body. Sometimes used in place of posterior.

Ectocranial: The outside surface of the bones of the cranium.

Endocranial: The inside surface of the bones of the cranium.

Epiphysis: A part or process of a bone that ossifies separately and later becomes fused to the main part of the bone.

Excavating in spits: The process of excavating soils in levels and even layers.

Extended: The position of a body when the extremities are laid out flat (not flexed).

Facet: A small articular surface. For example: rib facets located on thoracic vertebrae.

Faunal: Of or relating to nonhuman animals.

Final disposition: The arrangement of a deceased person's remains, such as burial, cremation, or scattering.

Flat bones: Bones that are typically thin and flattened in shape often with slight curvature. For example: bones of the cranium.

Flexed: The position of a body when the extremities are bent at the joints.

Foramen: An opening in a bone for blood vessels and nerves to pass through.

Foramen magnum: A large hole (foramen) in the occipital bone at the base of the cranium where the spinal cord passes through.

Forensic anthropology: A subdiscipline of biological anthropology specializing in the analysis of human skeletal remains in a medicolegal context.

Global positioning system (GPS): A network of satellites and receivers used to determine the location of points on earth.

Grid survey: A survey wherein two line searches are conducted perpendicular to one another, effectively forming a grid. For example, the initial search of a designated area traverses north to south and the second search of the same area traverses east to west.

Human remains: The physical remains of a human body including cremains, fragmented human remains, hair, and fluids, among other components. When human remains are believed to be commingled with other materials (such as soil or faunal remains), the entire admixture should be treated as human remains.

Inferior: The position of a bone or portion of the bone away from the cranium.

In situ: In place. It is best practice to document all items of evidentiary value in place (in situ).

Interjurisdictional: Occurring between or involving two or more jurisdictions.

Irregular bones: Bones that are neither long or short and often vary in shape and size. For example: the os coxae.

Jurisdiction: Territory within which a court or government agency may properly exercise its power. Or, the power that a court of law or an official has to carry out legal judgments or to enforce laws.

Lateral: The position of a bone or portion of the bone away from the midline of the body.

Law of superposition: A principle of archaeology describing the relationship between items in the ground wherein items located deeper are older than items located superficially. For example, in burials, items lower in the grave were placed before items located higher in the grave.

Line search: An organized search method of a scene where a group of people walk together in a straight line to identify and flag skeletal remains and evidentiary items.

Linear distribution: The dispersal of skeletal remains and evidentiary items appearing in a fairly straight line with items relatively close together.

Long bones: Bones that are generally longer than they are wide. For example: bones of the limbs.

Macroscopic: Visual to the naked eye without the use of a microscope.

Medial: The position of a bone or portion of the bone toward the midline of the body.

Medicolegal: Of or relating to medicine and law.

Medicolegal significance: Relevant to the medicolegal death investigation system; anthropologically, this term typically refers to human skeletal material of recent origin.

Midline: A line dividing the body into symmetrical left and right halves.

Morphology: The shape of a bone.

National Missing and Unidentified Persons System (NamUs): A national centralized repository and resource center for missing, unidentified, and unclaimed person cases across the United States.

Native American Graves Protection and Repatriation Act (NAGPRA): A federal act established in 1990 requiring federal agencies and federally funded institutions to return Native American remains and cultural objects to tribes.

Nonlinear distribution: The dispersal of skeletal remains and evidentiary items without organization with items usually spread far apart.

Osseous: A term used to describe bone material.

Ossification: The process by which cartilage turns into bone during growth and development.

Ossification centers: Where the ossification of cartilage begins.

Osteologist: A person who engages in the scientific study of bones.

Paired bones: Bones that are symmetrically located on opposite sides of the body (left and right). For example: the femora.

Palmar: A term used to describe a bone or portion of bone oriented toward the palm of the hand. Used only when describing bones of the hand.

Petrous portion (pyramid): The pyramidal-shaped portion of the temporal bone housing the inner ear. The petrous portion is the densest bone in the human body (other than teeth) and is often preserved in archaeological burials.

Plantar: A term used to describe a bone or portion of bone oriented toward the bottom of the foot. Used only when describing bones of the foot.

Plan view map: (scene map) A scaled map of the entire recovery scene from a bird's-eye view. A plan view map must include a scale, north arrow, key, and GPS coordinates of the scene.

Postcranial bones: All bones of the skeleton except for the skull.

Posterior: The position of a bone or portion of bone oriented toward the back of the body. Sometimes used in place of dorsal.

Primary burial: The original deposition of a body or bodies within a grave.

Prone: The position of a body when it is face down.

Pronate: Rotation of the hand and forearm so the palm faces back (posterior) or downward.

Proximal: The bone or portion of a bone positioned nearest to the trunk (midline) when in anatomical position.

Pythagorean theorem: The mathematical equation of triangulation ($a^2+ b^2= c^2$) used to construct the burial unit around a suspected grave.

Quadrupedal (pronograde): The type of terrestrial locomotion where an animal walks horizontally on four legs.

Reference points: Items or groupings of items of evidentiary value assigned a number beginning at one, or a letter beginning with A. Reference points are mapped, described in notes, photographed, and packaged together.

Repatriation: The process of returning human remains and associated funerary objects to the appropriate country, Tribe, or family.

Rose-azimuth board: A board with a compass dial used in rose-azimuth mapping. The center of the dial is the secondary datum of the scene.

Rose-azimuth mapping: A surface scatter scene mapping method where distance and degrees are used to measure items of evidentiary value. This method requires a compass rose and a measuring reel.

Secondary burial: A burial resulting from the removal of a body or bodies from the primary burial to another grave. A secondary burial may contain incomplete skeletons and/or the body may not be interred with elements in their natural position.

Secondary datum: An established point at a recovery scene from which all measurements are taken. This point is usually established by the scene investigator and marked with a piece of rebar or nail driven into the ground. The secondary datum needs to be tied into the site (scene) datum.

Semiflexed: The position of a body when the extremities are slightly bent at the joints or when only some extremities are bent at the joints.

Sesamoid bones: Bones that are embedded in muscles or tendons without direct articulation with other bones. For example: the patella.

Short bones: Bones that are generally as short as they are wide. For example: bones of the wrist.

Shovel skimming: An archaeological digging technique where a flat-edged shovel is used to carefully remove soil by scraping the ground surface in shallow levels.

Site (scene) datum: A fixed permanent point at a recovery scene used as the primary location point for the scene.

Skeletal material: Osseous, cartilaginous, and dental tissue.

Sketch: An informal drawing of a scene or components within a scene. A sketch is useful for note-taking but is not a substitute for the plan view map.

Skull: The term used for the bones of the head when the mandible is present.

Soil probing: An invasive technique using a soil probe to test the soil density in and around a suspected grave.

Spiral survey: A search method useful for a single individual where the surveyor initiates the search at the location of an item of evidentiary value and walks outward in a spiral to identify and flag evidentiary items.

Standard operating procedure (SOP): A written document outlining the steps required to complete tasks within an organization.

Sterile: The term used to describe undisturbed soils devoid of items of evidentiary value or excavation activities.

Subadult: An individual that has not yet reached the age of maturity. Often used synonymously with juvenile or immature.

Superior: The position of a bone or portion of the bone toward the cranium.

Supine: The position of a body when it is face up.

Supinate: Rotation of the hand and forearm so the palm faces forward (anterior) or upward.

Surface scatter: A scene where human remains and/or associated items of evidentiary value are dispersed across a landscape.

Taphonomy: Everything that happens to the body from the time of death to the time of discovery.

Trabecular (cancellous or spongy) bone: The spongy inner layer of bone.

Transverse foramen: The foramen (holes) located on the transverse processes of the cervical vertebrae.

Transverse process: The lateral projections of bone on the vertebrae.

Unpaired bones: Bones that exist singularly in the skeleton. For example: the sphenoid bone.

X-axis: Used in baseline mapping to document the distance of an item of evidentiary value from zero (secondary datum).

Y-axis: Used in baseline mapping to document the distance from the measurement on the x-axis to the item of evidentiary value. This measurement runs perpendicular to the baseline.

Z-axis: Used in baseline mapping, rose-azimuth mapping, and burial mapping to obtain the measurement of an item located above or below the ground surface. Items in trees, downhill, or within burials require a z-axis measurement.

Index

Note: *Italic* page numbers refer to figures.

For Product Safety Concerns and Information,
please contact our EU representative GPSR@taylorandfrancis.com
Taylor & Francis Verlag GmbH, Kaufingerstraße 24,
80331 München, Germany

Printed by Integrated Books International,
United States of America